float

Dear Janet,
Thank you for all the support
& love over the years & till &
beyond. From one writer to
another, stay afloat!
xx ☺

float

a novel by

JoeAnn Hart

Ashland
Creek
Press

Float: A Novel

By JoeAnn Hart

Published by Ashland Creek Press, Ashland, Oregon 97520

www.ashlandcreekpress.com

ISBN 978-1-61822-020-2

Library of Congress Control Number: 2012938513

This is a work of fiction. All characters and scenarios appearing in this work are fictitious. Any resemblance to real persons, living or dead, is purely coincidental.

Printed in the United States of America on acid-free paper. All paper products used to create this book are Sustainable Forestry Initiative (SFI) Certified Sourcing.

The quotation on page 90 is from *On Love, Aspects of a Single Theme*, by José Ortega y Gasset, translated by Toby Talbot, and used with permission.

"People Who Live" by Erica Jong, from *Becoming Light* © 1981. Used by permission of the poet.

Cover art by Karen Ristuben.

Cover and book design by John Yunker.

To Abby, Morgan and Wilder, the future of the world.

"To have faith is to trust yourself to the water. When you swim you don't grab hold of the water, because if you do you will sink and drown. Instead you relax, and float."

—Alan Watts

one

God Help Us.

The words, writ large in the sand, appeared on the beach after Duncan Leland's attention had already drifted. It was in the pink of the afternoon, at the end of another trying day, when he should have been attempting something spectacularly proactive to save his sinking business, such as scrambling numbers on a screen or gathering somber consultants around him, but instead, as was his habit, he was looking for answers outside his office window. The sky was clear and blue, the water calm. The serenity of the day mocked the economic storm raging around him. He was now, as Harvey Storer of Coastal Bank & Trust had so coldly pointed out to him that morning, officially underwater. He owed more on Seacrest's Ocean Products of Maine, Ltd., than the business was worth.

"True that," Duncan had agreed, "but only at this very moment."

"What else is there?" asked Storer.

A leveling silence washed over Duncan as his mind slowly emptied of words. He was opening and shutting his mouth like a fish when Storer, sitting across from him at the loan desk, leaned in closer.

"Duncan? What else do you have that might secure this loan?"

Duncan shook himself out of his trance, realizing that Storer's was a fiscal rather than a philosophical challenge. "It's all here," he said, half-standing as he slapped pages of the loan application down on the mahogany like tarot cards. "Look, in the spring, our new line of fertilizer hits the market, opening a revenue stream so robust it'll be like drinking water from a fire hose!" He displayed a spreadsheet thick with projections, but this banker, like the ones who came before him, remained unmoved. Duncan's vision of rosy profits in the future failed to overcome the devalued assets of the present, and in that moment he saw his business begin to slide away.

He'd left Storer's sterile cubicle in a funk and gone back to his office, back to the warm embrace of his chair and the tranquilizing effect of the harbor view. He fixed his gaze on the beach, a patch of rust-streaked sand so inhospitable it did not even exist at high tide, and let his mind fix on a plastic bag caught on a submerged stick. He watched the bag, alive with water, wash gently from side to side until his own currents of thought slowed to a listless tempo. After an empty space of time, the retreating tide abandoned both stick and bag to the land, and his hypnotic amusement was over. Looking back, he was sure of one thing: There had been no one on the beach, and there had been no mysterious message written in the sand. That was two things, but still.

He wondered if he might have been a witness to the event if the music hadn't ended. He liked to keep an iPod playing on the factory floor, on the theory that if he was asking his employees to spend their days cooking fish skeletons down to a fine powder, then he had better give them some background music to divert their senses. If nothing else, managing the sound system was one of the few enjoyable duties left to him, so when a cycle of early Beatles ended, he turned his back on the water view to deliberate at length between PLAYLIST #8 (Miles, Coltrane, and Rufus Harley) and PLAYLIST #22 (Dylan, Joni, and Steve Earle) before abandoning hope of coming to any decision at all. He clicked SHUFFLE in defeat and returned to his chair. When he looked back down at the beach, there, scratched into the sand, were the three-foot-high wobbly letters spelling out *God Help Us*. The surface was still reflective from its recent brush with water. The message faced the harbor, not him, so it didn't appear to be a personal accusation, more like a random act of prayer. Or not. Worst case scenario, it was written by an employee petitioning God on behalf of Seacrest's. But no matter who wrote it or what the intention was, it was a desperate message and a bad one for potential investors, should he ever have any. It had to go.

Down, down to the sea he climbed, taking the two iron flights of the fire escape to avoid his factory workers, who seemed to want so much from him these days, most of all an optimistic face on Seacrest's future. Gone, gone, gone. It was low tide now, and his heels sank into the wet sand as he trudged toward the words, his footprints filling with water behind him. With the tip of his black rubber boot, he proceeded to rub out the message, erasing the *d* first, changing *God Help Us* to *Go Help Us*.

"Better," he mumbled. More ecumenical, more in keeping with his Unitarian ancestry. Then he contemplated *Us,* that sweet plural pronoun of marriage. He rubbed it out. It had been the middle of August when Cora had asked for a little air, and here it was after Labor Day and he still hadn't heard back from her whether she'd caught her breath. He stood very still, trying to quell the sour tide in his gut. How had the solid continent of *Us* become the scattered islands of *him* and *her?* They had just wanted what everyone else seemed to have. "Is a baby really too much to ask for?" as Cora would say. "They're everywhere!"

He should have known that to have expectations was to court disappointment. Two years ago they'd decided it was time to add to their fund of general happiness, but nature had not taken its usual course in the bedroom. Was it her? Was it him? Or were they just a bad combination? But Cora, even-keeled as she was, wouldn't let them go there. "No finger-pointing," she'd said. "Let's just get the problem solved." And in July they began to take deliberate steps toward in vitro. At the very first appointment, he was asked for a sperm sample to test for volatility. He found the staff oddly humorless about the situation, and his jokes fell flat, but he got the job done. Afterward, it was he who fell flat. He froze in the hallway with the filled specimen cup in hand, locked in terror as if staring into a milky abyss. A nurse had to wrest the container from him, and from then on his marriage began to spiral down the drain.

The problem was this: Fertility treatment had led him to think about the dangers of replicating his family's genes, and those worries began to bloom like algae in a stagnant pond. The next thing he knew, he was debating whether it was right to bring children into the world at all, a world so overcrowded and polluted it sat on the brink of ecological extinction. This, in turn, led to questions about the meaning of life itself. "When we give them life, we give them death," he said. "What's the point?"

That had been it for Cora. "Enough thinking," she'd said through her tears. "It's time to act." Off to counseling they went, but they could not reach the line of salvage in that desolate terrain, with its boxes of tissues and anatomically correct dolls stored in a milk crate in the corner. Cora was particularly teary because she'd been getting estrogen shots in preparation for the egg harvest. Marriage counseling ended when he failed to follow through on scheduling an appointment, a chore the therapist insisted they take turns doing, a tactic that seemed like some kind of a test. He remembered the moment he stalled out. He had been, as was his habit, gazing out of his office window, watching the Hood Dairy blimp hover in the air above a distant beach. ENJOY HOOD ICE CREAM was printed on the rounded sides, sending him into a smiling reverie of dripping vanilla cones, sand buckets, and other childhood joys. "Enjoy it *all*," he'd said out loud. He continued to watch until the blimp turned inland, but instead of majestically disappearing over the horizon as usual, it slowly—ever, ever so slowly—dipped too close to the treetops. The navigation bucket got stuck in the branches, and it could not move. Engine trouble, he'd found out later. No one was hurt, but how could he make an appointment after that?

"What kind of a world is this where a zeppelin can just fall out of the sky?" he said to Cora. It was the day he'd gone to Portland to produce the specimen for the first attempt at implantation later that week, so he was particularly shaken up. "How can we bring a child into a world that hasn't even mastered nineteenth-century technology?"

Cora was as unmoved as the zeppelin. "Fuck the blimp," she said. She was a family therapist herself, and as far as she was concerned, his inability to make the appointment demonstrated not just his lack of commitment to the process but a lack of commitment to her and their future baby. Like a cruise ship, Cora was not easy to turn around once she was set on a particular heading. She started throwing ballast overboard. She sent Duncan away that very night. "Go to Slocum's for a few days to get your head on straight. You're too anxious to be around right now."

Their relationship had been sitting in dead air ever since. But that was not today's problem. His marriage would have to wait in a long line of tomorrow's problems because today he had to save his business. Seacrest's was letting in water at every seam, and it was all his fault. He had aimed too high. He should have opted for the cheapest solution he could get away with a few years ago when the EPA mandated the installation of pollution controls, but no—in the spirit of the careless prosperity of the times, he'd gone trolloping to where the woodbine twineth and borrowed too much money for a complete modernization of the plant, making it as clean and tight as a toolbox. The banks were crazy to loan him so much money. How much profit, really, could be had from fish waste? Seacrest's, whose business was to process marine waste into feed and fertilizer, used to be known, along with all the other gurry or dehydration plants on the coast, as the smelly stepchild of Maine's fishing world. Now the renovated plant was almost odorless. The industry had come a long way since his great-great-grandfather Lucius Leland's time, when gurry—the finny bones and entrails left over from cleaning the day's catch—was unceremoniously dumped into the harbor, only to wash up on shore later in the day. Lucius was originally from bustling New Bedford, but he'd dropped anchor in Port Ellery in the name of love for a local lass and soon saw wealth where others saw garbage. Using the money he'd raised touring the Midwest with a sawdust-stuffed whale in a boxcar, he built a factory to dry and grind up the fish scraps for livestock feed. The first thing he processed was his whale. The pet food industry soon became a major buyer as well, and business boomed for more than a century, but in the last few decades they'd had to branch out just to keep up. Duncan's father developed their unique fish fertilizer, and more recently Duncan had added kelp to the recipe after watching Cora gather seaweed from the beach for her garden.

Kelp. He looked at *Go Help* in the sand, then changed the *H* in *Help* to a *K* and added an exclamation point.

"*Go Kelp!*" he shouted, then looked around, but there was no one to hear. Not even the gang of seagulls patrolling the water's edge had paused to consider his outburst. As was too often the case these days, his words made sense only to him. *Go Kelp!* could be the name of his new retail line of soil amendments, if there was a future for them at all. Before the expensive renovations to the building, he'd always sold his fertilizer in barrels to companies that resold the powder in small bags under their own pricey labels, but as the bills came flooding in, some daft accountant said that the only way to recoup his capital expenditure was to leave the safe harbor of wholesale and set out into the deep waters of retail. Which meant more money out the door. His marketing investment had been huge, and the product was still not launched. Worse, competition was darkening the sky. A dehyde down in Massachusetts had contracted with key fish processors for their waste and was already selling eco-sludge directly to the planting public. Another company in northern Maine was peddling lobster-shell dust and getting as much play in the gardening magazines as a dazzling new rose. He hadn't acted fast enough in making the transition. The words he'd overheard in a bar ten years ago, soon after he took his father's place at Seacrest's, came back to him now: "Duncan Leland run a business? He couldn't run a bath."

One of the seagulls bounced closer with an eye toward a blue shell near his foot. Duncan kicked the mussel to the bird so it could see for itself that it was empty; then, with a start, he realized that there were no footprints on the beach other than his. How was that possible? Someone had written the words without walking on the sand? He looked around, then up. He was lost in troubled thought when a ship's horn sounded, frightening the seagulls into the air with hysterical shrieks and a slow flapping of wings.

All but one. There was always one.

The large black-backed gull had a loop of a six-pack holder stuck in its beak and around its neck, so that the sharp plastic dug into the sides of its face. The rest of the holder was bunched up around its head, and two of the loops formed glasses through which the bird stared at him with red, burning eyes. One wing hung limply by its side, dragging in the sand. The poor bastard could hardly move without making things worse, and Duncan knew that feeling all too well. The kindest thing to do was to let nature take its course, but when the bird opened its beak in mute appeal, Duncan realized he was screwed. He'd have to give it a fighting chance or never face his friend Josefa Gould again. Josefa ran Seagull Rescue out of her backyard, a cramped space where the birds went to linger in pain before dying. He looked up at the factory. He couldn't see anyone at the windows because of the harsh reflection of the sun. But even though he couldn't see his employees, he could feel their eyes upon him, and in his mind he heard them laughing.

Let them. Wounded animals had to stick together.

He held his arms out, fluttering his hands, and as he edged slowly toward the injured gull he felt himself to be the ridiculous figure his employees thought he was. He could hear Cora telling him in the measured cadence of her profession that he was being paranoid, that he had the love and respect of all his employees. But this was not paranoia; how he wished it were. Ever since his father died, forcing Duncan to move back from New York to take over Seacrest's helm— his older brother, Nod, having laughed it off—he felt he was not meeting the employees' expectations of a Leland boss. Duncan had arrived at the tail end of a long line of rugged, blond male specimens who were athletic, competent, and self-assured on land and sea. He was none of those things. Baby pictures showed him as a happy towhead, but the years had darkened his hair along with his mood, until both were mud-colored. Behind his back, he imagined that his workers made fun of his coordination (faulty) and glasses (eyes too dry for contacts). He was tall, yes, but tall in a gangly, loose-limbed sort of way. His image was not helped by the fact that at the moment he wore a business suit tucked into calf-high muck boots. After he'd returned from the bank with an empty begging bowl, he was too tired to change into his work clothes of jeans and a sweatshirt. He'd removed his tie and tossed it up and over the ceiling fan like a noose, then slipped off his leather shoes and put on the wellies he kept in his office for slogging around the factory floor, but he'd done nothing to protect his navy Brooks Brothers outfit. What did it matter? He saw no future that included a three-piece suit.

Taking care not to slip on the amber blobs of jellyfish that had been stranded by the tide, Duncan feigned left and the bird bobbed right. Back and forth they went, tangoing their way slowly to the crumbling seawall where the gull could be cornered among the debris. If the harbor of Port Ellery, Maine, was anatomical, they now stood firmly in the appendix. The town, all red brick and shadows, was neatly centered in the groin between two intertwining estuaries that flowed into the harbor like crossed legs. Protected coves formed armpits, and piney islands spread across the skin of water like raised hives. Seacrest's sat off the harbor's irregular belly, in a small unnavigable loop prone to collecting trash. Blue rubber gloves and pieces of yellow rope were dashed twice daily against the seawall, then fell behind the dark, wet rocks. Twisted metal shrines of lobster traps had dug into the beach to become part of the natural landscape, but plastic water bottles and featherweight polystyrene coffee cups were the transient and windblown accessories. Some days the tide took it all away; other days it left it all behind.

The gull's options narrowed, and it turned its back to the wall, preparing to hold its ground. Duncan removed his jacket and held it aside like a toreador. The air blowing in off the harbor was cool, but the warmth of the sun on his back reminded him it was still technically summer. "It's not over yet," he said to the bird and moved carefully toward it, attempting a graceful drop of the jacket, but that required him to get so close that the gull was able to slash the tender part of his palm with the curved tip of its beak before trundling away.

"Damn!" Duncan squeezed his hand and looked up at the factory. He was sure he saw people move away. Would no one come to help him? Worse, would someone come to help and expose him as a leader who could not even catch an injured gull? It was equally unthinkable that they should see him walk away from a bad situation. He had to hurry. He took hold of his jacket and, with what he considered to be a superb show of agility, pounced on the bird. There ensued a whir of elbows and wings, and for a moment Duncan thought he'd lost him, but finally, kneeling in the wet sand with sea water seeping through the wool blend of his trousers, he managed to wrap the jacket over the bird's head. Darkness calmed it down while Duncan restrained its wings with the sleeves. He was breathing hard by the time he collapsed against a barnacled rock with the neat package of gull under his arm. "For a dying bird, you've got a lot of fight left in you," he said. He readjusted his glasses, then dug around in his pants pocket for his cell phone.

"Josefa, I'm on Seacrest's beach with a gull for you—bring a cage and a Band-Aid."

two

Josefa arrived lugging a dog crate with both hands while trying to keep a canvas tote from slipping off her shoulders. She was somewhere well over sixty, with thinning black hair and a complexion so pale it was as if her skin had been bleached colorless by the sun. Her eyes had long ago disappeared in folds of wrinkles, and she had a chin like a fried clam. In spite of this, she had the youthful, tubular body of a preteen and wore the Disney clothing of a toddler, making her seem helpless, which she was not. But even if he wanted to help her with the crate, Duncan couldn't stand up without losing the gull, who had worked its head out from under the fabric and was eyeing Duncan with evil intent. The bird had a noble head with a long patrician beak, and its neck feathers were ruffed up around its face from the ordeal. It was the first seagull Duncan ever saw that looked like a bald eagle.

"Blood on your shirt," Josefa said as she put the crate down.

Duncan raised his cut hand. "I was trying to help him, and he attacked me."

She smiled. "Good ... knows how to protect himself." She removed a pair of scissors from her bag and carefully cut the plastic loops off the gull's head while Duncan held it still. His own head was very close to the bird's back, and he could smell its musty linen scent.

"You're going to cut my lapel," said Duncan.

Josefa kept snipping. "He looks more ... comfortable in that suit than you," she said, using words with difficulty. She was easier around animals than people and had a hard time translating human talk into thought and back again. The widow of an employee who had died in a freak accident at the plant, Josefa had since patched together a meager living with life insurance, social security, and the occasional donation, all of which gave her the freedom to save seagulls full time. She patrolled the beaches every day, combing the wash and rocks for sick gulls, then monitored the streets for ones injured by cars when they dawdled too long over roadkill. She'd load them into her rusty van and bring them to her yard, where they stood staring at the fence, depressed and dirty, often dying just hours after being saved. Most people consigned her to the category of someone too strange to know, but Duncan had an exceptionally high tolerance for strange, so they had developed a loafing kind of friendship. She had, from what he could make out, half a dozen adult children and a small herd of grandchildren, but they had all moved to distant pockets of the country for year-round jobs and placid weather. She missed them. She missed her husband. So here she was, funneling her affection onto seagulls instead. "Love is an energy ... has to go somewhere," she'd once told him. "Bottle it up, nothing but trouble."

"The bird can keep the jacket," said Duncan. "I won't be needing a suit again until my funeral."

She looked up at the brick building, which had SEACREST'S OCEAN PRODUCTS OF MAINE newly repainted in glossy white on its side. "Old dehyde looks smart enough. Things that bad … on the inside?"

He twisted his upper torso around to admire the building. "It had better look good for all the money I poured into it. I'm in over my head in debt, and the banks have thrown up a headwind to any more credit until I pay off the renovation loan. They want their principal back. Now. I didn't even know they could do that."

"You didn't read the loans?" Josefa carefully eased the plastic off the gull, and it jerked its bruised head back in response.

"Loan agreements are as easy to decipher as the small print on a plane ticket. I guess I knew they had the right—I just never thought they'd do it. I don't know how I'm going to stay afloat. I don't even have enough money to make payroll on Friday."

"There's always Beaky," she said, struggling with the catch on the crate.

Duncan shook his head as if he were getting rid of water in his ears. "I'm over-extended as it is. I'd never get out from under a debt like that." In the local lending world, Beaky Harrow was known as a hagfish, an eel-like creature who burrowed into the flesh of dead and dying fish caught on lines.

Josefa shrugged. "Here … slide your friend in." She held the door of the crate open, and, with some bending of neck and compression of wing, Duncan managed to get the bird safely inside as he released his jacket. Josefa reached in and stroked the traumatized bird, murmuring gull-like noises. To Duncan's ears she sounded as if she were gasping for air, but the bird relaxed under her touch. He held out his jacket and inspected it for gull poop. Satisfied, he shook it out and put it back on, only a little worse for wear.

"You think someone did this on purpose?" he asked, picking up the six-pack holder.

Six-pack holders were part of the plastic armada that floated in the sea, but they looked like slow-moving snacks to the gulls, who bit at them and ended up getting caught by their own prey. Those were accidents, although his plant manager, Annuncia, would call them flagrant murder by irresponsible trashing. What was not so accidental was the lunchtime game that downtown workers played by holding the plastic six-pack rings out of their office windows to let gulls snatch them out of their hands. Humans were so cruel, the way they knew how to play on natural greed. Didn't the birds ever learn? Didn't they ever notice the fate of every other seagull that succumbed to the temptation? He'd seen gulls compete over a single holder, fighting over the very thing that would choke them to death.

Josefa secured the crate. "Don't matter how it starts," she said, removing a box of Band-Aids from her canvas bag. "It's the same bad end."

Duncan tucked the plastic in his pocket before settling himself back down against the rock, in no hurry to return to the office. Josefa retrieved a paper cup from her bag and walked down to the tide line. She splashed some water on her hands, wiping them clean on her pink-hooded Ariel the Mermaid sweatshirt before filling the cup. When she returned, she stood for a moment and scanned the beach.

"Speaking of bad ends … I found a knee. On Colrain Beach."

"Is this the beginning of a joke?" Duncan held his hand out and braced himself as Josefa poured salt water over his wound. "Ouch."

"Called the police. Weren't laughing like it were a joke. They guess it's Marsilio flotsam."

"Poor bastard," said Duncan. Marsilio was Slocum's brother-in-law, who went down in his lobster boat in the storm.

Josefa snorted as she dried his hand with the hem of her sweat-shirt. After she applied the bandage, she took a bottle of Gritty's Beer out of her bag and handed it to him. "For being brave."

"I wasn't brave," he said, twisting the top with a spritz. "I'm just saving my voice for Friday when my employees rise up against me."

She sat down with a grunt and opened a beer of her own. They both watched the foam rise from the top and spill onto the sand. "Dunc, the future's never what we think ... no use getting yourself wrapped around the propeller about it."

True that. Josefa's future could not have been predicted by anyone. Her husband, George, had been on Seacrest's loading dock directing gurry from a truck into the chute when he got dive-bombed by a gull. The new system had just been installed, and waste was no longer exposed as it went from truck to holding tank—hence, no vapors of rotting bones and entrails in the air. This made the EPA and the citizens of Port Ellery happy, but a frustrated gull, used to feeding on spillage, went into battle fury. George stepped back to wave him off and fell ten feet to the ground, onto his head, which did not in itself kill him. If every worker who fell on his head died, Duncan would have no employees left at all. But the truck driver panicked when he saw what happened, put his vehicle in the wrong gear to get out of the way, and crushed George against the factory wall. It was an extraordinary act of grace that Josefa continued to save seagulls, but she said the gull was just being a gull—it was the human who had the gift of conscious choice who'd fucked it up.

They drank in silence, gazing out on the water, which was calm, for water. Its surface undulated in pink and teal as it slurped under the docks of the industrial marina next door. But no matter how calm the water seemed, he knew. A storm could rise out of nowhere, especially as they moved into the fall. He slapped at a mosquito on his neck. The days were getting shorter. Complete dark was still a couple of hours away, but the sun was already hugging the horizon, creating a hazy, watery light. In a month's time, the end of the day would seem to take place underwater, but for now the sun's luster stirred up murky sediments in his brain. He'd always considered himself content, but ever since that day at the fertility clinic, everything—even an injured gull—had become an opportunity for questioning life.

"Why do you try to save the birds?" Duncan asked. "Why bother when your success rate is so low?"

She twirled her bottle close to her ear and listened to the suds inside. "'Cause there's always the one, the one who gets better and flies away."

"How many of those in your lifetime?" he asked.

"Dozen?" she said, without taking her eyes off the harbor. "Last success was Fathom, attacked by a dog and lost half a foot. He adjusted. Learned to fly and land. Time for him to go, I made a big thing of it, rowing out to the lighthouse … tossing him in the air. But I found him a week later with fishing line around his neck. I helped him again ... no use." She tightened her sweatshirt around her and took a sip. "I like to think of the ones I've saved, up there. I like to think they think of me."

"I'd like to think there was someone up there who thought of me, too," said Duncan.

They watched a few day boats straggling in from the sea, chugging loudly and expelling clouds of diesel, heading for the fish auction. Seagulls followed them in, screaming in a dozen loud languages, demanding that the crew start cleaning fish and toss them the guts, as they had for hundreds of years. But the fish were already cleaned and in the hold, and the guts were in barrels ready to be delivered by truck to his plant. In the name of improving the environment, the gulls had lost another food source. It was funny how heavily regulated fish waste was, which got snapped up so eagerly in the wild, and yet any boob could throw away plastic, which never disappeared.

"Why didn't something eat the knee, do you think?" asked Duncan.

Josefa shrugged. "All bone. Reminds me. I've got bodies for the chute."

"I wish you wouldn't do that," said Duncan. "I'm going to get in trouble one of these days."

"Stop being a worrywart, Dunc. You're within the law."

It was true; a few gulls were allowed into the fertilizer mix because the regulators understood that a certain number of seabirds would end up in fish waste. The seaweed was riddled with gull body parts. Some days it seemed as if the birds molted wings as easily as feathers. He was allowed up to three percent "other" organic material in the dark powder, as long as it did not contain heavy metals or toxins. Josefa could not possibly dig enough graves for all her failed rescues, so she sometimes threw them down the waste chute into the grinder, the first step toward dehydration. When George was still alive, he used to bring the bodies to work with him in an insulated container, and Duncan still thought twice before opening a beer cooler at a picnic.

"That's how I want to be buried," said Duncan. "No commending to the sea, no ashes scattered in a daisy meadow, but here at the factory. Wrap me up in a sheet and drop me down the chute. In time, some gardener will spray me on a prize-winning pumpkin, and I'll have made the world a better place."

"Amen to that," said Josefa, and she shook her beer bottle to make sure it was empty before putting it in her bag.

"Speaking of amen," said Duncan. "I didn't come here to save a seagull. I came down to erase a strange message someone wrote in the sand. It gave me the willies."

Josefa looked over to where he was pointing with his bandaged hand. "You really trawl for things to fret about. What does it say?"

"It said *God Help Us*," said Duncan. "But I've changed it to *Go Kelp!* What do you think of that as the name for the new fertilizer?"

"As a slogan, I like the first one better." And then she stood up and wiped the sand off her pink sweatpants. "Come on, let's take care of the bodies … before Annuncia and Wade shut down the works for the day."

Duncan pulled himself upright and steadied himself against the seawall. His hand hurt, and the air on the wet seat of his trousers chilled him to his core. His knee ached, too, but that was probably sympathetic pain for the lobsterman awash in fragments. He thought of his father, lost at sea, his body never recovered from a sailing accident. Cora often worried on Duncan's behalf about this lack of closure over his father's death, but he didn't mind. It was better to have him gone altogether than to have to bury a single knee.

"Duncan," said Josefa. "Wake up and help."

He took the crate from her and felt the gull slide to one side, throwing him off balance for a moment. Josefa adjusted her rescue bag over her shoulder, and as they headed up to the parking lot they passed dark wreaths of sea grass left by the tide.

"It's like stepping on graves," Duncan said.

"Not particularly," said Josefa. She gave him a sideways glance. "Might want to think about moving out of your mom's house and getting back with your wife. Your brain is beginning to take on water."

"Cora doesn't want me back until … " And then, as if a spigot was abruptly shut off, the leveling silence returned to his head, draining him of thought. Until *what?* As his skull emptied of thought, he felt a sharp pang of worry, way off in the distance, and wondered if this was the first sign of the family madness.

three

After a few days of frustrating calls and meetings with loan officers, Friday arrived, and Duncan made payroll in spite of them all. Not, as he would have liked, through any financial heroics but by withdrawing the money out of his personal account. He wouldn't be able to outrun the tide too much longer, since Cora had set money out of his reach for the fertility project earlier that summer. After signing off on payroll, he spent the rest of the day staring out the window, half-expecting another message to appear in the sand.

"Mr. Leland, I'm locking up," called Wade from the first floor.

Duncan nodded, then realized too late that Wade couldn't hear a nod and was already heading up the metal stairs.

"Why is it so dark in here?" Wade stood at the door, grabbing at the air until he found a cord, and an overhead fixture came on with a fluorescent tinkle. Duncan stared at Wade, this bringer of light, whose eyes were too close together and favored one side of his face, like a flounder. His arms were roped with veins and purpled with tattoos. He was one of the many men at Seacrest's who had begun his working life on the sea but got tossed ashore when the National Marine Fisheries cut his boat's fishing quota to three days a month. Now he was Seacrest's head of maintenance. A janitor.

"You go," said Duncan. "I'll close up."

Wade stood at the door, staring at Duncan. "Want to come to supper?" he asked. "Clokie's got a lobster stew on the burner. Bet we have a baby lying around you haven't even met."

Duncan smiled. "Thanks for the offer, but some other time. I told my mother I'd pick up dinner so she and Nod could work on racing tactics."

Wade gave a wry smile. "Wish 'em luck." Then he raised his hand in farewell and went back downstairs, the sound of his steps echoing, then disappearing altogether.

The door slammed, and the building was empty. Duncan remembered being in the factory after hours when he was young, playing among the old tanks and wooden ladders with Nod while their father arranged the orders for the next day, and then they'd sail back home together in the catboat, his father's good-weather commuter vehicle. If it was dark, Duncan would lie flat on the bow with a red and green light to make them legal. As their father raised sails and adjusted the rudder, he tried to scare them with stories of sea monsters and ghost vessels, but they only laughed at the thought that anything could go wrong while they were all on the boat together, floating between worlds. Their mother would meet them on the dock *alcoholic ?*

and scold them for walking into town without telling her, but she didn't mean it. She was only covering up the fact that she hadn't realized they were gone.

It was getting late. "On we go," he said as he stood up and gathered himself together. After setting the building's alarm system, he closed the door firmly behind him, then climbed into his blue Ford pickup truck, the only vehicle left in the lot. He drove a couple of blocks to Manavilins as the sun set, bruising the sky with color. When he pulled into the parking lot and turned off the ignition, the engine coughed a couple of times before it finally died. Along with all his other unmet responsibilities, he was overdue for a tune-up, but it had waited this long; it could wait some more. It could all wait. He leaned his head back and closed his eyes, offering his freckled neck to an unfeeling universe. His windows were open to the evening air, and through the thick exhaust of the restaurant's deep fat fryer he could smell the salt-heavy Atlantic. All around him, life went on. Motorcycles ratcheted into reckless gears; fully loaded freezer trucks hit potholes that tested their suspensions. Gulls squabbled at the Dumpster. His spine tightened when a ferry scraped against a piling as it docked. It was a world awash in menace, and he didn't want to get out of the truck. A car horn shattered his thoughts, and his eyes shot open.

"Duncan Leland." The voice came from the gray-and-black Mini Cooper that had pulled opposite him, so that the two driver's side windows faced each other.

Duncan shook his head, not denying he was Duncan, but to imply he didn't know who this man was, all scrunched up in his shell.

"Beaky Harrow." The man leaned out his window, and Duncan groaned in recognition. Beaky's face was pinched and ageless, with a mustache like a bit of dark seaweed. His brown hair looked dyed and was gelled flat to his head. Bones must have been missing from his

like death
Grim Reaper

back because his neck did not quite appear above his jacket collar. A beige, sock-like animal sat on his shoulder and stared at Duncan. It wore a small pink harness.

Duncan leaned away. "What *is* that?"

"Meet Fingers. My ferret. I'm glad we caught you, Mr. Leland. I was hoping we could talk business. I understand you could use a little." He punctuated each sentence with a little snort.

"A little … " Duncan could see what was happening. Had Beaky found out that payroll had come from his own savings that day? Certainly so. Did he know how much—or little—was still available? Of course. He wouldn't be here otherwise.

"Shall we talk?" Beaky's eyes were set far apart, like a crab's, and it was hard to tell just where he was looking.

"That's kind of you," said Duncan. "But I don't need to talk. I'm really not in the market for your business." Duncan tried to say this lightly. He did not want to make an enemy of this man, just decline his favors.

Beaky raised himself from his seat and stretched his arm to create a bridge to Duncan's window, and the ferret shimmied across it and in a moment was on his steering column. Duncan meant to scream but nothing came of it, and by the time he made a grab for the animal, it had climbed up the front of his shirt and was trying to burrow behind his neck. When he pried it from his person, he was surprised that its warm body went limp in his hand. He'd been expecting a fight, but instead it arched its head up and stared amiably and intelligently at Duncan as if they were old friends.

"Look at that," said Beaky. "Fingers likes you."

"Take it." Duncan held the ferret out of the window and dropped it into Beaky's waiting hands. Beaky kissed the ferret on its forehead before returning it to his shoulder.

"Drowning men try to fight off their saviors, Leland, but we're trained to knock them out to get them ashore. We do whatever it takes." He put the car in drive. "When you change your mind, call me. My number is in your shirt pocket." *oh my gosh !*

Duncan put his hand to his chest and felt a business card.

Beaky smiled as he turned out of the parking lot. Duncan watched him disappear into the night, trailing two streaks of red light. His vanity plate read WEASEL. Duncan's financial crisis was now officially blood on the water, attracting bottom feeders and scavengers alike. He felt himself sinking slowly into the deep cold, where the light grew weak and blunt noses bumped against his ribs.

oh no !

Duncan abandoned his truck for the relative safety of Manavilins to wait for his dinner. Rather than take a seat, he stood at the takeout counter and read the blackboard. Along with the usual strange dishes, he noted the market price of lobsters. Cheap. Too cheap. Poor economic times had brought a halt to the purchase of luxuries like lobster, so the market was glutted with them. The major cruise lines had cancelled millions of pounds of orders for the season and were serving cheap farmed shrimp from Asia instead of lobster in their surf and turf. He picked up a copy of *New England Fisherman* to take his mind off his financial woes by reading about others' woes. Above the general noise of the restaurant, he heard a thickly accented voice rise from a booth.

"I am willing to make a contribution to nature, but nature must be willing to make a contribution to me first! Who is going to pay for me to change my nets?"

Duncan pressed his glasses hard against his face, as if that could block out the words. No matter which way he turned these days, his business problems lay in wait for him. This particular problem was Kendrie Ottejnstein, captain of a 100-ton South African vessel fishing out of Port Ellery for the herring season, and there he sat, trapped by Annuncia, whose physique was as solid as if she'd been poured in a foundry. Kendrie was a fish she'd been trying to land for a long time, and all she had to do to block his exit from his booth was pull up a chair. Aside from her job managing Seacrest's, she was an organizer for Green Fish, a group that promoted ecologically caught seafood. She was constantly haranguing captains like Kendrie—a paying Seacrest's client—about conforming to practices that respected the fisheries, such as proper net size to limit bycatch, the inadvertent capture of one species while trying to fish for another. By law, the bycatch—which was almost always dead, and, if not dead, dying—had to be thrown back into the sea. It couldn't even be given to Duncan to dehydrate, which was a truly sinful waste of an already depleted resource. Duncan understood the long-term consequences of dirty fishing, but with Seacrest's on such shaky legs at the moment, this was hardly the time to alienate clients because of it.

"It's cheaper to pay the fines than to change my nets," continued Kendrie. "You know how much that costs?"

"Do you know how much it costs not to?" asked Annuncia. She spoke with controlled motions of her hand, as if she were trying to keep from hitting him. "Healthy fisheries are good business, good for everyone. If the fish disappear, so do we."

"I'll be here," he said, his mouth full of coleslaw.

"No, Kendrie, not you." With this she tapped him on the forehead, and he gave her a serious look of warning. She pushed her chair back with a purposefully grating sound. "You may be clever, Kendrie, but you're not very smart."

Duncan hid behind a pillar so Kendrie wouldn't see him and

cancel their contract on the spot. The week before, the captain of a factory trawler left Seacrest's for a waste processor in Portland to get away from Annuncia's public attacks. She accused him of scraping the bottom of the ocean floor clean with his trawl, the marine equivalent of clear-cutting rain forests.

"Duncan!" Slocum called from the kitchen. "Put a piece of lemon in your mouth!"

Duncan picked up a wedge from a bowl and stared at it. Manavilins was owned by his buddy Slocum Statler, whose bread and butter was the fry plates, but he dreamed of making a name for himself in gastro-aquatic wonders, as he called them, and flew a pirate's flag in the kitchen. He kept up with the latest food trends, with a special interest in molecular gastronomy, while closely adhering to a New England fish shack menu. Often this meant a liberal hand in substituting one ingredient for another. He was known to stuff shrimp with breadcrumbs made from almond cookies, and he kept a tank of live eels in the courtyard for making pie. The calamari calzone wasn't half bad, if you could get past the disturbing menu notes: *Squid are generally recognized to be smarter than dogs. Endangered status: Zero. Because of warming waters, squid have surpassed humans in total biomass on the planet.*

"It's a test," Slocum said, wiping his hands on his apron as he approached the takeout counter from the kitchen. He had an ancient-mariner gleam in his eyes and a full, squared-off beard and walrus mustache, probably in violation of the health code. It made him look like an Old Testament prophet, which made people trust him more than they should. He was wider than Duncan but just as tall, and it was this height that had bound them together in elementary school. They saw life from the same perspective, above the fray and into the future, full of hope. When Duncan left Port Ellery for St. Mark's Prep in New Hampshire, he thought he'd never return. After graduating from Columbia University with a degree in chemistry, he got a job managing a perfume lab for Revlon and thought his life would be spent in New York City, touched with glamour and excitement. But his father, who worried that living among strangers for so long would prevent Duncan from seeing himself through the eyes of others—a powerful tool, his father believed, for making sound, ethical decisions—had often tried to lure him back to Port Ellery. He finally succeeded with his death. Through all this time, Slocum had kept his dreams, no matter how daft, as Duncan slipped blindly into family expectations. He couldn't even remember what it was he once wanted to do with his life.

"A test of what?" asked Duncan.

"Lemon juice makes introverts salivate more than extroverts. This is for Clover's kid's science project. Open." He squeezed the lemon on Duncan's tongue. "Now don't swallow for a minute."

Clover was Slocum's sometimes girlfriend, who wore tight pleather jeans low on her hips, with a huge belt buckle centered on her pelvis. They'd met when she rode through town with her motorcycle gang years ago and have continued happily in this way for years, her coming and going whenever. Right now, she was in New Mexico while her preteen son, Harley, was staying with Slocum above the restaurant. Harley's father and Clover had never married, but when he died in a bar fight, she'd had his penis ring refitted for her finger, and Slocum often cited that as proof of her capacity for love. He also praised her mothering skills because she often left Harley at Slocum's for months at a time while she was on the road, to give him some stability.

"Time to get with the program, Kendrie," Annuncia said to the red-faced South African. "You might call yourself a captain, but you don't know dick about fishing." With that, she stood up slowly and walked away.

"Time's up," said Slocum, brandishing a flashlight. "Tip your noggin and let's get a look." Duncan opened his mouth for inspection, and while his head was bent back, he read the hand-lettered sign tacked over the counter: NO TRANS FATS USED IN COOKING. What the sign didn't say was that Manavilins used lard for frying, and Slocum often claimed he'd use whale blubber if he could get his hands on any. He believed that fat was the secret to the success of the species. Humans were not just the fattest primates, they also had ten times as many fat cells as would be expected in any animal of its size, which, to Slocum, pointed to one obvious conclusion: Humans were descended from aquatic apes. And, he believed, they needed to maintain those fat deposits for when—perhaps not so far in the future—the rising tides of global warming forced Homo sapiens back to the sea.

"Hmm," Slocum said at last. "No response." He gave Duncan a worried look, then smiled. "We'll have to preserve you in a specimen jar and bring you to the science fair—the non-responsive wonder."

Annuncia appeared at Duncan's side. She was still in her work clothes. Her red smock, with SEACREST'S embroidered in white on the pocket, strained at the hips and was streaked with black fish powder. Her bushel of dark hair was pulled up under a tight red snood. "Hull-sucking sea worm," she said, turning back to face Kendrie, who did not look up from his mountain of onion rings. "There are fishermen who make a living fishing, and then there's an industry that wants to make a killing," she said even louder. When Kendrie refused to rise to the bait, she picked up her takeout bag. "Don't look at me like that, Dun'n."

"We need every customer we can get right now, Annuncia. Don't single him out for killing off the human race. You're as subtle as a pile driver."

"Whale balls. Puddingheads like Kendrie, they've got to

understand what the stakes are. It's not like we can go somewhere else when we fuck it all up. *This* band of temperature, *this* mix of oxygen—it's all we can live in, and it all depends on the ocean to keep it stable. Kendrie's Neanderthal skull can't compute that saving the ocean means saving his own sorry ass."

"Can this wait until *our* business is a little more stable?" Duncan whispered.

"Dun'n, don't compromise yourself for money."

"I have nothing left to compromise myself for."

She looked around the restaurant. "Where's Wade? He's giving me a ride home."

"Here!" Wade stepped out of the walk-in cooler behind Slocum. After work, he sometimes ran fish from his cousin's boat to local restaurants. He wanted to save family fishing boats in the same way that family farms had become a national cause. He was so disgusted with the corporately owned industrial fleet that he frowned on Seacrest's accepting its fish waste, which was substantial. Between Wade's local fishing and Annuncia's green fish, Duncan felt as if the financial health of Seacrest's was far down on his employees' lists of priorities.

"We're leaving, Dun'n," said Annuncia. "Come on, Wade. See you Monday, boss."

"Wait." Wade picked up a Support local fishing bumper sticker from a pile on the counter and handed one to Duncan. "I know you'll want one of these. To save the fishes." And with this he slapped his heart.

"Of course," said Duncan, and he moved to put it in his pocket, but Wade pulled it from his grasp.

"I'll put it on the truck for you on my way out," he said. "No problem."

Duncan cringed. Yes, local boats needed every extra

consideration to survive, but so did he. He hoped Kendrie, or any of the other factory boat captains, would not recognize his truck.

Annuncia and Wade smiled at him as they turned away, but come next Friday when there was no paycheck, they would eat him alive. He wanted to reach out and pull them to his chest so he could point to the crumbling edge of the cliff on which they all stood. But that would only cause panic, and God knows he already had plenty of that.

When the door closed behind them, he looked around the restaurant, as long and narrow as a shipping container, filled with the comforting warmth of human bodies. Young lovers dipped fried oysters in tartar sauce and brought them to each other's mouths; children licked ketchup from white paper cups and got it on their noses; married couples eyed dishes sprung from Slocum's misplaced imagination, smiled, and dared each other to go first. They were happy. Duncan could be happy. He should take Josefa's advice and devote his energy to getting back with Cora and let Seacrest's sink or swim on its own. He could not play God; he could not part the sea. And besides, maybe next week the banks would reconsider. After all, wouldn't they rather keep him as a customer they could continue to suck dry than lose him to bankruptcy? He felt light and free at the thought, as if he were floating above his earthly troubles. He smiled as he saw Slocum pack up his order, he smiled as he handed him the credit card, and he kept right on smiling past the point when his card was rejected.

"Sorry," said Slocum, handing it back to him.

Duncan ran his thumb over the raised, useless numbers on his plastic. The bank must have found out that he'd paid out of pocket for payroll that day, and to make sure he didn't put it on his card the following week—which he'd been considering—they must have canceled it altogether.

"I'm supposed to cut it in half," whispered Slocum. "But you keep it. Pay me whenever. And wait." He held up a batter-coated finger and called to a waitress. "Bag up a special for Duncan here."

Duncan adjusted his glasses as if it had all been a matter of faulty vision. Either an embarrassing silence had swept across the room or else he had a case of hysterical deafness. Slocum placed a bag on top of his box. "Pulpo gallego! That'll cure what ails you." He lowered his voice and put a hand on Duncan's shoulder. "Call me, my friend, we'll get you back on course. Remember—a dead calm comes before a new wind."

Duncan gave him a sickly smile and left. In a time like this, if all his best friend could do was to give him some oily octopus and a maritime platitude for comfort, then the end could not be very far away.

four

Balancing the grease-stained bag of pulpo on the box of calzone, Duncan climbed the irregular steps of the wraparound porch of his childhood home, the octagonal beast that had come down through his mother's side of the family. All was dark except for the third floor, whose glow extended up into the glass cupola that topped the roof, like a baby beacon to match the lighthouse at the curved tip of Batten Cove. When he paused at the door to straighten out the sea-grass welcome mat with his foot, the fibers clung to his sole. The mat created more debris than it caught, and yet it stayed, year after year, deteriorating but not going away. His legs became immobile, and he could not move. As the heat of the food dissipated into the air, he felt his own body cooling down with it. How had he regressed to this? Neither he nor Cora had intended that he go live with his mother. He wasn't even sure she knew he was here. She'd have a field day with that, but he could not continue to live above Manavilins. Sleeping on Slocum's sofa, numb from the barstool remedies for marital woes pressed upon him by friends and wrapped in a blanket of fryer fumes, he felt himself sliding back into the stupor of college life. Every night he seemed to sink deeper into emotional time, until one day he went to his mother's house to do his laundry and never left. Now it was beginning to feel normal, and he worried he might never find his way out again.

A mosquito buzzed his ear. "On we go," he said, with weak determination. He grabbed hold of the unpolished knob as he pushed his shoulder against the door, a rough-hewn slab that looked like a boat hatch. Its ornate keyhole served many purposes—decoration, spying, letting in the northwest wind—but locking was not one of them. It had no key. According to family lore, his mother's great-great-grandmother, Ethel Tarbell, asked to be buried with it so she could let herself back in "later on." It wasn't that she was crazy enough to ask—which, by all accounts, she most certainly was—but that old man Tarbell was daft enough to grant her wish, and for generations the house stood waiting for a ghost that never arrived. No one thought to have the lock replaced or to have another key made, but after his recent encounter with Beaky Harrow, security was much on Duncan's mind. The only deterrent to intruders was the fact that the doors and windows in the house were usually swollen shut from the damp sea air. With one practiced shove, the door released with a start, and then he closed it behind him with a kick. He'd offered to take the door off its hinges and plane it, but his mother refused, claiming that the kick forced people to knock the sand off their shoes.

"One shoe," he said. "It gets the sand off of one shoe. What about the other?"

"Oh, Duncan, dear," she said, with a laugh. "The things you think about."

So the house was always filled with sand. Mrs. McNordfy, the cleaning woman, came twice a week to push the small dunes around with a broom, abrading the teak floors white before she sat down for a two hour mug-up with his mother. The Oriental carpets were heavy from the weight of the sand, but by his mother's reckoning, this was a good thing. It was only half as much as it could be! "If you live on sand, you're going to live with sand," she always said. Ethel had built the house sometime in the 1860s on this sandy basin surrounded by a ring of stone outcroppings. It was during a brief period when architects promoted octagonal homes in the belief that they were not only more economical but increased sunlight and ventilation to boot. In reality, they did exactly the opposite. The rooms themselves were not octagonal, which meant the interior was a confused warren of wasted triangular space and halls, leaving most rooms with only a single window clouded with blown salt, making them dark as well as disorganized. Few octagonal homes remained standing today, and the ones that did were both a curiosity and a cautionary tale.

And yet, for all its faults, the house could be lovely, especially at night, when moonlight illuminated the romantic architectural details—porthole gables, shapely balustrades, and an ivy-covered dovecote. It was strong daylight that revealed a house that looked as if it had been built by pirates. The exterior was covered in rounded shingles that overlapped like scales, with so many of them loose or curled it looked as if it had a fish disease. The building had lost a few foundation stones, like missing teeth, but that had given it a strange stability, allowing rogue storm tides to come and go underneath without causing significant damage, though, like most things, it all depended on a person's definition of the word. His mother believed only total annihilation could be considered real damage; everything else was just regular maintenance. Bits and pieces of the house had been torn off by wind and water over the years, replaced with inappropriate styles and patched with whatever was on hand. Old masts served as joists, fishing nets replaced trellises, and briny driftwood was fitted and nailed to fill in the blanks. Duncan had been begging his mother for years to get a structural inspection, but she waved him away, and the house mocked him by staying firmly in place. It was no use even trying to get things properly repaired because she was proud of its strange ruination. "Shows the world we can survive any disaster!"

That remained to be seen. Duncan reached his hand out blindly for the Chinese porcelain lamp on the hall table, tripping over a pile of canvas shoes and a sail bag, but he managed to keep dinner safe. Working his way to the kitchen, he zigzagged through the dark rooms, turning on a series of iron floor lamps as he went, like marks on a course. There were no wall switches. The only overhead lighting in the entire house was the dust-glazed Venetian chandelier in the dining room, which was all blue-green glass frills, designed to look like seaweed. It could only be turned on by standing on the walnut table underneath, which was inlaid with marquetry compasses and other nautical motifs that popped out with every footstep. It was missing its North compass point altogether.

He switched on the electrified whale oil lamp on the mantel in the living room and was, as always, briefly startled by a single eye staring at him. The eye belonged to the marlin mounted over the beach-stone fireplace. The tail was rotting along the edges, and the once brilliant silver scales were dull with age and smoke. His mother had caught it in the Bahamas during her honeymoon decades before.

She had fought the fish on the line for five hours and was severely dehydrated when she finally pulled it in. Then she scratched herself on the fin, bled profusely, and got nauseous. As soon as she finished posing with her fish at the weigh-in, his father rushed his young bride to the emergency room. She'd won the tournament but spent a feverish week in the hospital, and it was the last time she ever set foot on a moving boat. As much as she wanted to be out on the water, she blacked out the moment she approached a gangplank. After that, she threw her life into being onshore navigator for her husband, Brendan. When he died, Nod took over the tiller of the bunged-up catboat, and she managed his racing career, such as it was. Duncan did not sail anymore, and his mother called him a nonstarter. Cora suggested he had psychosomatic sympathetic seasickness, but it didn't make him ill. He just didn't care for being on the water anymore, which set him apart from most of the community who regarded the sea as an extension not just of the land but of themselves.

When he got to the kitchen—a stark, stuccoed affair built for servants—he took off his jacket and began to open cabinets and drawers, the sound of which drew his mother's Newfoundland shuffling into the room.

"Chandu!" said Duncan as he took out some tarnished silverware. "No one feed you yet?"

Chandu sat and drooled. Of course not. Dogs had discovered centuries ago that to live in comfort it was only necessary to feign affection for humans, but they had apparently not reckoned with sailing season. Duncan scooped up some kibble and filled a bowl, then crouched next to Chandu as he ate. The dog spent his days on the water's edge, staring out to sea, ever hopeful for a sinking ship. "Old man," Duncan whispered, and patted him on his back. His thick black fur was matted and smelled of the tide. After washing his hands, Duncan turned his attention to human food, but first he had to move from the counter the empty wine bottles, which gathered in corners and under tables waiting for his mother to refill them from wooden casks in the basement. Great-Uncle Fern, Ethel's son, had gotten it in his mind to raise silkworms and planted fifty mulberry trees on the property. When the trees were big enough, he sent to Japan for cocoons, and they hatched into millions of worms, all of whom got to work on the business of spinning. Then came a nor'easter that blew the worms into the sea, so Fern had to content himself with the berries. He took up wine-making, hence the pyramid of casks in the basement from which his mother still drank. It was a sticky liquid, fermented from slightly unripe fruit. Duncan would rather eat the worms, but his mother loved the stuff and had ramped up her consumption in the years since his father died.

Cora thought his mother was an alcoholic. "Wine has drowned more people than the sea," she'd say after another woozy dinner with her mother-in-law, but Duncan knew better. Great-Uncle Fern was no vintner, so the mulberry wine had minimal alcohol content. It was not much more than stale juice. It certainly did nothing to relax her. On race days, she hunkered down in the cupola with her binoculars and her jelly glass of mulberry wine, her nostrils puffed up in excitement like sails. She tried to give direction to Nod by running signal flags out on a pole, but he was always too flustered to look up for help. Poor Nod. He was out to sea in more ways than one. The onslaught of hormones at puberty had acted as poison to his system. Something had gone wrong, but no one, least of all Nod, could say just what. Cora called him NQN—Not Quite Normal—but that was an opinion, not a professional diagnosis. His mother insisted Nod was fine and didn't need help. He spent one miserable year at boarding school and never went back. He attended Port Ellery Regional High instead and refused to go to college. He'd sometimes helped his father down at Seacrest's, doing inventory or processing orders, but other than that he never held a real job or had a girlfriend. When Duncan lived in New York, he could never get Nod to visit. Finally, when Nod was in his late twenties, he made plans to move out of the house, but then their father died, and he felt he could not leave his mother. The only thing that made living back at home bearable for Duncan was the knowledge that at least he'd once left it.

He put the calzone in the microwave, then opened the refrigerator for bottled water. Standing in the wash of cool light, his thoughts turned to his vial of orphaned semen in the fertility clinic freezer. He closed the refrigerator without taking anything out and stood there with his forehead on the door. The appointment for implanting the fertilized egg had been scheduled for the week he'd left home. The day had come and gone without a call from Cora, and he knew she'd given up on him. It was just as well. Any child of his was bound to be unbalanced.

The microwave timer dinged and pulled him back to shore. He got the calzone out, and as he cut through the crust, small tendrils oozed from the cheesy filling and curled in on themselves. It was a far cry from dinner with Cora. They used to cook elaborate meals together; she'd taught him to chop and sift, to stir and have patience. She educated his palate, explaining how subtle differences in seasoning made big differences in the finished product. "Taste this," she'd say, holding a spoon of some new dish to his mouth. "Close your eyes and tell me how it makes you feel."

He took his glasses off and wiped them. She'd make a great mom.

After Chandu finished his kibble, Duncan let him outside through the back door, then started upstairs with the tray of food. The third floor had its own staircase, which was tight and winding, narrowing as it went, making him feel as if he were being forced through a nautilus shell. He passed a plaster niche in the wall, which, according to family lore, had housed a wooden saint that crumbled away to dust the night Great-Aunt Cecilia died of a broken heart when her sailor never returned from Barbados. Love notwithstanding, the entire house was crumbling away. Powderpost beetles gnawed at it night and day, leaving small piles of sawdust under all the furniture and rafters. His mother had replaced the saint with one of the many sailing trophies won by his father, and in it she stored Duncan's caul, the withered snot of birth sac considered lucky for sailors, protecting them from a death from drowning. Nod had arrived tangled in his umbilical cord and hence no caul, but Duncan was born so lethargic that he couldn't be bothered to break his ahead of time and was delivered encased in his egg, floating in the middle like a yolk. When his mother left the hospital, she held the boxed caul in her lap as his father wheeled her to the car. A twelve-year-old candy striper walked behind them, carrying baby Duncan in her arms.

"Shouldn't the caul be in the boat?" he once asked her when he was old enough to wonder what it was and why it was on the stair landing. "We're not likely to drown in the house."

"Of course we're not going to drown in the house," she'd said. "We've got the caul!"

While the caul was busy protecting the house, his father slid off the boat one day in a squall and drowned. Duncan sometimes wondered if he should have just ignored his mother and put it in the boat himself. But then if he did that, he'd be buying into her wacky belief in the caul to begin with. There was never a right answer where she was concerned.

When he got to the top of the stairs, he slipped off his shoes as if entering a temple. The third floor was different from the first two stories in that it was not divided into strange little rooms but had been gutted to create one huge, well-lit space. It was smaller than the other floors because it gave up footage to the widow's walk that circumnavigated the house, making it look like Miss Havisham's wedding cake. French windows faced out in every direction, and any surface that was not glazed was paneled in teak. On one of those spaces hung a photograph of his father in a seashell frame, fixed with a medal and the insignia from his uniform. His parents had known each other since childhood but had not fallen in love until he joined the Navy. She still kept his uniform under their bed. Faded racing pennants hung from the beams, and one wall held a trophy case displaying the family's glory, the mounted silver boats and urns won by his father or grandfather, his aunts or uncles, his cousins or in-laws, and the many variations thereof. There were no trophies won by the living. It was a room where the present was measured against the past and had come up empty-handed. But it was not through lack of trying. The focus of the room under his stockinged feet remained the same. Beautifully painted in marine paint on teak floorboards was the coastline of Port Ellery. The map had been commissioned by Ethel Tarbell, who paid a local teenager two dollars to recreate the harbor as a teaching aid to her children. The young artist signed and dated it in the far corner—*Benjamin Bellamy Dodge, 1875*—and then moved out West to create the luminous American landscapes he was to become famous for. This floor was his only surviving New England work. Museums made increasingly frequent inquiries about buying it, but his mother ignored their pleas. "No oyster ever profited from his pearl," she'd tell them before hanging up.

With envy Duncan eyed the floor, whose fortunes had been rising as Seacrest's had been sinking, and he contemplated the fleeting nature of business compared to the eternal value of art. The vaguely anatomical shape of the harbor beneath his feet was as recognizable now as it had been to his ancestors, with only the slightest alterations. Over the years, family members had sketched in new dangers, such as a sunken boat or a new shoreline due to erosion or rising water levels. Great-Aunt Hilda had penciled a toothed eel where she claimed to have seen a sea monster while rowing out to check her lobster pots. On the shore, fish sheds had been overlaid with honeycombs of condos, but Seacrest's still sat in the little loop off the inner harbor, its stack a landmark for sailors. Black cans and red nuns and other important navigational markers were repositioned as needed, while isobars in a fine teal line marked the depths. Dotted lines indicated the different tides, and at the far end of the room were the words *Aqua incognita.*

The hills around the harbor were included in Dodge's portrait, too, along with the town graveyard, where crosses had been added over time due to natural causes or when the family called a missing sailor dead, as they had done for his father. On the hopelessly distant shore was his real home, where Cora sat, refusing to call him back to where he belonged.

Neither Nod nor his mother looked up as Duncan walked across the water, stepping on green islands with names lettered in black archaic script. He knew enough not to get near the fleet, the dozen or so foot-high, felt-bottomed boat models being maneuvered around the floor with a velvet-bumpered tool, a cross between a push broom and a croupier stick.

"If the wind comes in from the southeast, you've got to head up towards the lighthouse, then work your way around Parker's Island on the lee side," his mother said, tapping Nod's blue boat along. She wore, as she so often did, canvas ducks and a tailored shirt with the Boat Club burgee knotted like a scarf around her neck. Her feet were bare and perfectly pedicured in red. "Like this." She moved swiftly across the harborscape, expertly prodding the little boat between the shore and the island, then gave it a firm shove with her stick out to the center of the room, where it skidded a few feet until it finally rested at the head of the pack. She leaned on her stick with both hands, her face pink with satisfaction. She'd once been a redhead, but the bright color had softened with age to a shade of orangey-gray, which she kept in a long braid that fell down her back like a serpent. Her nose was pronounced, and the tip of it glowed when she was happy, as she was now, when winning was still possible. The race—and her life— was perfect as long as it stayed in her head and in this room, which went a long way toward explaining why she had not left the property in close to a decade. At first, everyone, Duncan included, explained away her self-imposed house arrest as an expression of deep grief when his father died, and, while odd, it was perfectly understandable when judged against the family baseline for "normal." Soon what was once a temporary derangement became the new norm, especially since no one called her on it. Cora marveled that Duncan never even tried to get her out. "It's hard to say who's the crazier," she often said with a laugh.

"But what if Roger tries to follow me in *Dragon's Teeth* and blocks my wind?" asked Nod, who spoke, as always, through rising bubbles in his throat. He was tall like Duncan, but his shoulders were so bowed he seemed inches shorter, and his clothes were too big, which only added to that impression. He wore racing shorts and a green collared T-shirt emblazoned with his boat's name on the back—*Ariel*. He had gone prematurely bald, and his hair was a black sickle above his neck, framing a head so sun-damaged it was as spotted as a trout. He had a clean-shaven face that added to his overall monkishness. He'd been born with an anomaly on the edge of his ear of which he and his mother were inordinately proud: A gill, a very small pinpoint of a hole that was an evolutionary throwback, like webbed fingers or a stub of a tail. The two of them claimed that in the same way the caul protected her, the gill would protect him from a watery grave. They shared a strange, isolated existence that they constructed with myths and truths of their own making.

If this was Nod's first choice of any life he might have lived, it had not seemed that way when they were children, when he was bright and engaged with the wider world. Cora had once pointed out that addicts were stalled at the age they started using their substance of choice, and it did seem that racing had kept Nod a perpetual adolescent. Lately Duncan began to wonder if that's how she thought of him, too, as stuck in his life. If she thought of him at all.

Nod motioned at the floor with his stick. "I'll have enough trouble finding air behind the island."

His mother swung her stick and whacked *Dragon's Teeth*'s little white hull. The boat skidded sideways across the map and ended up at the far side of town, near the dump. "Blow him out of the water with speed and cunning." She tapped her temple with her stick. *"Speed and cunning,* my boy! Put some lift in your sails."

Nod took on a slack expression, as if he were already accepting his defeat. He put up with a great deal of abuse from their mother. Once, when he had not bailed out the boat to her satisfaction, she made him carry around two buckets of water for the rest of the weekend so he could see how heavy water was. It never occurred to him to just say no.

"I'll get my head handed to me if I cut across his bow," Nod mumbled.

His mother set the boats back up at the starting line and sighed. "Let's begin again. The wind is from the southeast, the tide is high but going out. What do you do?"

As his mother and brother played out their imaginary race, Duncan flipped open a table and set down the food. There was no real furniture in the room, only drop-down tables and seats from the wall, as on a yacht. There was a Murphy bed for when his mother stayed up all night plotting, but Duncan always imagined her up in the crow's nest, sleeping upside down like a bat. To get up there, she had to ascend to a gibbet in the center of the pitched ceiling, using a rope ladder that hung on a clip. The only free-standing piece of furniture, if you could call it that, was the bible stand in the shape of a boat's prow bolted into the floor, where sat the Log, the handwritten family record of nautical conditions and race results going back a century or more. Duncan settled down, then picked up the container of marinated octopus—or pulpo, as Slocum called it—and took a tentative bite, which made his mouth pucker. Too much vinegar. He hoped it was vinegar—who knew with Slocum? He gazed outside as he chewed, watching the pillar of light from the stone lighthouse sweep across the lawn, a beacon meant not so much to guide boats in as to tell them to keep away from this place of danger. He swallowed, imagining tentacles as they slithered down his throat.

Nod turned to Duncan as if suddenly awakened and opened his mouth just as the stick on his shoulder got caught in the rope ladder. Nod couldn't be within a mile of ropes without getting tied up in them, and therein lay his fatal flaw. He had never won a race because of it. While Nod tried to untangle himself, Duncan used the opportunity to grab their attention. "This is probably the final week of Seacrest's Ocean Products," he announced. "As you two are on the board, I thought I'd let you in on it first."

"Oh," said Nod, removing a rope from around his neck.

"Mmm," said his mother. She had a rolled-up nautical chart under her arm and was inspecting the instruments on the wall, including two working barometers that she was constantly comparing. She also consulted a broken barometer, which always pointed to bad weather so that, according to her logic, they would never take fair winds for granted. Or, as Cora often said about her, "You don't need a weather vane to see which way the wind blows."

"Don't you two care?" Duncan asked. "This is the family business we're talking about, and it's going under."

"Nonsense," said his mother. "It's just a bit of chop. Pull your sails in, you'll be fine."

"I will not be fine," he said, irritated, as always, by her combination of daft optimism and bullying. Not to mention that he'd had it up to here with sailing metaphors. "The bank won't give Seacrest's more credit, I don't have any of my own, and there's no time to find investors willing to put up money for dried gurry. A loan shark approached me tonight. That's how bad things have gotten."

From his cat's cradle of ropes, Nod looked at him with an uneasy expression, as he always did when forced to envision the world outside his own strange kingdom.

"If your ship doesn't come in, swim out to it!" his mother said without looking up from her fleet.

"Maybe we could take a mortgage out on the house," Duncan ventured. Even after Boat Club dues and property taxes, there was still family wealth, but the bulk of it was the house itself. He looked pointedly at the painted floor. "Or something."

His mother stopped her examination of instruments and looked at him. "Are you mad?"

"Why not? Seacrest's is a good investment. Dad's company. Grampy's. Don't you want to save it? Think of old Lucius. Their initiative shouldn't be allowed to just trickle away."

"This is no time," she said, using the words she used to derail any conversation she did not like, then gave a red boat a little push toward the western shore. Seacrest's was, after all, not her family's business. She had only married into it and felt no sentimental attachment. Her family, the Tarbells, had made their fortune by introducing glass fishing floats to America in the 1840s, launching the industrial fishing era by making it possible to deploy much larger and more efficient fishing nets. In retrospect, it was probably a very mixed blessing.

Chandu started barking in the yard. "Let him in, Duncan, dear," his mother said, dismissing him with a wave of her hand before turning back to the arrangement of teeny boats on the floor. "Look at this situation now, Noddy. At last, we have a firm hand on the tiller!"

Duncan opened a French door and stepped out onto the widow's walk to see what the dog was barking at. He stared down the great distance to the ground and saw Chandu, a black shape against the moonlight reflecting off the harbor, which was flat and glassy in its stillness. He could smell the salt marsh in the distance. Tall cedars, almost human in their posture, stood guard at the Drop where the lawn ended. When Duncan was growing up, the house was fifty yards from the Drop, but now it couldn't be more than thirty. Rocky steps and an iron railing zigzagged ten feet down to the beach. The rail had been reset three times in his lifetime as the edge of land moved closer to the house, and it was not long for its current position either. The freak tides were coming more often, jumping the bluff and reaching the house once or twice a year now. Duncan voiced his concerns, of course, but to his mother erosion meant she could watch the races from a closer perspective. It would not be too many years before the quiet spot in the yard where the family pets were buried got washed away. He heard an owl cry, then saw it drop out of a cedar as it swooped across the lawn. The sight startled Chandu into silence, and he turned to sway slowly back to the house.

Duncan went back into the war room. "Eat the calzone before it goes cold," he said. "I'll let Chandu in."

"Leave our rations there," his mother said, and she began reading out loud from the Log. "On this day in 1911, the wind was coming in at twenty-three knots from the southeast. You see that? Great-Uncle Torkle managed to place second in the Huntington Cup in spite of that."

"Duncan, wait," said Nod, who was hanging the rope back on the ceiling hook. "I saw you on YouTube today. You! On YouTube!"

45

"YouTube?" Duncan looked up from putting his shoes back on. Nod, who had no job, spent his day surfing the Internet for anything to do with Port Ellery weather that might give him an advantage in the race. He also maintained electronic correspondence on a number of networks dedicated to sailing and the Boat Club. LISTSERVs served as his social life.

"It was smashing," Nod said, clearing his throat. "You catching a seagull like that. I sent it out to everyone."

"Duncan, dear," said his mother, her eyes still on the configuration of boats on the floor. "If you spent more time in the office, paying attention to business, and not outside playing around with birds, maybe Seacrest's wouldn't be in the trouble it's in now."

Duncan closed the door without answering, passing his caul as he went downstairs. After letting in Chandu, he locked himself in the library where Nod kept his computer, prepared to have a good long look at himself as others saw him.

five

The Batten Cove Boating Club was exclusive, but it was not fancy. It was sided with plain brown clapboards stained white with salt, and its only prominent architectural feature was a screened-in porch that ran its length. Duncan sat there on Saturday afternoon, alone in the shadows, to watch Nod race, an activity as exciting as observing the movement of crabs in a tide pool. After three hours, the fleet was still bobbing along out beyond Fletchers Island on water becalmed as Jell-O. The only boat with a pulse was not even in the race; it was a dory rowed by Rheya, Slocum's sister. She was a decent chef, better than her brother in that her dishes were innovative while still being recognizable, and she often hired herself out on yachts, being handy crew besides. Or it's what she used to do until she married Marsilio Collodi, who insisted she stay home and cook just for him. And then he was lost in the storm the week before. Every day she circled the spot in her dory where her husband's vessel had been found, turtled and empty. Duncan refocused his binoculars on her pregnant stomach, Slocum's much anticipated niece or nephew, who would now be born fatherless. He wondered if the police had told her about the knee Josefa had found on Colrain Beach, but maybe they wanted to wait for DNA results before breaking the news. Hope was such a useful emotion. He remembered having it once.

Chandu, lying near the screen door, groaned in his sleep and kicked all four legs out as if he were swimming. Duncan tried to recapture an image from a watery dream of his own the night before, but it sieved through his mind, and—as so often happened when he slept in his childhood home—he'd woken up seasick. He really had to get out of that house.

With a start, Chandu lifted his head but was still connected to the floor by a line of drool. He and Duncan watched as the Phinneys and Coles crossed the lawn on their way to the clay tennis courts. Chandu dropped his head to the floor with a thud, and Duncan leaned back in the wicker chair, trying to make himself invisible. The springs in the upholstery pushed against the cotton padding, and he felt the pressure keenly, no matter how he adjusted his position. Peter Phinney silently mouthed words to the others, like a fish, then Mallory Cole, Seacrest's lawyer, wiggled his hands at Duncan in a fair imitation of someone trying to catch a seagull.

"Go kelp!" shouted Miriam Phinney, and they all laughed.

Duncan shifted again in his chair, causing it to molt fine white flakes of paint. He had prayed that Nod had not shared Duncan's YouTube seagull performance with their entire known world, but so much for prayer. He waved gamely and tried to maintain a posture of strained dignity as he lifted his binoculars to his eyes and watched as the wind picked up. The little boats with their outspread sails dispersed like seagulls. He had nothing to be ashamed of. The video had not been shot by an employee spying on him from the factory window, as he originally suspected, but by members of an art collaborative out to recreate the sand installations of Adoniram, the preacher's son, Port Ellery's only other famous artist besides the floor-painting Dodge. In the early 1970s, Adoniram was a well-known conceptual performer, and his grainy film clips were still shown at universities around the country, inspiring young artists, a few of whom, armed with grants and theories, had formed the New Adoniram Project, of which he—Duncan—was currently the featured work. The original Adoniram clips were posted on the site, showing the artist as a full-bearded young man in cutoff jeans and dark hair that hung in his face and rippled down his bare back. With a cigarette clasped between his fingers, he wrote nonsensical phrases in the sand with a stick—*Toil Tear, Adversity or Lamb,* and *Failure Flight Fortitude*—creating the sayings for the arrangement and beauty of the letters rather than any meaning. Then, as the moon played with the sea, water washed over the words, erasing them forever. He filmed these installations, then sped them up, condensing an eleven-hour tide cycle down to sixty seconds. He worked with and against the clock, "as do we all, in the end," quoteth Adoniram. "To no avail." The curator's text explained that aside from the obvious impermanence of worldly existence, and the meaninglessness of the written word, Adoniram was expressing his belief that we have to learn the same things over and over again, in our own lifetimes and the next. Old souls don't get wiser. Generations pass nothing on. We learn nothing.

God Help Us was Adoniram's last sand installation, created in 1976 when he washed his hands of the human experiment altogether and took off in a handmade boat to Europe in a work he called "In Search of the Miraculous." The craft was found nine months later off the coast of Ireland. His body was never recovered, and so he was transformed into a piece of ephemeral art himself. Duncan did not wonder that Adoniram got lost, what with all that hair in his face. He was twenty-eight when he died.

To recreate *God Help Us*, the NAP conceptual artists used the same location as Adoniram had, directly in front of Seacrest's, originally chosen for its industrial taint. And, like Adoniram, they had arrived by a flat-bottomed skiff, leaning out from the boat to write in order to protect the pristine canvas of sand, which explained both the lack of footprints and the wobbly handwriting. The artists had been rowing back to the mother ship to wait for the tide to recede a bit more before filming when they saw Duncan change the message. They took some footage, which led—certainly to their joy and amazement—directly to the dance of the seagull. Then they posted it on YouTube as a promotion for the reenactments and as an example of the transformative power of art.

Duncan let the binoculars hang from his neck. The wind was gone. It was the third leg of the race, and Nod had managed to trail half his lines in the water. The wonder was not that he had never won a race; the miracle was that he never killed himself in the process. Right about now, his mother would be throwing herself against the glass in her cupola like a trapped bird. It was strange the way she behaved as if defeat were an unknown quantity in her life. Aside from competitiveness to the point of instability, she suffered from a chronic case of unrealistic expectations. She transmitted her debilitating disease to Nod. Every week they still both expected to win in spite of what past experience had to teach them. Maybe Adoniram was right. We learn nothing.

The good news was that the officials would have to call the

race soon even if no one crossed the finish line. Nod wouldn't have lost because no one would have won. It usually worked the other way around—as long as he was in the race, the rest of the sailors were never last, which made Nod one of the more popular members of the Club. No matter how late he came in, he was greeted with a hero's welcome, with drinks and cheers all around, which tempered his chronic state of loss. Racing had given his life meaning, such as it was, and as pathetic as it might have seemed to some, it was more than Duncan had at the moment.

Judson Drake—Duncan's stock broker when there had been stocks to broker—walked across the lawn toward the boat ramp and waved as if he were innocent of any YouTube. Duncan held his breath and waited. Judson was never innocent of anything. Just before he disappeared down the ramp he turned around, cupped his hands to his mouth and shouted, "Go Kelp!" Then he continued to the launch boat, his shoulders shuddering with laughter.

Duncan's humiliation was now complete. He was not art, as he had begun to think of himself; he was an idiot. Judson's voice traveled over the water as he joked with the launch driver. The boat puttered past the old stone pier, which was half submerged like the spine of a sea monster. At high water, it was a profound danger when its jagged stones were invisible to the navigator's eye, but the Club felt it kept out the amateurs and weak of heart, and so it stayed. The launch continued to the outer edge of the mooring field where *L'ark* floated like a swan. The glare of the low sun played on her brightwork mast as the vessel rocked, sending bursts of light up and down the shaft. Among the many lovely yachts in the tranquil cove, she stood out for being the most elegant. She was a vintage Q-boat, all brass and beveled glass, thickly enameled in Prussian blue and as sleek as a thoroughbred horse, at many times the price. Judson was insanely proud of her even though he didn't have time to actually sail, but he often came out just to sit, sometimes even spending the night on her linen-covered bunks. Most of the yachts of this caliber were owned by people in the financial industry, like Judson, and very few by their clients, like Duncan. Lately though, he'd heard that Judson was having trouble holding onto her. Business was that bad. He'd already let go of his captain and cook when the market crashed, and while he still managed to hold on to his precious boat, he rarely sailed her. He barely even knew how. The only time he'd gotten out this year had been when Nod volunteered to take him for a two-day shakedown cruise in the spring. Nod much preferred the freedom of a one-man vessel with a simple sail, but he was adept at big-boat sailing, so he offered to captain for the weekend but would not cook. For that, he took on Rheya, who could work the lines as well. Marsilio was not happy about that, and it was the end of Rheya's working life at sea. She didn't put up a fight because she soon found out she was knocked up, yet another local pregnancy that made Cora both wistful and determined.

A trio of men walked past the porch steps, discussing the price of boat slips in Miami. They were headed for the Club's office to arrange for their vessels to be pulled and delivered to their winter homes. It was that time of year when, one by one, the migratory cocktail set stepped through the seasonal mirror and into the alternate reality of Florida. Soon the waterfront crew would pull the floats, and maintenance would board up the diamond-paned windows of the Club, and with it close another avenue of hope that he would run into Cora, or at least mingle with her friends who might speak well of him. But she'd kept her distance, sticking close to their wooded neighborhood on the other side of the bay.

The screen door slammed, and Duncan looked up. Osbert Marpol appeared as a flat silhouette against the outdoor light. "It's 'mud, blood, and green grass beyond,' eh Leland?"

Osbert, a gaunt man in his sixties, had a stone-and-gravel company somewhere inland. He was not just from out of town but out of state as well. He'd showed up in Port Ellery in the late nineties from Rhode Island, during a time when there'd been a shake-up of mobsters in that state, which led to speculation about his past. He seemed to have no use for sailing or boats but managed to get himself nominated for membership. His smooth-shaven face was as pale as a polyp and so deeply lined it seemed drawn in with a pencil. A thin slither of black hair was pulled back in a one-inch ponytail, streaked with gray that was concentrated at the temples, like two white volutes. He was not cozy with the other members but used the club as a place to bring construction clients for drinks, its exclusivity being a strong financial aphrodisiac. The Club had no food service outside of the snack bar, but, as if to compensate, it maintained a very full bar, featuring an enormous stuffed albatross that hung from the high-timbered ceiling, its wings spread in flight. Many lucrative deals had been consummated under that bird.

"Blood?"

"An old Brit war saying," said Osbert. "Rereading Churchill's memoirs. Mind if I sit?" He held a knobby walking stick, sort of like a sheleighly, and used it to point to the rocker next to Duncan.

Osbert had never done anything but nod politely at Duncan before, so this sudden intimacy must be the result of the video. He'd become an official curiosity. "I ought to start charging people to stare at me," he said, flipping his hand to the rocker. "I'm not doing an encore, if that's what you're hoping."

Osbert chortled as he stepped over Chandu to take a seat. "You were very impressive." He had a corrosive voice but maintained a pleasing smile. The split-cane rocker creaked as he arranged himself to face Duncan, smoothing the contours of his fitted gray suit. He rested his walking stick on the floor but did not take off his sunglasses. "So was your pretty little factory."

"True that." Duncan examined the hinge of his binoculars. The video was good advertising, and if Seacrest's future were more promising, he would even post it on his own website. If he had to look like an idiot, he might as well do it for the sake of his company. "It looks great from the outside."

"I'm told things aren't quite so perfect on the inside."

Duncan removed his glasses and stared directly at him. "Who said that?"

Osbert took a thin cigar out of a case from his inner jacket pocket and tapped its end on the arm of his chair. He leaned in closer, so that Duncan could see his reflection in his Ray-Bans. "You shouldn't be so defensive, Leland. 'Our greatest glory consists not in never falling, but in rising every time we fall.'" He leaned all the way back in his rocker, which squeaked as if he had crushed a nest of mice. "Churchill." He looked up at the porch ceiling, then he rocked forward and held his position, level with Duncan's head. "Annuncia tells me that you work miracles with fish garbage."

"You know Annuncia?"

"I like to keep up with the working waterfront, and she does not keep her opinions to herself."

Duncan wondered what else Annuncia told him. In her enthusiasm for her cause, she might be courting danger. He leaned back in his chair and feigned indifference. "Seacrest's turns seaweed and fish frames into fertilizer. It's hardly a miracle."

"Fish frames?"

"The seventy percent of the body left after filleting, including the scales and entrails." He smiled. "Even eyeballs." He lifted his binoculars to check on Nod, and it took him a moment to realize that the ocean had become small, focused, and radically foreshortened. Osbert watched with undisguised amusement as Duncan flipped the binoculars around, then kept them there longer than necessary to cover his embarrassment. The boats were back to floating around in a cluster, except now the dory was gone.

"Seventy percent," said Osbert. "That's a lot of leftovers."

Duncan let the binoculars rest against his chest and put his glasses back on. "Seacrest's used to dehydrate the usable scrap for pet and livestock feed, but most of it still had to be towed out to sea in a barge before we found a way to process all of it."

"It's expensive to tow and dump anything, isn't it?" Osbert said thoughtfully.

"And not even legal anymore, if it ever was." Duncan nodded at Syrie Shuttlethwaite, who'd just come onto the porch with her teeny bit of a dog under one arm and a vodka tonic in her hand, bringing the fresh smell of lime with her. He'd known Syrie since grade school. She'd been his hometown honey in college. If he'd returned to Port Ellery instead of staying in New York, they probably would have married. She sat on the wicker sofa and crossed her legs at the ankles. Most of the women of the Club had already given up their light dresses for corduroy skirts, but not Syrie. She wore a zebra-print dress with a green silk jacket and sling-back pumps. Duncan noticed that women who were recently divorced, like Syrie, exuded summer about them all year round. Would Cora soon be showing cleavage in the middle of the day? Maybe it was Syrie's business that made her radiate with pheromones like that. When she'd divorced Lance a couple of years ago—an academic man Duncan could never understand and had never liked—she started a phone-sex wake-up service from the family den, recording a new suggestive message every day. Hers was not a seductive voice, but it had a carrying quality that translated well on the phone. What was originally a local operation had expanded across the state, and she was even hiring new voices. How was it that she could make a success out of nothing but a few dirty words, and he couldn't make a dime with a ton of fish flesh?

"You wouldn't want to do anything illegal, would you?" Osbert crossed his legs and flung one arm over the back of the chair, and Duncan felt the springs of his own chair dig deeper into his bottom.

"We are completely legal," Duncan said. "In fact, the costs of legality have nearly sunk us. I spent all that money for emissions controls in time for fish landings to go down because of tighter regulations. No more fish, no more fish waste."

"That's bad," Osbert said. He looked out at the water, keeping the unlit cigar grasped between two knuckles. "But you could make fertilizer out of anything, couldn't you? I just read that a Swedish biologist developed a method of burial that turns the human body into organic matter in weeks."

Duncan was not sure if he was supposed to laugh. "Well, the thing is, our profit margins are so small that the raw material has to be free to begin with. In fact, most of the big boats pay us to take the gurry off their hands. We also have a nice seaweed product. But it doesn't launch until spring, and we're a little unsure of the market."

"We must never confuse the invisible hand of the market with the hand of God, Leland. Certainly you can dehydrate *any* sort of waste?"

Again, Duncan was not sure what this man's point was. "It has to have high organic value, and it has to be from the sea." Duncan waved the binoculars at the water. "There's a moratorium on non-marine use on the waterfront"—he snorted—"as if fishing were coming back. I can't even sell the building for condos."

Osbert put the cigar in his mouth and stared back up at the ceiling as he rocked. They were silent for a minute, and, other than the squeaking of the rocker, the only sound was the soft wash of water hitting the rocks.

"What's the biggest piece of garbage your machinery can handle,

Leland? Maybe we could do some business together."

"Whatever biomass fits through the chute." Duncan held his hands out about two feet apart. "It goes down to the grinder, then off to vats of emulsifier to dissolve before being dehydrated into dust." He paused to consider what sort of disposal issues a gravel company could have. "It can't handle stone," he said uncertainly.

"But bone," Osbert said, tipping the rocker forward toward Duncan and expelling his breath in his direction. "It could do *bone.*"

Duncan leaned back. "Well, it does fish bone. There used to be a big market for the bones to make mucilage, but those days are gone."

"Oh, the little brown bottles of glue in kindergarten," said Osbert, closing his eyes. "With those soft rubber tips. I can still remember the smell." He inhaled deeply.

"I can still remember the taste." Duncan smacked his lips.

Osbert opened his eyes and stared out into the distance. "I loved kindergarten. I remember Miss Hildenfisch leaning over with her hand over mine to show me how to make my alphabet." Then he turned and looked at Duncan as if he was just remembering he was there. "So, Leland, when the gurry gets loaded into the chute, who sees it?"

His question implied something unwholesome, but Duncan gave it serious thought. "The whole operation is fitted and sealed now so that nothing can be seen—or smelled." He did not say that, with the right key, you could also open the hatch and drop in, oh, say, a couple of dead birds. It would have been disastrous if the New Adoniram Project camera had followed him and Josefa to the other side of the building and filmed their dark work. They had to be more careful from now on, what with people running around with phone cameras and YouTube accounts.

"Leland, we might be able to help one another," said Osbert. He held the cigar gently, as if he were protecting a long, firm ash. "After all, fish aren't the only fish in the sea." He smiled at his own joke.

A gun went off, and Duncan nearly sprang out of his chair. The race was over. He settled back, removed his glasses, and lifted his binoculars, this time paying attention to which end was what. When he got the fleet in focus, it was as he suspected. After four hours, no one had crossed the line, and the race was over. No winner and no loser. Good for Nod.

Syrie Shuttlethwaite loudly flipped through a magazine. "There are plenty of fish in the sea," she said, dipping her oar in. Porch etiquette declared that if you could hear a conversation, you were included. "If they caught lesser-known fish, there'd be plenty of waste for everyone."

"There's no demand for the odd fish," Duncan said. "Besides, it costs money to refit a boat for different species, and it's a big risk if the fish doesn't catch on with the public. Slocum still has to explain what pollock is to tourists."

"The problem isn't with the pollock, it's with Slocum," said Syrie, closing her magazine with a sharp slap. Chandu looked up at the noise, as did her own little dog, who had been sleeping on her knee. It was so small it was more like a cat in drag and could have balanced on the tip of Chandu's nose like a biscuit. "You know I adore the man, but the way he cooks, he makes fish sticks taste like an alternative species."

"Maybe *we're* the alternative species," said Osbert, staring out to sea.

"At least he tries," said Duncan, defending his friend. "He wants to do something different at Manavilins. He wants people to experience seafood in all new ways."

"New is good, isn't it, Duncan?" said Syrie. She picked up her drink and fished a slice of lime out of it and tossed it in his direction. It landed at his feet with a splat. Was she flirting with him? Or was she still carrying around some residual anger over him leaving so suddenly way back when? The fact that he could never read her went a long way toward explaining why he bugged out when he did. With Cora, they were usually surfing the same tide, and if he didn't understand her actions, she was happy to explain her thoughts and his as well. She sometimes accused him of being as tightly shut up as an oyster, but he much preferred to have her interpret him than to try to untangle the mess that was his inner world. But lately she'd been saying he had to learn to sort things out on his own, so he could pass it all down to his kids, and therein lay his problem. He didn't even know where to start.

Like now. Was new good or not? Thankfully, he didn't have to respond to Syrie because two racers entered the porch talking loudly as if they'd been in high seas all day instead of the calm harbor.

"I say you should be penalized," said Tim Roland, stepping over Chandu. "Passing a foot!"

"We weren't sure, and what if we'd been wrong?" asked Jerry Fadiman. "We would have lost the race for nothing!"

"But you weren't wrong. It was a *foot*. A human *foot*. Does that mean nothing to you, Fadiman?"

"Foot, schmoot. The rules say you have to stop for anyone that has fallen off your boat—they say nothing about stopping for an unknown foot. The committee boat went back for it when we told them. I think we've done our duty."

"The race was called," said Tim, throwing his hands up. "You could have spent all day retrieving the foot, and you wouldn't have lost an inch in the standings."

"We didn't *know* the race was going to be called, did we?" said Fadiman. "We'd *all* do everything differently if we bloody well knew the future."

And then the two men disappeared to the bar, both trying to get through the door first, their discussion having turned to a race five years ago when someone hadn't stopped to help a windsurfer blown out to sea, and the penalty exacted for that. The racers had a very strong collective memory.

"That's horrible," said Syrie, and she pulled her own two feet closer to her.

"Josefa Gould found a knee the other day on Colrain," said Duncan. "They suspect it's Slocum's brother-in-law, who went down in the storm. Must be his foot, too."

"Why would he be in little pieces from a drowning?" asked Syrie. "Sounds like a shark."

"Bodies," Osbert said, shaking his head. He put his cigar back in its case, then picked up his walking stick and used it to stand. He adjusted the crease in his pants and examined the wafer-thin watch on his wrist. "I'd like to come down and have a look at your operation, Leland. Why don't I swing by on Monday, see the place, take you out to lunch? We'll go to Manavilins!" He raised his stick to Judson Drake coming up the lawn, back from his conjugal visit with *L'ark*. "I have to talk to Judson. See you Monday, Leland."

He bowed to Syrie. "My dear."

And then he stepped over Chandu and was gone before Duncan could either agree or disagree. Duncan watched as a few more racers disembarked from the launch, balancing sail bags the size of futons on their shoulders. Others were already rolling out their mainsails on the lawn to dry as they talked about race rules and the foot. Nod was still at the mooring untangling his ropes and would be for a while. Usually he'd be at their own dock, but the rusty chains that held the float at their pier gave way in the storm, and it still hadn't washed up.

Syrie got up from her sofa and dropped down upon Osbert's vacated seat as if she were a nymph sinking onto a lush mink throw.

Duncan was acutely aware of being alone on the porch with

Syrie. She was not pretty in the usual way—her face was mostly lips and chin, but the whole package was quite appealing. It always had been. Chunks of gold hung from her ears like figs and made her eyes sparkle. Did she think he was available? He knew how Club gossip swirled and eddied around every little disturbance in the social waters. His separation from Cora must be causing all sorts of speculation. They probably made more sense of it than he had. "Nice weather," he said finally.

"We'll pay for it," she said, talking slowly, as if she were charging him by the minute. "I saw you on TV." Her movements were unhurried and deliberate as she slipped off her shoes and crossed her legs. "Nice moves with that seagull. You were a real hero."

"Not TV, exactly," said Duncan. "YouTube."

"No, real TV. You were on the local news this morning. 'Area businessman rescues seagull'—and then they showed you dancing with it. They interviewed Josefa to ask how the seagull was doing. It's still alive, thanks to you."

Duncan looked out over the cove. Nearly invisible skeins of shore birds swooped close to the water and up again, driven by a communal sense of urgency as they prepared for their trip down south. He envied them their fixed routine. He wished he had somewhere to escape to. "I hope they happened to mention that it was art," he said, not looking at her. "It wasn't just me being ridiculous." He turned toward her to make his case and was struck by the intensity with which she was looking at him.

"Indeed," she said, shifting in her rocker until she showed nearly all that was possible of her legs. "They also interviewed the adorable college kids who were running the project. Who knew so much theory could be wrung from so little art?" She sipped from her straw and watched him over the lip of her glass. "What is it that Osbert wants to wring out of you?"

Duncan shrugged. "I'll find out on Monday, I guess. Do you know him?"

She pressed her lips together and looked up without moving her chin. "I wonder about him."

"What do you mean, wonder?"

"He seems so normal, and then he doesn't. And his only friend that I can tell is Beaky, that little guy with the rodent."

"It's a ferret, not a rodent," said Duncan. "His name is Fingers."

Syrie shuddered slightly. "At any rate, Osbert seems to have a mysterious disposal problem." She leaned in closer to Duncan and put her mouth to his ear. "Like the mob," she whispered. She sat back in the rocker and ran her fingers along the pearls at her neck. "I'd just be careful."

Duncan turned to watch Osbert fold himself into his black Mercedes, and when the car door shut he could barely hear it. It was the silence of luxury engineering. It was funny how he had never noticed the benefits of wealth until he had none. Nice cars, big homes, and pots of money weren't everything, but they helped a person get through the day. He wondered how far he would be willing to go to get back to all that. Would he take Osbert's garbage, whatever it was? What did it mean to be tainted by the mob these days anyway? Everyone was corrupt in one way or another. So what if Osbert was involved in the illegal dumping of toxic waste? Or medical waste. Or worse. Was Duncan supposed to be such a saint while others who were not shackled by honesty and integrity got rich around him? It was, after all, his business to clean up the mess of others, to take what wasn't wanted, all the useless parts, the guts and tainted flesh, so that he could transform it all into something useful. Back to the earth with you! Dust to dust.

Whatever. It wouldn't hurt to hear Osbert out on Monday. He had nothing better to do. And he was in no position to refuse a free lunch.

There was a commotion at the side of the building. Two police cars tore into the drive, blue lights flashing, followed by an ambulance whose wheels shot bits of marble gravel into the air as it skidded to a stop. Chandu stood up and barked.

"I don't know why they're in such a hurry," said Syrie. "There's no point trying to resuscitate a foot."

And with that, Duncan felt one of hers upon his.

"I've got to go home," he said, standing up so quickly he almost fell on her. Chandu, anxious to join the emergency outside, pushed open the screen door with his nose, and Duncan slipped out with him. Syrie's laugh continued to echo on the porch and in his mind, long after he was actually out of range.

six

When Duncan and Osbert walked into Manavilins on Monday, the entire staff and a few customers, including Dr. Zander, Bear Peterson, and a postal worker who should have been out on his route, froze in nonchalant poses around the counter. Duncan immediately regretted his choice of restaurant before remembering it wasn't his choice. Osbert was calling the shots. Duncan asked the waitress for a booth in the back; Osbert insisted on a table by the window and got it.

"I like to see what I'm eating," he announced as he settled in his chair and rested his stick on the floor.

haha!

"A mixed blessing," said Duncan. "Maybe if you took off those sunglasses, you'd see better."

Osbert pointed to his eyes. "Extreme sensitivity."

"All the more reason to sit in the back where it's dark."

"And miss this?" Osbert held his hand out to the industrial waterfront right outside. A Whole Foods reefer truck was trying to back up a narrow passage to an aluminum fish warehouse, stopping traffic both ways. Cars sulked on their horns as two men shouted at the truck driver to turn the wheel to the left and swing to the right with such animated signals they looked as if they were doing calisthenics.

Duncan sat down. What downtown lacked in natural beauty, it made up for in drama. He looked around to see who might be lurking in the dark recesses of the booths, but he couldn't identify anyone because they all seemed gripped by a sudden interest in their menus, nearsightedly so. He had hoped not to give his meeting with Osbert any particular significance, but their lunch seemed to have turned into a spectator sport. It had been worse at the plant that morning, when his employees had fawned all over Osbert. Annuncia must have told them about his financial interest in Seacrest's because they treated him like the golden messiah of job security. Wade led the way, holding aloft a droplight to illuminate hidden corners, discussing the stainless steel grinder and emulsion tank in intimate detail, while opening closets and bins for close inspection. Employees gathered in tense knots to watch their progress, and Duncan felt the weight of the community upon him. Every time employees looked straight at him, he imagined them to be mouthing the words, "Don't fuck this up." He might own Seacrest's, but they were the ones who depended on it. If it closed tomorrow he might continue to bob along, but they would sink into chronic unemployment and borderline poverty.

As Osbert examined the menu, Duncan tried to arrange his legs under the table. He wanted to be comfortable for this exchange, but even that seemed impossible. His knees grazed hardened wads of gum attached to the underside of the table, and one leg of his chair was shorter than the others, making it tippy. Osbert replaced the laminate menu back in its chrome holder. "Let's get on with it, shall we?"

"On we go." Duncan spread his hands out on the varnished table to clear an imaginary space between them. Under his palms, gouged deep into the wood, he felt the lobster-pick carvings of crude hearts, oaths of love and profanities. *History.* Years of Port Ellery history. He could not get away from it. The walls around him were painted pearlized green, shimmering like water and hung with buoys, plastic lobsters, nets, and glass floats, so that he could not forget that the city's life turned at the fragile intersection of commerce and the sea. If he refused this business transaction and let Seacrest's go under, the local fishermen would have to contract for their wastes at a gurry plant in another town, at greater expense. Once they were doing that, they might as well sell their fish there, too. Then they might as well stay. The leakage would continue until the bucket ran dry.

Duncan glanced at the familiar menu and put it back. As high in calories as it was, the only safe thing to eat from Slocum's kitchen of deep-sea horrors was a standard fry plate. He wiped his hands on his jeans and wondered if he ought to have put on a suit. He wore a tweed jacket that needed pressing, maybe even fumigation, since it was the jacket he kept in the closet at work. In comparison, Osbert smelled of leather and shaving cream and was so crisp he seemed to have stepped inside his black suit without disturbing the fabric. His silk tie was nearly invisible against his shirt, both in subtle variations of lavender-black, and his batwing collar was so starched it was a wonder he did not choke. Just looking at him made Duncan's own throat constrict, and he put his hand to his neck.

"Let's order so we can begin," said Osbert. He took a cigar out of a case in his jacket and placed it carefully next to his knife and fork like another utensil. The sun slipped behind a cloud outside, making the restaurant's fluorescent lights pulse harder, casting Osbert's face in blue. Maybe it was better to let Seacrest's die than to sup with the devil.

Duncan glanced over at the pass-through window of the kitchen, looking for Slocum. A man was staring back at him. Duncan tried to look past him, and the man waved.

"Is that Slocum? He's lost his beard."

"It's a wonder you could recognize him," said Osbert. "I suppose context is everything."

Slocum nudged Marney, a waitress who had so much metal on her face it looked as if she'd fallen into a tackle box. She gathered water and bread in both arms and hurried toward their table. Slocum followed, walking swiftly over the raw floorboards, his apron flapping like wings.

"Gentlemen," said Slocum with a grand sweep of his hand. His sandy hair was sooty, and his watery blue eyes glowed under burnt eyebrows. "May I suggest a starter?"

"Slocum, what's happened to you?" asked Duncan. "Where is your beard?"

Slocum touched his stubbled chin and smiled. His lush walrus mustache still stood but was singed at the ends. "I was heating up a mountain of jellyfish this morning, and they burst up something good. Full of mystery, they are!"

"And volatility," said Osbert.

"We should be so lively," said Slocum, and pinched a burnt end of his mustache. Cooking accidents were not rare events in his life. He did not even have all his fingertips, so what were a few lost hairs in the march of gastro-aquatic progress? His ambitions were high. Aside from hoping to invent a world-famous dish, he also envisioned an underwater restaurant in which to serve it. He'd heard of one in the Maldives, where the dining room was surrounded by coral reefs and bright, jeweled creatures of the sea. But Port Ellery was not the Maldives. What would diners see here in the harbor, if the brown tint of the water ever cleared enough to see anything? Rusted anchors, oil drums, abandoned moorings, scary pieces of ill-fated boats in which mottled gray fish hid in the shadows? It would be an experience, all right, just not the one Slocum was dreaming of.

"We should indeed," said Osbert.

"Learn something new every day, keeps the blood moving." Slocum glanced down at his left hand, which was missing half of his pinky and the tip of his index, the result of learning how not to open clams with a cleaver. "Yesterday I heard about a new life form. The *symbion pandora*, a teeny trisexual dude who lives on the lips of lobsters." He touched his own lips. "Three sexes. Think of that," he said, looking off into the middle distance before snapping back to the present. "So what'll it be? Shall we voyage off-menu today?"

"Chef's choice for the both of us, three courses," said Osbert, even as Duncan frantically tried to signal *no*.

Slocum was all fired up. It was not often that someone was reckless enough to say those words to him. He pushed his singed hair back from his face. "As the fish yearns for lemon juice and clam dreams of the batter, I go to my stove!"

"God help us," said Duncan as Slocum retreated to the kitchen.

"That's an interesting phrase," mused Osbert. "My father used to call people he'd given up on as a 'hunk of God help us.'"

They listened to the back door slam. "Great. He's gone to the eel tanks," said Duncan. "Giving him freedom was a dangerous thing to do, Mr. Marpol."

"You've got to take risks in this world," said Osbert. His glasses were as slate-colored as water and just as unfathomable. "Plus, it made him happy. He won't forget I did this for him. You lived with Slocum not so long ago, didn't you?" He picked up his cigar and rolled it between his fingers.

Duncan paused, alarmed that Osbert had explored the hidden marshes of his personal life. He'd done no research at all on Osbert, as if his rumored connection with the mob told him everything he needed to know. But he realized now he knew absolutely nothing. "For a few days," he said, coughing his words into his freckled fist. "I'm out on the Cove now."

"Your mother's house."

Duncan bristled. "The family home."

"You know, Leland, you're not intended to live on a life raft. It's only supposed to get you away from a sinking ship."

"Is that your buddy Churchill's saying?"

"No," said Osbert. "In your case, it's a popular observation."

"Well, my marriage isn't sinking," said Duncan. "It's only floating at anchor for the moment."

"Be that as it may, Seacrest's anchor is dragging. A dangerous situation. You're lucky I'm here to help."

Before Duncan could formulate a response, he heard something large and wet being slammed repeatedly against the building, the sound of which only added to his distress. He reached for his red plastic water glass and knocked it over, flooding the table and causing cubes of ice to spin away. Marney came running over with a towel. Densch, the busboy with a jawline beard, appeared with a fresh glass. They were keeping a very short lead on him. Everything was put to rights in a minute as Osbert watched with acid amusement.

When the workers disappeared, Duncan spoke in a low voice. "I don't need help."

"Beaky tells me that's what you'd say," said Osbert. "But we know otherwise, and so do you. Here's the deal. In exchange for a chunk of money that would put Seacrest's back on its feet, I need you to dehydrate something for a side business of mine."

"Is Beaky your partner in this side business?" asked Duncan. "I hear he—and you—are not always—I don't know what you'd call it. Legitimate."

Osbert tapped his cold cigar on the wicker bread basket. "We fill in the trouble spots that are not being served by the usual commercial enterprises. As Ezra Pound once said, credit is the future tense of money. Consider me your future."

"I see," Duncan said. He should never have let things get as far as lunch, letting himself be pushed around by the prevailing wind. He used to be so good with details and planning, taking control and managing his life so that nothing happened without his consent, but now—now he found himself too close to the rocks, and he had no one to blame but himself. "As I told Beaky, I don't need that sort of help. I might not be able to pay it back, and I don't want to live in fear."

Osbert leaned forward in his seat and pointed the cigar in Duncan's face. "You are already living in fear, Leland. You might as well make it worth the effort. It's fortitude or failure at this point." He leaned back in his chair, and the two men stared at each other. Duncan felt the leveling emptiness coming on, as if his head had lost its ballast.

"I own a small trash company that serves a few wealthy communities north and west of here," Osbert continued, idly scribbling on the table with his cigar as he spoke. "It meshes well with the quarry, seeing as I can always use landfill. We started charging extra to customers who wanted to separate out their kitchen wastes for us to compost. Makes them feel good about their impact on the earth, and we have a little extra cash in our pockets. Trouble is, the composting isn't going as well as we'd hoped. All we got was rats and rot and a citation from the health department. The program has proved so popular we're afraid of getting caught burying it all at the quarry."

Duncan took a sip of water and felt blood returning to his brain. "So you are doing something illegal then?"

"Not completely truthful, let's call it. It's going to biodegrade in the quarry eventually—it's just not the closed circle the customers are led to believe. You're the missing link that will close that circle. You transform fish waste—why not garbage?"

"I don't want to become a garbage collector."

"The world is divided into garbage collectors and garbage producers." Osbert smirked. "You find this sort of thing distasteful, I can tell, but you don't have a choice. If I stood up and walked out of here this minute, you couldn't even pay for lunch."

"Slocum would let me put it on a tab," said Duncan, pushing himself away from the table. "I can get by without you."

"Your employees can't. They don't all have mommies out on the Cove to run home to when things get choppy."

Duncan took off his glasses and concentrated on wiping them on his napkin to keep from saying something he might regret. But what could he say in the face of an obvious truth? He could feel the hot breath of the pack on his neck. While his guard was down, Slocum placed a dish in the middle of the table.

"Picorocos!" Slocum waited for a moment as the two men contemplated the four beaked shells sitting on white fists of meat. "Giant barnacles from Chile," he explained. "Tastes just like crab." As he pushed Duncan closer in, there was a small explosion in the kitchen, and he hurried back to his stove.

Duncan put his glasses back on and watched Osbert lift a barnacle with his fork and spoon and place it on his bread plate as gently as a baby. He stabbed the insides with a lobster pick, winning a shred of barnacle, then smelled it before putting it in his mouth.

"Not exactly like crab," he said as he chewed. "More like bottom paint." He put his pick down and reached for his water. "You should take a lesson from your friend," he said with a wince, and his eyes filled with tears. "You've got to keep trying new things in this world. Innovation and daring are the keys to success." He drained his glass.

"They can be the keys to ruin just as easily." Duncan lifted a barnacle by its shell, considered it for a moment, then put it back down again. "Slocum's experiments are rarely successful. Sometimes they're deadly."

"He hasn't killed anyone yet," said Osbert. "Which is more than I can say for a lot of people. As for Seacrest's, Annuncia will make sure that no matter what gets poured down the chute, the product will remain consistent. She said we can add fish waste to the garbage and call it Surf 'n' Turf. A new hybrid marine product, so you still comply with maritime zoning."

"You two have really worked this out." He reached for his lobster pick.

"You trust Annuncia, don't you?"

Did he? It was true that she would never do anything unethical, but she was not above doing something illegal in the name of keeping the oceans clean. She would want to process as much waste as possible, no matter the source, to control what seeped back into the water table. But she really had no way of knowing what was in it. What if it wasn't residential garbage at all but toxic or medical waste, the disposal of which were extremely lucrative enterprises when legal, more so when done in the dark of night? What if it was something worse than that? He thought of the knee on Colrain Beach.

"Soup's on!" Slocum announced, arriving with two steaming bowls. The fumes rose to Duncan's nostrils, and he felt his lungs contract.

"Eat up," said Slocum, as he gave Duncan a slap on the back.

"It's new. Can't wait to see your reaction."

"We're honored," said Osbert, and he picked up his spoon.

Duncan was less honored but dipped his spoon in anyway and brought it to his mouth without touching it to his lips. He thought of Slocum's trisexual parasite that lived on lobster lips.

"Mmm," Duncan lied as he put the spoon back down. "Very interesting, Slocum. Anything I've ever heard of?"

Osbert fished around in his bowl and produced what looked like limp pieces of skin. "Jellyfish?" he ventured.

Slocum winked at him. "The slippery suckers that've been washing in with the tide since the storm. You need buckets and buckets, and you have to condense them without letting them explode." He touched his singed mustache.

"How do you know they're not poisonous?" asked Duncan.

"The usual way," said Slocum, picking up the plate of picorocos. "Trial and error." And with this he went back to the kitchen, and Duncan continued to go through the motions of eating. Outside, the gulls began to screech as they gathered at the Dumpster, waiting for lunch. Amazingly, there seemed to be no higher rate of gull mortality in the Manavilins parking lot than any other place in town. He thought about Kelp, his rescued gull, who was now a minor YouTube celebrity. One of Josefa's sons had set up a website so gull lovers everywhere could trace Kelp's progress and make donations to the cause. Everyone wanted to save Kelp. Why was it that the only person who wanted to save Seacrest's was Osbert, who came shrouded in suspicion? *wrong word*

"This is very good!" Osbert said, obviously surprised. Duncan watched him eat so he could keep pace with his pretend eating, and when Osbert finished and pushed his bowl aside, so did he. But before they could continue their unpleasant discussion, Slocum arrived with two large plates, which he put down in front of them with a great deal of ceremony.

"Starry gazey pie," Slocum said, wiping his hands on his apron. "The dish of kings."

"Eel pie," said Duncan, who had seen this sort of thing emerge from Slocum's kitchen before. "From the Middle Ages," he explained to Osbert.

"No, it's not," said Slocum in an offended voice. "I just killed those eels. And they're not slime eels either—they're the real eel."

Osbert smiled. "Churchill was very fond of eel," he said. "Henry the First died of a surfeit of them."

"Surfeit?" asked Slocum. "How is that prepared?"

"It means an excess," said Duncan. "As in, 'He who dies of a surfeit is as dead as he who starves.'"

Osbert studied Duncan intently. "Very nice," he said. "You're not as thick as you make out to be, are you?"

Again, Duncan pushed his chair back to leave, and Slocum pushed him back in. "We won't have to worry about too many eels, surfeit or otherwise," said Slocum. "It's getting harder to find them, what with the worldwide eel decline. Global warming. You wouldn't know it by looking at them, but they have a very narrow comfort zone."

"I have a very narrow comfort zone, too," Duncan said, trying to push back against the chair, held firmly in place by Slocum.

"What is this?" asked Osbert. With his fork he poked at the eel head arranged on top of his wedge of pie, looking at a piece of star-shaped pastry nearby. A sharp little tongue of pimento stuck out from between its circle of teeth.

"The eel is gazing at the stars," said Slocum. "That's why it's called starry gazey." He touched the eel head on Duncan's plate. "They're closely related to humans. That round mouth? He uses it to attach to his prey and suck the life out of it." Slocum opened his mouth and made a perfect round just like the eel's. "There aren't many species with round mouths, but we're one of them."

With this disturbing thought, he picked up Osbert's empty bowl and left Duncan's full one, as if he still expected him to eat it. Duncan glanced longingly at an order of fried clams and onion rings at the next table and wondered why, if Slocum could produce such reliable, tasty fare, he continued to experiment with odd ingredients and complex techniques, reaching for some elusive goal. Slocum was still standing behind them, looking out the window, transfixed by the waterfront, where lobster boats swayed at their berths and cranes pointed to the sky. "We should all gaze at the stars now and again," he said, before heading back to the kitchen.

"Do you believe, Leland, that a man's crust is formed at an early age?"

Duncan watched as Osbert cut into his pie as meticulously as a surgeon.

"Or do you think change is always possible? Do you think, for instance, that you could stop pondering your own mortality long enough to consider actually living?"

Before Duncan could open his mouth, the little bell on the restaurant door tinkled and, with a blast of wind off the water, in walked Syrie. She shook her hair free of her chiffon scarf, and the small dog under her arm shook its head as well. Syrie's face glowed when she saw Duncan. He was surprised and a little frightened. He could still feel the smooth touch of her foot on his at the Club. It had brought back vivid memories of their past physical relationship, which had been fiery in a way that only youth could have fueled. This made him worry in a whole new way about his marriage. He missed Cora. He wished she would call. He wanted to go home.

"There she is!" said Osbert, half standing as she approached the table. "Syrie, I'm afraid I've scheduled back-to-belly appointments today, and I'm not quite done with Mr. Leland. Sit and charm us with your company."

At this Syrie laughed with a shake of her shoulders. "Back to belly. That sounds intriguing, doesn't it, Duncan?" She wore tight black pants and a blue silk cardigan with buttons in the form of seashells, clothes meant to attract attention to the body, so very different from how Cora dressed, in a style that could best be described as mismatched. Sneakers with skirts, sweaters with shorts, reds with oranges, and plaids with anything at all. Hats with everything. And yet, the package as a whole worked, even at her office, where she threw a thin shawl over her shoulders and looked like the wise and patient therapist she was known to be.

Duncan stood up uneasily, causing his fetid soup to slosh out of its bowl and onto the table. He threw a few paper napkins on the spill. Densch, pushed by Slocum from behind, came running over with another chair for Syrie, and they all sat down. Osbert returned to his lunch.

"Eel pie?" asked Duncan, edging his plate toward her.

"Thank you, no," she said, leaning away, clutching her dog to her bosom. "I don't eat parasites."

Duncan stared at his plate. The eel stared back at him, with its round human mouth, so he picked it up to turn its face away, but when he saw that the neck was a hollow socket, he could not resist. He forced it over his right index finger, then began to speak in an eely voice as he flexed his finger. "Help! Help! Global warming is making me ill!"

Osbert stared at him for a moment with what Duncan thought was a glimmer of a smile, but no. Osbert suddenly leaned over and yanked the head off Duncan's finger and flicked it across the room, where it skidded to a dark corner. If people hadn't been watching them before, they certainly were now. "Don't play with your food, Leland."

Duncan stared at him. If he let him get away with this bullying now, it would never end. He was still the boss—Osbert was only a potential investor. "Don't tell me what to do," said Duncan, and he reached over to Osbert's plate and took his eel head and put it on his finger.

"You must behave like a man of business, Leland," said Osbert, barely moving his lips when he talked. "Or you are wasting everyone's time."

"The oceans are heating up! Eels are dying, I'm dying … " said Duncan, letting his voice trail off as the eel head drooped on his finger. He smiled at Osbert as he removed his finger puppet and put it in his jacket pocket to keep him from taking it back.

"I'll wait next door at the coffee shop," said Syrie, standing. "It doesn't seem like you two are finished with your discussion."

"It's quite all right, my sweet," said Osbert, reaching for her elbow to pull her back down to her seat. "As Churchill said, 'I like a man who grins when he fights.'" Then he returned to eating as if nothing had happened, but Duncan knew that blood would stay in the water.

"What are you doing here?" he asked Syrie.

"Osbert is financing my expansion." She used her wrist to push back a wisp of blonde hair.

He wondered why Syrie had warned him about Osbert if she was ready to do business with him herself, but that was not something they could talk about in front of him. "Osbert certainly has his finger in quite a few pies," said Duncan.

Osbert turned to Syrie. "The Seacrest's pie, too," he said. "We've just agreed in principle." He went back to eating without even looking at Duncan, and in the following silence the deal was done. Duncan had neither agreed nor disagreed but had let the deal wash over him.

"I was just talking to Chief Lovasco," said Syrie, stretching her feet under the table, causing Duncan to twist his body away. "He says they've confirmed that the foot the racers found on Saturday belongs to Marsilio."

"Belonged," corrected Duncan, and he looked over at the kitchen. Slocum would shed no tears for the man, who was known to be unfaithful to his sister.

"DNA come in?" asked Osbert, finally moving his plate aside and wiping his lips with his napkin.

"No," she said, pausing to scrunch her face up. "His head was pulled up in a flounder net this morning."

Duncan felt ill. "In the water all week and still identifiable? Not eaten away?"

"Dental records, I'm sure," said Osbert. "Teeth are tenacious little bastards."

"They're trying to figure out if he died during the storm … or not," said Syrie, as she played with the tiny edge of cobweb lace on her collar. "It seems the foot was sawed off at the ankle, not snapped off by a propeller."

"They used to tell the time of drownings by when the watches stopped," said Duncan, "but they're all waterproof now."

"He wasn't wearing a watch," said Osbert.

"How do you know that?" asked Duncan.

There was a dark silence during which Osbert picked up his cigar and put it back in its case. "It's what the man's wife told the police. It was in the paper. You do read, don't you? Or do you just play with eel heads?" He took his napkin off his lap and retrieved his stick. He turned to Syrie and gestured at the wall with it. "Shall we go next door for coffee?"

Syrie stood up by way of an answer and shook her clothes back in place.

Osbert rose like an iceberg. "I'll settle lunch on my way out,

Duncan, and I'll have papers sent over later today for you to look at. They're all made up."

All made up. Their partnership was not five minutes old, and Duncan hated him already. He stood to shake hands, and it felt like holding a mackerel. Syrie leaned across the table and kissed Duncan on the cheek. He felt her tongue on his skin, and then he felt it slide to his lips, which made him jerk back, bumping the table and spilling more of the soup. Syrie turned and flounced to the door, laughing to herself. He noticed one or two people turning their heads to look at them, and he quickly busied himself sopping up the soup. When he peeled away the thick layer of napkins, the varnish came off with it.

He stared at Osbert's perfectly suited back at the cashier's station by the door. Osbert removed a roll of bills from his pocket like plunder and was beginning to count out the money when he suddenly pitched forward and grabbed the counter. His walking stick fell to the ground with a loud clatter. Duncan could not see Osbert's expression, but he could guess. Right now, the soup must be burning through the lining of his stomach.

"Osbert!" Syrie shouted as he dropped to the floor, knees first, then forehead, before folding up on himself completely. The dog barked.

Slocum and the staff came running out from the kitchen. Marney called 911 on her cell phone, then stood next to Duncan, shaking. He held up his bowl. "Could I get some of this soup to go?" he asked, and she looked at him as if he had two heads. Off in the distance they heard the first siren. Slocum threw open the door to wave them down, and a wall of wind pushed into the restaurant, blowing Osbert's wad of ten-dollar bills around the room in a storm of money.

going to use Sloc's proof (8 copies) in a new product?

great scene! very very visual

seven

The contract landed on Duncan's desk later that afternoon, as promised, even while Osbert was still in the hospital having his stomach pumped.

"For your viewing pleasure." Beaky bowed from the hips, and as he bent forward his ferret slid off his shoulder and leaped to the desk. Duncan took a swipe, and it was gone in a flurry of fur. The air was heavily perfumed with ferret musk.

"I've got to hand it to Fingers," said Duncan. "It takes a lot of B.O. to overpower rotting fish." He cracked open the window and was instantly fixated by the blinding glare of the sun on the water. A trawler made a black shape against the light as it pulled into Petersen's Marina, surrounded by a white mist of gulls that had followed it in from the sea.

"Lovely, isn't it?" said Beaky.

"Yes," said Duncan, not expecting someone like Beaky to appreciate the beauty of anything other than money. "No need to wait. It's going to take a while."

Beaky picked up the ferret from the floor. "It would be a shame if all the pretty fishing boats started to disappear just because you won't sign the contract."

Beaky tucked Fingers in his jacket pocket and turned away. Duncan listened to his retreating steps on the stairs that led down to the factory floor, and above the din of the machinery he heard Beaky call up to him. "Leland! You have until tomorrow!"

Duncan started humming "Tomorrow" from *Annie*. Maybe he'd build a playlist around it for the factory. Then his problems would be over because they'd lock him up. He felt a strong pull to the window but resisted the urge and sat down at his desk, determined to tackle the contract. He arranged the manila envelope in the exact center of his desk. DUNCAN LELAND was penciled with precision on the envelope. He touched the "D" with the tip of his finger. The lead point had dug in deeply, like engraving on a tombstone. He pulled the contract out of its envelope and let his eyes wash over the words, which were typed in an unusual, severe font, but his brain could not process the information they were meant to convey. The more he focused, the more the words floated beyond his grasp, drifting about his mind like the wreckage of a foundered ship. Everything—the lines and paragraphs, the subheadings and punctuation, even the page numbers—seemed like sad, isolated units yearning to join together in some grand design. And yet they composed a peculiar beauty that made him forget for a moment his agonized situation.

He felt he was in one of those modern art museums Cora used to bring him to, where he understood nothing but left changed in spite of himself.

She was always so good for him that way, exposing him to the new and unusual, asking him to see the world with fresh goggles. She was a native New Yorker, a single Upper West Side child raised by her divorced mom, who'd become a therapist after Cora's dad abandoned them both to find fulfillment on an ashram in California in the late seventies. Cora had been finishing her own master's of social work degree at NYU when she met Duncan on campus. He was there to recruit students for lab experiments at Revlon. He gave her a bag of free makeup samples, and they became inseparable. She introduced him to foreign movies, exotic food, obscure books, alternative music, and other cultural goodies. Gift baskets for his brain, she called them, as if she were fattening up his intellect for marriage.

And what did she get out of their marriage other than managing his anxieties? She hadn't even gotten a baby, though she often told him how grateful she was that he'd brought her to live by the sea, so fully immersed in the natural world, so different from the one she grew up in. They were a good match that way, she'd said—she brought urban culture to the marriage; he brought the water. But now that she lived here, maybe there was nothing left for him to do.

"Enough." He shook off this dangerous heading and got down to business. He read what he could manage of the contract, then faxed a copy to Mallory Cole's law office and called to ask him to do a quick once-over. While he waited for him to respond, he stood at the open window and breathed in deeply. Next door was Petersen's Marina, which did not cater to the yachting crowd as other marinas in town did but serviced the commercial fleet, supplying ice and diesel and doing complete haul-outs. It had always been in a state of picturesque decay but lately seemed to be in unromantic decline, surrounded as it was by rotting pilings and sinking floats. At the dock, two pleasure fishing boats were in line to be pulled for the winter. It was not exactly a rush. Usually in September boat owners were clamoring to get out of the water before a nor'easter did the job for them, but last spring many of them couldn't afford to put their boats in for the season. So much unemployment, and yet no one could enjoy their free time. He watched Bear Petersen, grandson of the founder, supervise a lobster boat being run up on the ways to have her bottom scrubbed. The hull, dripping with water, was thick with sea vegetation and barnacles, and the boat seemed to groan with world weariness as it settled into its cradle. He wondered if Bear, who sometimes relaxed in a dress and heels in private, ever felt trapped in the family business. He wondered if the cross-dressing was a way of accepting it and rejecting it at the same time. He'd asked Cora what she thought about it once, and she'd only shrugged. "It fills a need."

He looked at his watch. "Come on, Mallory, call back already." Since he could not calm his mind with the view, he rifled through the bookshelf for something to distract him. Among the faded vinyl binders of maritime regulations, he found his father's old copy of *The Little Prince.* He let the book fall open in his hands, to a passage that was underlined twice: "If you want to build a ship, don't drum up people together to collect wood and don't assign them tasks and work, but rather teach them to long for the endless immensity of the sea."

His father used to read those words aloud to him, preparing him for when he'd be running the business. But he never went into specifics. How did one go about making an employee long for fertilizer? When the telephone rang, he picked up the receiver, which was redolent of fish, and he had to pry a hardened whiting scale from the plastic. He wondered if Annuncia had been poking around in his office again.

"Duncan," said Mallory, with barely suppressed laughter. "Rescue any gulls lately?"

"This week I'm just trying to save myself."

Mallory cleared his throat and put on a lawyerly voice. "Basically it says here that the garbage company can make unlimited deliveries of nitrogenous materials—at night—in exchange for a loan sufficient to carry Seacrest's through the next six months. If at the end of that time Seacrest's is unable to repay the principal, the company will be transferred to Osbert."

Duncan took off his glasses. "You know how it is around here. Should I sign it?"

"Depends on how desperate you are. There are a lot of risks. You'll have more processing and maybe more profit, but only if you can actually sell the new mix to the public. Would people really want to spread other people's garbage on their gardens?"

"Would I have to tell them what it was?"

Mallory whistled. "Maybe there's some wiggle-room in the truth-in-labeling laws."

"In the meantime, I'll have marketing come up with some other word for 'garbage.'"

"One more thing," said Mallory. "On page three, near the bottom? I'd get rid of that 'death clause' if I were you. Never get yourself in a situation where you're worth more to an investor dead than alive."

"True that," said Duncan. He'd seen the clause, a disturbing little proviso that Seacrest's would go to Osbert if something happened to Duncan—something like death. "I'll talk to him and call you back later."

"Screech!" said Mallory, in a bad imitation of a seagull, before hanging up in laughter.

Duncan dialed Osbert's cell phone number slowly, as if he were moving through mud.

"Leland," said Osbert, answering his phone himself, sounding as crisp as ever in his hospital bed. "Have you signed?"

"My lawyer says I have to cross out the death clause."

"Bosh," said Osbert. "It's all boilerplate, a standard inclusion to prevent you from killing yourself in order to keep the factory in family hands. What are you leaning on your lawyer for? You're the boss—you can do what you want."

"I can't do what I want because I don't know what I want."

"You do know," said Osbert. "Go deeper. The answer is there. Live, Leland—take a chance. Don't be afraid until you have to be. Beaky will pick up those papers tomorrow at noon."

Osbert hung up. After a few moments in which Duncan did not quite know where he was, he slid the unsigned contract back into the envelope and closed the metal clasp. He needed another opinion. If things fell apart and he lost the business to Osbert, he didn't want all the blame to fall on him. He slumped back in his chair and listened to Playlist #18 (early Stones and late Beatles, including some *Sergeant Pepper*) before locking up the office. Ringo's "Octopus's Garden" continued to echo in his brain, and he made a mental note to delete that song from the list. If he did not solve his company's financial situation, he would soon have plenty of time for projects like fine-tuning his music. It was about a week's worth of work, which was as far into the future as he could plan. Beyond that be sea monsters, as the ancient cartographers used to say when the world was small and flat.

"A board meeting," he blithely announced to Annuncia as he was leaving the plant with the contract in one hand and a one-gallon olive oil container in the other, but she would have none of that. She took one solid step sideways and blocked the metal door with her formidable self, waiting for an answer. With her bullet-shaped body draped in a red smock and topped with a snood, she looked like the red nun, one of the navigational buoys in the harbor. It was how he often thought of her, anyway. After his father's death, when Duncan's family expected that he'd return to Port Ellery to run Seacrest's, it was Annuncia who drove to New York to convince him that he could do it. It was Annuncia who'd then talked him into staying in Port Ellery when he realized, yes, he probably could do it, but he didn't want to. Once he was resigned to his fate, it was Annuncia who sat him down in the office and showed him how to navigate the turbulent currents of the business. More recently, she'd helped guide them through the renovation of the building and encouraged him to expand into retail.

But all those decisions had brought him and Seacrest's nearer to ruin. It was time to start seeking counsel elsewhere, even if it was only his mother.

"What's that in your hand there, Dun'n?" she said.

"Soup," he said. Duncan had asked Marney for the jellyfish soup because anything that could lift varnish off a table and stop a man dead in his tracks might have a few commercial applications. Jellyfish had become more abundant than ever due to warmer waters and the overfishing of their predators and competitors, crowding everything else out. If he could find a lucrative use for one of the species, he would have a constant supply, and the fishermen would be happy to have them gone from the waters. So little was known about them, nothing was impossible. For his current needs, he knew that jellyfish were inefficient as fertilizer because of the huge quantity needed to dehydrate into a single spoonful of dust, being 99 percent water as they were, but after seeing how they had exploded in Slocum's face and then produced a soup as strong as turpentine, he thought they might have potential for a solvent. After the ambulance had left with Osbert, Marney had funneled the pot of Slocum's jellyfish soup into an empty olive oil can for Duncan and poured the rest down the sink. "Better than Drano," she said as she pushed him out the back door, one step ahead of the health inspector. She'd been through this drill before.

Annuncia stared at the can as if she could see through steel. "The soup that about killed Osbert?"

"Shh," he said and put a finger to his lips.

"You don't intend to do yourself in, do you, Dun'n?"

"Not this way," he said. "I'm sort of a coward when it comes to gut-wrenching pain."

There followed a pointed silence during which Annuncia seemed to be contemplating his cowardice in all its manifestations, but she let it pass. "What's that in your other hand?"

He inspected the manila envelope as if he were surprised to find it in his possession. "Some paperwork."

"It's the contract from Osbert," she said. "Are you going to sign it and save us, or not?"

Wade, who had been heading toward the loading dock, stopped to pick up a broom and started mechanically sweeping around the few square feet in which they stood.

"It's not an either-or situation," said Duncan. "If I don't sign the agreement, there are still ways to save the business." He looked around the empty factory. The stainless steel tanks had stopped churning for the day, and the cement floor was wet from a rinsing. He looked at his watch. "Where is everyone? The shift isn't over yet."

"We got through early, and rather than let them sit on their hands for a half hour, I sent them down to the beach to pick up plastic crap. Don't change the subject. Tell me about this other 'or.' You have payroll for Friday?"

"To pay to have the beach cleaned? No wonder we're in trouble."

"Let me worry about whether the work gets done and when."

"What 'Nun is getting at," said Wade, who had stopped all pretense of sweeping and was now leaning on his push broom, "is that for things to stay the same, we gotta change. Think long. Like 'Nun here sending workers out to collect the plastic 'fore it taints the fishes." With that, he slapped his heart. "No fish, no fish guts, no Seacrest's."

"Survival means more than just the survival of the business," she said. "Who else but you can take the world's mess and transform it into something useful?"

"Annuncia, don't I have enough pressure right now without adding the weight of a world on me? I can't do everything."

"Do something," she said. "Look past the tip of your nose. As your dear mum would say, keep your hand steady on the tiller and your eye on the horizon."

"I'm trying to see dear mum right now," Duncan said. "If you'll just move aside."

"Why?" asked Wade. "She wouldn't take notice of the factory 'less you strapped a spinnaker on the roof and pushed the building into the sea to see how fast it'll go."

"And Nod," added Duncan. "He's on the board, too. I have my responsibilities."

"Your responsibilities are misplaced," Annuncia said. A worker, one of the few apparently not out gathering garbage off the beach, puttered toward them in a forklift, heading for the loading dock. Annuncia stepped aside to let the machine pass, and Duncan slid out the door.

"Go ahead, go talk to your 'board,'" she called. "But come back tomorrow with a signed contract, or none of us will be working by the end of the week."

Duncan wanted to point out that no one was working now, but he kept his mouth shut in order to make a smooth escape. He felt their eyes on his back as he climbed into the pickup and drove off. What was the point of pretending he was still deliberating? He knew he would sign the contract, and not just because Annuncia told him to but because there was no other way to save Seacrest's. Deep down, in spite of his ambivalence, he wanted to save it. Embarrassment was stronger than fear. He could not relinquish the company without a fight and still hold his head up in town. And maybe, just maybe, if he took care of one responsibility (Seacrest's), the other (his marriage) would fall into line. He felt lighter just thinking about it. In fact, the farther he drove away from Seacrest's, the better he felt about its future, so much so that he decided he would no longer wait for Cora to call. He would risk rejection and call her to discuss their own future. He fumbled for his cell and tried her office number.

"Duncan! Oh, what a relief. You've called."

"I think we're saved," he said, positively giddy.

"We are?"

"I've found a temporary partner for Seacrest's. He wants to process some garbage in exchange for enough money to carry us over until we launch the new fertilizer line."

He waited for her to be happy for him, but when she finally spoke, it was in a voice touched with repressed rage that took the wind out of his sails. "Seacrest's?" she said. "What about us? You haven't seen or talked to me in three weeks. Three long, important weeks, and you don't even ask about the biggest thing in our lives."

Duncan started bailing with both buckets. "I thought you were supposed to call me when you were ready to have me back." The light turned red, and when he stopped short a car screeched to a stop behind him. "Can I? Come home?"

"Home?" He heard her take some breaths. Was she crying? "I don't think that's a good idea. I need to relax, and you'll just want to throw a panic party. You're getting me very upset right now as it is."

"I know, I've been such a wreck. I thought I was going to lose Seacrest's. But that's all going to change."

"I'm sorry you're having such a rough time of it," she said. "But do you really have nothing to say? *Nothing* to ask me?"

What? *What?* He'd already asked to come home. What else was there?

He heard her sigh. He imagined her sitting in her office at the back of their house, a cozy room with teal curtains that let the sun shine through like water. She would be at her desk. Their orange cat, Dabs, would be curled up on the chair opposite her, like a reclusive client. Before he'd called and interrupted her life, Cora would have been making notes about the last client or reviewing them for the next. Behind her on the wall was a framed print of a quotation by the Spanish philosopher José Ortega y Gasset, which more or less acted as her family counseling mission statement:

> The type of human being we prefer reveals the contours of our heart. Love is an impulse which springs from the most profound depths of our beings, and upon reaching the visible surface of life carries with it an alluvium of shells and seaweed from the inner abyss. A skilled naturalist, by filing these materials, can reconstruct the oceanic depths from which they have been uprooted.

He was the alluvium she kept turning over in her hands. "What do you think it says about me that I'm with you?" she had asked early in the summer while they were waiting in the clinic's office. "It says you like a project," he'd said, with a laugh. She didn't laugh back. "When we have a baby, Duncan, that will be my project. Our project. Think you can stand that?"

He'd squeezed her hand and pulled her close. "I can't wait." Soon afterward, though, the business had started going down and so had he. He needed Cora, but she was immersed in the minute changes of her hormones and could not be reached. He'd always depended on her to tell him about himself. Now she wanted him to figure it out on his own. It was like a pop quiz at school, only he didn't even know what the subject was.

The light turned green, and he lurched forward.

"Okay, never mind," she said in defeat. "Tell me about this garbage. Did you do a feasibility study or risk assessment?"

"There's no time," he said, a little sick to find himself sounding like his mother. "I have to make payroll this week or go under. I can't draw on our own money to pay for it again."

"No! Don't even think about it. We need every penny now more than ever."

"Then let me get the business stable so we can concentrate on us. Isn't that what you wanted me to do when you sent me away? Clear the decks?"

"I thought you were going to Slocum's for a few days so I could relax. Now I hear you're living at your mom's." He heard her shuffle papers. "Although that might not be a bad thing. Revisiting the past might help you step into the future."

He pulled over to the side of the road because he could not keep driving and have this conversation at the same time. He forgot to signal, and the driver behind him leaned on his horn as he passed. A gray Mini Cooper. He recognized Beaky Harrow and felt a damp chill run through his body. What did everyone want from him?

"Can we talk about this in person?"

There was a hollow sound on the other end of the line, and he thought she'd walked away from the call. "Duncan," she began again, a little tearily, "right now I just can't take care of you. You

have to take care of yourself. As for me, not that you've asked ..."
And then she paused. In a swift, terrifying moment he wondered
if someone had told her about Syrie kissing him at lunch that day.
Or seen her foot on his at the Boat Club. Then, in an even more
terrifying moment, he wondered if she had a Syrie—a male, virile
Syrie, willing and able to do what Duncan could not—and that was
what she wanted to tell him. It was a confession he did not want to
hear. He pressed on his horn.

"Someone's telling me to move," he said over the sound. "I'll
call you later." And then he clicked the phone shut.

He rested his head on the steering wheel and felt his sweat
against the cold plastic. A truck rumbled by full of empty clam shells
from the processor, and when it hit a pothole a shell bounced out
and landed on his windshield with a sharp crack. He sat upright and
touched the damage, a sparkling circle of shattered glass the size of
a dime. "One more thing to repair."

Two of his employees walked past the pickup and stared at him.
He smiled and waved cheerfully at them as if nothing was the matter,
then started his engine and pulled out into the traffic. He could not
stay where he was.

eight

Duncan was so turned around by his conversation with Cora that he was suddenly unsure of his ability to navigate. "Water on my right, water on my right," he said to himself as he drove, a silly mantra when all he had to do was stay on Shore Road. While he lamented the shipwreck that was his marriage, he mourned the equally disastrous changes in his old route. It was no longer the road of his blissfully rudderless youth, when this long stretch was the somewhat wild and untamed curve of the bay, dotted with signs of warning—SWIM AT YOUR OWN RISK and CAUTION: STRONG TIDES—which had only encouraged recklessness. This area had once been so sparsely settled that as kids he and Nod could walk the few miles from their house to their dad's office without ever taking their feet off the rocks. Often that meant racing to get to town before an advancing tide forced them up onto the civilization of the sidewalk. How they had loved the damp band of earth that was neither wholly sea nor entirely land, a constantly changing landscape that offered their prepubescent souls new, exciting dangers to overcome. They had felt themselves gifted at avoiding the perils of the seaweed slicks; they had leaped across the cracks and crevices with ease, even grace, and had waded unafraid through tide pools full of barnacles and crabs. They had stepped over lobster traps and avoided the many minefields of trash. They were masters of their world, demigods of the water's edge.

But their infinite kingdom was gone. They'd be arrested for trespassing if they tried that today, if it was even possible to climb over, under, and around all the new docks and fences. The shoreline had been rapidly built up over the recent years, and now, as fast as it had all gone up, it was coming down. He passed the unfinished "Lightkeeper's House," as the developer called it, a plywood mansion with a fake lighthouse attached. The protective plastic that had once covered the raw wood had blown away in shreds, waving like battle standards. Another ruin in the making, like so many others along the stretch, abandoned during construction due to the homeowner's or builder's financial apocalypse. The wrecks were signs of a lost civilization, like pagodas in the jungles, soon to be smothered with vines and inhabited by gangs of monkeys.

He stopped by the side of the road, between two houses where there was still a window to his old world, and got out of the truck. He put one foot on the guardrail and looked out at the water, which rose and fell as methodically as a breathing chest. Rheya was out there, rowing her dory listlessly around and around, as if she could not rest until all the parts of her husband were together again.

A gray Mini Cooper drove by, and Beaky waved from inside his little shell of metal.

"Leave me alone!" Duncan shouted as it disappeared down the road. Would this be his life if he signed the contract, constantly being watched and supervised? What would be his life if he didn't sign?

He got back in the truck and sped off, turning wide onto Cean Avenue, his mother's street. Years ago, long before he was born, it was Ocean Avenue, but the "O" had cracked off the end of its hand-painted sign, so it became Cean Avenue first by custom, then by law. It was pronounced *keen*, as to wail loudly. He turned into his mother's driveway, killed the ignition, and sat. He closed his eyes. Over the sound of the surf slapping the rocks, he heard his mother's voice, as sharp and piercing as a gull's, carping at poor Nod down by the water. Duncan pulled himself out of the truck, taking with him the manila envelope and the tin gallon of soup.

He paused in front of the house. Usually he would get to the backyard by the wraparound porch, but he and Nod had just stored all the lawn furniture on it before the fall winds arrived to blow them away. Instead, he used the ratway, a narrow path squeezed in between the house and the neighbor's high stone wall. Zoning would not allow a house to be built that close to the property line today, but there was so much about the structure that was grandfathered in, it might as well be a boat in dry dock for all that it conformed to modern building code. Even the porch railings, which canted inward like a ship's rails, were more nautical than domestic.

The ratway was overhung by hairy evergreens, casting him in a green underwater light. The trees had been planted on the other side of the wall decades ago by the abutters and left by subsequent owners as a barrier against the irregular life of the Lelands. On his left, open latticework concealed the crawl space under the porch, and he kept his eyes averted for fear of spotting furry things creeping among the terra cotta towers of flowerpots and stacks of storm windows, beyond which lay the foundation of the house, the crude heavy stones upon which all the rest depended, and upon which the old house had teetered during gales, always—amazingly—managing to set itself right in the end. And behind that wall of stone, in the cellar, lay Great-Uncle Fern's casks of mulberry wine, on which his mother depended. Beneath Duncan's feet, the path crunched with layers of sea glass, the dumping place of a century's worth of family beachcombing. As a hobby, Cora made whimsical mobiles from sea glass and sometimes scoured for pieces from the path because the supply on the beach was so rapidly dwindling. It had once seemed an unending source of material, but now, between the change to plastic and the ban on dumping, sea glass, that perfect collaboration between man and nature, was becoming a relic of the past.

Well, weren't they all?

At the end of the ratway, a stone arch spanned the house and the wall, and he had to duck to get out from under it. It wasn't until he stood up straight in the open expanse of the backyard that he realized he'd been holding his breath. He felt dizzy as he looked around. It was getting late, but the sky was blue, and a rising sea breeze moved through the branches, flickering the sunlight in yellows and greens. The season was changing, and it was change at its most beautiful—unlike his life, which was change at its lowest ebb. Keeping to the edge of the yard, he passed the grotto made by his Great-Aunt Hilda in her youth, where she had pressed seashells, fish bones, and seaweed into concrete, creating a fossilized ocean cave, complete with hidden piping that dripped water from cement stalactites. He paused at the still, black pool full of pine needles, where insects made ripples and clouds of gnats hovered over the water. Off to the side sat a streaked verdigris marine monster with a scaled tail, webbed toes, and a somewhat human head from whose nostrils spurted water in the summer, when someone remembered to turn it on from the house. Duncan reached in his pocket and tossed in a penny. "Cora," he said out loud, and then headed for the Drop.

At the top of the stairs was the last remaining mulberry tree, old and twisted and hanging by a root-toe to the land as it leaned precariously toward the sea. In late summer, the tree rained buckets of treacly berries to the ground, where they attracted yellowjackets and birds before being tracked into the house, darkening the floors and tinting the rugs. One tree could not produce enough to make more wine, but his mother was able to scavenge a few quarts for a cloying jelly that she and Nod lathered on toast. Duncan looked down at the beach, and there they were, messing with the inflatable's outboard motor. He reached for the iron railing to start his short descent down the Drop, and with each footfall on the loose stones, bits of rubble tumbled to the beach below. Halfway down, a gnarly wild cherry tree had sprouted from the crevice of the rocks and served as a newel post. He wondered how it stayed alive in such inhospitable earth. As it was, it was twisted and contorted, a third the size of its kin near the road. "What a difference a good home environment makes," Cora once noted. As he neared the bottom, he passed the spray zone where seaside goldenrod and beach pea held the earth in place. Judging from the visible tops of the stone pilings where Uncle Lloyd had kept up his herring weir, it was mid-tide. Duncan wondered how the market for herring was these days. He had to start thinking of what he would do for work if he could not make Seacrest's fly.

Chandu met Duncan at the bottom of the steps, and the two of them walked gingerly along the shingled beach toward his family, who did not look up. They were near the jetty, whose ramp was hanging limp in the water with no float attached. The rubber inflatable was beached because of it and seemed to be going nowhere, if their carrying-on was any indication. Around the crescent tip of beach, Duncan heard the rattle of chains and the sound of moorings being pulled at the Boat Club basin. A screaming seagull passed overhead and released a mussel, shattering the shell and splattering its occupant on the rocks. A half dozen gulls arrived to fight over it. "There's never any shortage of animals willing to share in the profits of others, eh Chandu?"

The dog whined in response, and Duncan saw that his front paw was tangled in fishing line. As he stopped to free him of it, he took in the sheer amount of garbage that had washed up lately. Detergent bottles, lobster buoys, beach chairs—the tide of garbage rose and rose and never seemed to ebb. Annuncia told tales about a flotilla of plastic trash the size of Texas rolling around in the South Pacific, and seeing how much there was just on this small patch of land he could well believe it. "A million seabirds," he'd heard her scold a boat captain recently. "One hundred thousand marine mammals and sea turtles, dead by ingesting our plastic every year. If I hear again that you've lost a deckload of fish bins and you don't go back to get them, you're going to join them."

Another satisfied Seacrest's client.

"There you go, old boy," he said, and he held up the filament for the dog to smell. Duncan remembered how he and Nod used to string line they'd scavenge off the beach with fish vertebra they'd collect at the high-tide line and make presents of them for their mother. She wore them still.

"Duncan, dear," his mother called. "Stop talking to the dog and come help us!"

Nod stood unsteadily in the rubber dinghy, which was half in the water, half out, with the outboard motor end in. His mother stood on the rocky beach and directed Nod's pulls on the starter rope. Duncan had a moment of déjà vu, remembering this scene from years before, except it was his mother and father bickering over the motor. Nod should be arguing with a wife about the boat, not his mother. Duncan tried to remember if this was what his parents' relationship had been like, and if his father had been forced into a life of racing through her thwarted ambitions. He seemed not to care so much about winning but liked being out on the water and enjoyed the camaraderie of other sailors. She was the one who insisted he come home to sail every day at lunchtime for practice, and he was so good-humored and eager to please her, he usually did, through most all types of weather. It was on one of those sails he had disappeared forever.

"If we knew what was wrong with it, we could get it started," said Nod. He kicked an empty Clorox bottle that served as the inflatable's bailer.

"Duncan, you get in there and give it a good pull," his mother said.

Duncan did not move. He was mesmerized by the sight of a bird eating another creature. "I think that's a crow eating a baby crow."

His mother looked over at the gruesome scene and sighed. "Every mother struggles with the impulse to both raise her young and eat them."

"They do?"

"Duncan, dear, will you please snap out of it and help get this started?"

"Remember that tame crow that used to take spoons out of the kitchen and hide them in the boat shed?" said Nod. "Maybe they're related."

"I can't pull any better than Nod," Duncan said. "I came down here to talk to the both of you about this proposal for Seacrest's. I've found a way to keep its head above water for a few more months, but there are risks."

"This is no time, Duncan."

"We've got to get this started first," said Nod, clearing his throat.

"Tighten that screw there, Nod." His mother squatted down and pointed a finger at the motor.

Duncan was jealous of the freedom that insanity gave his mother and brother. They didn't have to worry about the future of Seacrest's or, for that matter, any future at all. Still, he had to make an effort to make them understand, but he could see he was not going to get anywhere until the dinghy was working.

"Is the gas can full?" he asked.

"Of course it is." Nod picked up the red can, which was attached to the motor by black tubing, and shook it to prove there was gas. But there was no sound. Nod unscrewed the cap and looked in. "Huh," he said.

"You carried the gas can down from the house without realizing it was empty?" Duncan asked. There were some men, like his brother, who should be protected by law, like fish and game. Was it any wonder he still lived at home? Then Duncan remembered that he was living at home, too. Was this how people saw him? Incompetent and not fully aware of the world around him?

"Duncan, dear," said his mother. "Run back up to the house and get the other can out of the shed. Nod has got to retrieve the float."

"There is no other can," said Nod. "I left it at the gas station."

"Someone found the float?" asked Duncan.

"The Club called," said his mother. "It washed up where they want to store their ramp. Why don't you go siphon some gas out of your truck?"

"No," he said. If he agreed to it this time, they'd never get gas from the outside world again. "It's siphon-proof."

"Nothing is siphon-proof," said his mother. "If it can go in, it can come out."

"We might as well wait until tomorrow," said Nod. "By the time he returns with gas it'll be too dark to bring the float back. I need to get enough for the car, too. I'm planning a trip."

"Read this," said Duncan, handing his mother the manila envelope. She pulled the papers out and gave them a quick glance. In the dim light she seemed younger by decades, and he had a vision of how she appeared to him when he was a kid, when her hair was bright red and her face had the rough beauty of a woman too distracted to cultivate her looks. She was very much out in the world then, going to stores, parties, even traveling a bit. She had friends; she had a life outside of sailboat races. Normal, he always thought, but what did he know? He was her child, and there was no distance between them yet for him to question such a thing. Looking at her now, though, he remembered how her eyes, large and bluish-green, were always a mystery, the way her pupils never stopped moving and never settled, not even on him.

"What's the problem?" she said as she put the papers back in the envelope. "You need money and he wants to give you money."

"Osbert Marpol is not the most virtuous man I've ever met."

She handed him back the envelope. "As J. P. Morgan said, you can do business with anyone, but you can only sail a boat with a gentleman. I wouldn't sail with this man, but you're just doing business."

"Mom, you don't sail with anyone," said Duncan, folding the envelope into the pocket of his windbreaker. "Does that gas can have a filter?"

Nod looked in the opening and nodded. "Why?" he asked.

"Let's fire up Slocum's soup du jour. It's pretty volatile stuff. You never know."

Nod and his mother agreed. One of the few things he appreciated about his family was that they never questioned even the most absurd comments or actions. If Duncan believed that soup could combust, well then, go to it. He popped the cap of the tin can and peeked in, sloshing it around to see how many solids were in it. But it didn't slosh. It *was* a solid.

"Or not," said Duncan. "Nod, do you have your splicing knife?"

Nod unclipped his knife from his belt and tossed it.

Duncan flipped the instrument open and poked holes around the bottom of the container with the marlinspike while his mother and brother stared at the engine.

"I guess I'll drive out tomorrow and get that gas can," said Nod, and he began to put things back to rights on the boat.

Their mother stood up straight and wrung out the tip of her braid, which had dragged in the water. "Coming back up with us, Duncan?"

Duncan stuck the blade in the perforated can and started slicing the metal from hole to hole, and as he did, it crumbled in his hands. The soup must have begun to burn through the can before it solidified. "I think I'll stay here a bit and watch the sun go down."

While Duncan continued to work on the can, Nod and his mother pulled the inflatable up the beach and tied it to a metal eye cemented into a rock. Duncan freed the hunk at last and held the amber substance in his hands. It was not sticky, and it didn't even smell.

"Knife," said Nod, and Duncan handed it to him. He was about to turn away when he stopped. "That's a great new video of you on YouTube with an eel finger puppet."

"Oh, no," said Duncan. "Not that." Someone must have shot a phone video during his fight with Osbert. He reached into his pocket and felt around. He had taken his jacket off when he got back to work without emptying his pockets, and now the little head was rank. He let his thumb rub up against the teeth before tossing it overhand into the water. As soon as it broke through the surface, dark shapes came swimming toward it, and it disappeared.

"Noddy, wait," his mother said. "I forgot to record the water temp for the Log." She took a small thermometer tied to a piece of string out of her shirt pocket and dipped it in the water. "Fifty-three degrees," she said. "Still warm. Hmm." She stood for a moment studying the instrument like an oracle at Delphi, then put the thermometer back in her pocket. "Don't stand there thinking too much, Duncan. You know how you get." And then she and Nod headed for the stairs. Chandu swayed slowly behind them, in hopes of dinner.

"No, how do I get?" he asked, but she didn't look back.

Duncan turned the solidified hunk over in his hands. He looked up at the seagulls flocking in uncoordinated groups across the sky, flying to the islands where they slept. Off in the distance, he could see the lights coming on around Port Ellery, doubling itself in the water's reflection and making it twice as lovely. He wondered if he called Cora whether she would pick up the phone again, but he knew it was hopeless. He'd blown his chance. A wave of yearning for her washed over him, as intense as the first moment he'd fallen in love.

He hit the hunk of solidified jellyfish against a rock a few times as if there were some answer to his life to be found inside, but it did not break. It didn't even chip. He batted it around a bit as the tide continued to recede, leaving behind the garbage of modern civilization. Almost all of it was plastic, which would never change, never go away, only keep building up and up until they were trapped alive, living and dying in an indestructible world of their own making.

He held the amber block in his two hands and wondered.

nine

Whitecaps rolled in sideways from the ocean, little waves hello from a storm tossing around in the Bahamas. A chill wind cast a mist over Seacrest's beach—not enough to make Duncan close his office window but enough to soften the world. It might be mean weather for September, but inside he was radiating a tropical front. Everything had gone along swimmingly since he'd grabbed the lifeline from Osbert a couple of weeks before. In that time he'd been able to convince himself, through the usual means of daydreams and self-delusion, that his temporary yoke of indebtedness was going to work out just fine. All signs pointed to Yes: The eel puppet video had become a darling of the global-warmites and was actively drumming up business thanks to Nod, who created a YouTube account linking the gull and the eel back to the company. Orders for the spring season were pouring in from nurseries around the country for Go Kelp! And once these retailers were customers, the sales department could hook them on the new hybrid fertilizer, Surf 'n' Turf, when it was introduced, the thought of which got Duncan so excited he trotted downstairs to the factory floor to be part of the fun. His marketing consultant was even considering putting Duncan's picture on the label, but they could not do anything at all until they got the formula stabilized. The garbage—or *garpost,* as they agreed to call it—arrived in the middle of the night, and Osbert's employees took care of it all. Duncan never saw Osbert, who seemed to have crawled back under whatever rock he'd come from. By morning, the grinder and emulsion had done its job, turning garbage into slurry ready to be dried. That day's batch had just finished coming out of the dehydrator, and Annuncia was beaming at the contents of the barrel like a parent at a newborn. Duncan joined her, and they sighed together in contentment.

"To create the Surf 'n' Turf mix, I decided to keep the finished lines separate until the last minute for better quality control," she said and clasped a fistful of light gray powder. "So this is pure garpost."

"I like it." Duncan smiled. "I like it even before we blend it with seaweed. There's something special about it."

"Then," said Annuncia, letting the powder drift back to the barrel, "if regulators think to have a closer look, it'll be easier to deep-six the garpost if it's kept separate."

"What could the regulators find?" asked Duncan. "What is there for us to worry about?"

"No worries." She took a rag out of her smock pocket and wiped her hands clean. "It's just hard to keep the nitrogen level under control sometimes. We just want to keep our ducks in a row."

"These ducks," said Duncan. "Are they … legal?"

She put her rag back in her pocket and turned to him. "Don't fear change, Dun'n. Change can save you. When was the last time you talked to Cora?"

"I'm not sure what that has to do with anything," he said, but under her gaze he continued talking. "She needs a little more space."

"Space?" she said, staring at him. "Seems a funny time for space."

She delivered this in her flat, uninflected tone, difficult to interpret. Whatever it was she meant, she did not wait for a response—not that he had one—as she flipped on a generator and turned her back on him. He watched her recede down a corridor, toward Wade and his clipboard. Duncan absently dipped his hand in the barrel, letting the smooth powder run through his fingers like sands of time. He put it to his nose.

"Amazing. Barely smells like garbage."

~

An hour later, in the truck, he felt a momentous headache coming his way. He turned off the iPod, which had cycled to PLAYLIST #16, made during his Philip Glass period, which sounded like a piano being pushed down the stairs. Was his life so ordered when he'd made that list a few years ago that he could so easily absorb chaos? He swerved slightly to avoid a plastic trash bag that had fallen into the street. It was pick-up day, and downtown was littered with garbage. Most of it, including the trash bags themselves, was plastic packaging. What was needed in this world was a product that could stand up to use and then dissolve to no harm in a damp landfill.

Jellyfish, along with whatever Slocum had added to the soup, might just be the raw material to make that happen. Duncan had sent the hunk of solidified soup to his old college roommate, Trevor, at the state lab, and he was titillated enough to ask for more samples to play with. Duncan and Slocum were going to the beach at low tide that afternoon to gather ingredients to make another batch of "soup."

But first he had to drop off his truckload of donations for Josefa. People had been leaving all sorts of things at the plant for Kelp and the other rescued seagulls: Cases of sardines, medical supplies, stuffed animals, and, most important, checks. Leaf peepers swung through town to see the beach where Kelp had been saved, with hopes to meet Duncan, the gull's savior. Wade kept them out of the factory but profited from them by selling photocopied, handwritten directions to Josefa's for $2.00 a pop. "A public service," he called it, and in a way it was. The city's streets had been laid out in the 1700s on top of mule paths, then randomly marked as one-ways, so getting into the center of downtown was a challenge even for natives. Duncan wished he had one of those maps now as he found himself on multiple dead-ends, often driving against the traffic as he tried to navigate the inner world of Port Ellery, a grim corrective to its public face of beaches and clam shacks. Narrow streets rose up sharply from the water, joined at the top to create a high mound of old brick buildings. Altitude had protected them from the sea over the years, but the salted wind and reflected sun had aged them. A wet day like this gave them a dark luster. Josefa lived on the other side of the hill, where the newer housing—meaning built sometime in the last century—looked older still. Vinyl clapboards were chipped and bent back, exposing foil innards, and satellite dishes sprung from eaves like warts. Dirt yards were landscaped with swing-less playsets, and the only color in the neighborhood came from plastic flowers at the Madonna bathtub shrines. As he circled the streets, lace curtains opened, then closed, and he felt himself being scrutinized. With some sense of accomplishment, at last he pulled up to Josefa's, a single-family home that was this side of complete dilapidation and had the acrid smell of penned birds. The lawn was white with droppings. On the locked, chain-link gate, there was a sign: SHH: KELP IS SLEEPING. Josefa was nowhere to be seen, but Duncan heard her dogs barking inside. In the course of looking for sick gulls, she often picked up other needy animals, especially in the weeks after Labor Day when the summer people left, abandoning their pets. She found homes for them all eventually, but this time of year she still had a full house of dogs, cats, cockatiels, guinea pigs, and even a ferret. He thought of Beaky Harrow's ferret and shuddered. When he climbed down from the pickup, he noticed a half dozen cats sitting in the branches of a tree, as solid as sandbags, looking him over.

He took his cell phone out of the zippered pocket of his windbreaker and dialed Josefa. She opened the upstairs window, and even though they were only twenty feet apart they continued to talk on the phone. "Mrs. Delaney called to say you were on the way," she said. "So did Mr. Potts."

"And then you locked the gate?"

"Oops," she said. "No ... forgot. They won't leave us alone."

"They?"

"Kelp's fans ... dear souls. Money's pouring in through the website. If this keeps up ... I'm going to have my dream. A proper seagull rescue home." She looked wistfully down at the yard. A blinding white cockatiel came up behind her with a flurry of wings and settled on the windowsill. Josefa did not believe in cages in the house, and even the ferret ran free.

"I have money for you, too," said Duncan. "Does that let me in?"

"Goody," she said, and she clicked off the phone. She brushed the cockatiel back into the house with her arm and closed the window.

As he waited for her to come down, he examined the yard. A few gulls were in cages, but most of the others were just limping around, dragging a wing or two behind them, trying to maneuver around the piles of flotsam Josefa had assembled over the years. It was a maze of buoys and lobster pots, tangles of driftwood and buckets of sea glass. There was a mountain of seine nets—ghost nets, she called them, the ones that floated loose to entangle porpoises and diving gulls. She took what she could off the beaches so they could not be washed back out again, then found homes for them during tomato season as trellises.

The door to the house opened in an explosion of dogs who stormed the gate. Two little ones still clung on as Duncan stepped inside, his arms full of cases of sardines. Josefa pushed the dogs back with her foot as she latched the gate again. "What are you wearing?" asked Duncan.

She pulled the bottom edge of her baby-blue sweatshirt out so Duncan could admire the words Go Kelp! superimposed over a soaring gull.

"Nice advertising for both of us," said Duncan. "I'll sponsor the next batch."

"Look who's talking money," said Josefa.

"It's nice having money again. I just hope it stays this way. You're doing pretty well yourself." He set down the sardines and pulled a wad of envelopes out of his pocket, filled with checks.

Josefa took the envelopes and splayed them out like a hand of cards before putting them in her back pocket. "My daughter, Lavinia ... the architect? Wants to come home ... make her name by designing my 'facility,' as she calls it. She sees a white building with arched wings to create shade for the outdoor cages."

"Seems like a lot of design for a place gulls will come to die."

"You'll be glad for good design ... when your time comes.

Maybe it'll be all that matters." She pushed the dogs back into the house so she and Duncan could move the supplies in from the truck without them running away. "We'll even have a crematorium. No more chute funerals."

"It's all about disposal, isn't it?" He carried the sardines through the yard to the storage shed while Josefa brought bags in from the truck. He put the boxes down and picked up a sign—WOODEN BUOYS, $10.00. "Since when have you started to sell your collection?"

"When people started to buy it," she said, pawing through a bag of stuffed animals. "Selling eel, too." She pointed to a white five-gallon bucket up on a cage, out of reach of the dogs. Scrawled on the bucket were the words EEL PUPPETS—AS SEEN ON TV, 2 FOR $5.00.

"Gross," said Duncan, peeking in. "Old, dried-up eel heads."

"You made them a hot commodity. I get them for free down at the dock ... dry them out in the sun. Kids love them. The heads don't hardly smell after a while." She picked one up and gave it a good sniff, but there was no trusting a nose that lived with that many animals. She put it down and showed him a box of white and gray feathers. "Their favorite is still seagull feathers." She lowered her voice. "I say they're all from Kelp."

"How is my boy?"

"Oh ... he's fine."

"Can I see him?"

"Duncan, when you've seen one seagull ... you've seen them all."

This was not like Josefa. Usually she bombarded him with the minute differences between individuals. He looked over by the fence, and in the finest of her cages was a gull and a thickly lettered sign reading KELP.

"There he is," he said, and walked toward him.

"Oh ... Duncan," she said, then turned to busy herself with creating order in the shed.

Duncan squatted next to the cage and greeted the bird, which stood in profile, looking rather noble with its blunt beak. He thought of the bird's beginning, its dramatic break out of its isolating shell to discover itself in a cozy nest with other young gulls, with doting parents who brought food, and, in time, independence, showing it how to lift its wings and leave that nest, off to lead the life of a bird, floating over land and sea, swooping like an angel. To think that a creature so intricate and grand could be brought down by a lowly piece of plastic.

"Hi, Kelp," he said. The bird looked at him with its yellow eye, turning its head from side to side to bring him into its vision, appraising him with no recognition. Some gratitude. It moved a step closer to the wire and tilted its head with a look that read: *Food?* When it saw that Duncan had none, it turned its back. Its feathers were dirty, and the injured wing still hung limp by its side. There was not much that could be done for these injured birds. If they weren't already in shock when they were picked up, aggressive treatment might stress them into it, a point from which very few returned. Sometimes the only thing to do was to give them a quiet place to wait it out and hope they would heal themselves, which seemed to be the ticket for Kelp's head. The area around the beak where the six-pack holder had dug in was completely healed over. In fact, the feathers had even grown in ... Duncan considered the wing hanging by its side and thought back to when he held the bird under his arm. He was sure the bad wing had been on the left. This gull's injured wing was the right. He stood up and turned to Josefa.

"That's not the gull I saved."

"Isn't it?" she asked, continuing to stack boxes.

"No," he said. "It's not. Unless he healed one wing and then broke the other."

She put her finger to her lips, leaving her work to join him by the cage. She looked around and spoke in a whisper. "I have something to tell you, Duncan. It didn't heal … Kelp died."

Duncan looked at the bird and felt a silly twinge of sadness. Even though he knew the chances were slim, they were chances nonetheless, and now they were gone. "Then who's that under the sign that says 'Kelp'?"

"Let's call him … Kelp the Second. You have to swear, Duncan … not a word. People will lose enthusiasm. I won't ever get the new place."

"You're lying?" Duncan asked. "About a stupid seagull?"

"People have gotten very attached … no one can know." She reached her hand through the cage, and the gull pecked at it. "I'm on the alert for gulls that look like Kelp … or can be made to look like Kelp. I'm going to need one in a few weeks that's only a little injured … so I can tidy him up and set him free. I've talked to the mayor about calling it Kelp Day. A national TV station wants to cover it."

"Josefa, I'm sort of surprised."

"Why? A little lie … to benefit an entire species? It's not like I'm taking the money to go live in Aruba. Keeping Kelp 'alive' is going to help everyone. New clean housing, medicine, veterinary care … a flight cage … all the things I could never afford. Hard to be in a position to want to help … only to have your hands tied by lack of money. We'll bring seagull rescue to a new level. I have a crew of volunteers now who search the beaches and help … feed and clean. I've been swimming hard to keep up with the tide … now I want to float in with it."

Duncan put his hands in his pockets and made fists. Of all the people he knew, Josefa had seemed the most honest and trustworthy. What did it say about the human species if even she could be tempted by money and fame? "It's the thin edge of the wedge, Josefa."

"Think about the greater good … speaking of which." She

turned away, back to the storage bin, and took out a lumpy trash bag. A webbed claw broke through the plastic. "Could you dump this at Seacrest's?"

"No!" Duncan said. "With all those tourists hanging around waiting for me to rescue another gull, you want me to dispose of one?"

"Two," she said. "It was a bad day. That's why I put the 'closed' sign up ... so I could move bodies around. Go ahead. Do it after closing. Who's to know?"

"I'll know. And lately everything that I know, the world soon knows. I couldn't even drive here today without a constant report on my progress. I can't do it."

And yet he followed Josefa out of the yard and through the gate to his pickup, where she dropped the bag in the cargo area. "Duncan, I've never seen a man fret so much over the silliest things ... it's a couple of dead gulls. Give them a useful afterlife."

"Josefa, I'm worried enough about what's going in the mix as it is. It's not all coffee grinds, eggshells, and apple peels. Annuncia says the nitrogen is spiking like a slaughterhouse floor, and a few chicken bones wouldn't cause that." He looked around and lowered his voice. "I worry, you know, it being Osbert, that there are things that shouldn't be there."

"Such ... as?" she asked.

"What if he's looking for a place to dispose of bodies? Think of Marsilio. How does a simple drowning pull a man apart like that?"

"Oh, Duncan ... you are a suspicious bugger. Marsilio probably just met his end with a clean chop of the boat propeller. You go from oblivion to paranoia ... don't you have any middle ground?"

"Something is going on. This night delivery thing, for one. If it were all above board, it wouldn't have to be done in the dark."

"Nonsense," she said. "Osbert's company gathers garbage during the day and disposes of it at night. Simple." She turned to go back inside, then stopped. "How are you … and Cora doing?"

"Why does everyone keep asking me that?"

"Winter's coming … time to hunker down with your mate."

Duncan looked down at his feet, and they seemed a long way off. "I'm not sure she wants to hear from me. We haven't talked in a while. I think … I think there's someone else." He looked at Josefa to watch her reaction, and he thought he saw a flash of knowledge cross her face.

"If you don't ask, you won't know."

"That's it. I don't want to know. 'What the eye doesn't see, the heart doesn't grieve over,' as Uncle Torkle used to say."

His wife, Aunt Bert, had cherished her yellow parakeet, Tim, and because of this, Uncle Torkle checked its cage every morning before Aunt Bert woke up. Once every couple of years, he'd find it on its back with the little feet sticking up. Then he'd just pick up the cage, say he was bringing the bird to the office for the day, and come home with a new yellow parakeet. He did this throughout their entire thirty-eight years of marriage. Aunt Bert believed she had the world's longest-lived parakeet, but Torkle intercepted her letters to Guinness. Tim finally died for good soon after Torkle died, there being no one to keep up the pretense. Aunt Bert bought herself a green parakeet to replace them both.

When Duncan told this story to Cora years before, thinking it was a touching example of a loving marriage, she only shook her head. "Enabling is practically a genetic trait in your family, isn't it?" she'd said, and he still didn't know exactly what she meant.

Josefa sucked her lips in concentration. "If you won't talk to her … write a letter. A love letter."

"I don't think she wants to hear from me."

One of the seagulls squawked, and they both turned to look at it. "Good-bye, Duncan … do what I say."

The mist changed to spitting rain, and he put his hood up. Josefa went back into the house, joyfully welcomed by the dogs, with their muddy paws and muzzles caked with seagull dung. She loved them anyway, and her love for them would find them homes. He heard the door lock, and he looked over the yard to the cage that held the false gull. Poor Kelp. After all that effort to save him, he'd died anyway. But Duncan knew that going into it. It was hard to pin too many hopes on life, considering its competition. He stood for a moment as the wind funneled up the hill from the harbor. Then he picked up the bag of dead birds and threw it in the back of the truck.

ten

It wasn't until the next day that Duncan was able to get back to the office and write to Cora. After he left Josefa and her seagulls, he'd spent the afternoon with Slocum gathering jellyfish on the beach, then labored through the night at Manavilins, boiling them up in industrial stockpots as Slocum added fistfuls of what he called his "proprietary ingredients," the dusty roots and stems he gathered along the roadside over the course of the year. Rather than, oh, say, open a book and find out what a plant was useful for, or not, he liked to just play with them in the kitchen. "Nothing worse than preconceived notions to botch creativity," he claimed. It would be up to the lab to sort it all out and identify the plasticizing elements. Duncan's head still hurt from breathing in the fumes, no doubt the cause of his disturbing dreams before dawn. He was underwater, slithering armless along the trashy sea bottom, moving in and out of shopping carts and oil drums, nudging bits of plastic with his nose to see if they were edible. On the shore, a repellent sea creature sat on a pier looking down at him, like an unformed turtle without its shell. He came across a small overturned hull, its shiplapped planks undulating with algae. An octopus sat on top of it and acted as a hinge, bending itself back to reveal the insides of the broken boat, and there was his father, serene and confident as always, huddled in the ribs of the vessel like a soft-bodied clam, and then the dream ended. Duncan lay awake for the rest of the night, listening to the sound of mice tunneling through the eelgrass insulation in his bedroom walls.

He sat down at the desk and clicked on PLAYLIST #24, a collection of love songs, to put him in the mood. Marvin Gaye. Bonnie Raitt. Dave Matthews and even, God help him, Barry White. From a sheaf of creamy paper tied with a blue satin ribbon, he pulled out a piece of stationery as thick as leather, with his name embossed in navy at the top of the page. It was Aunt Ned's college graduation present. "For serious business," she'd said, but this was the first time he'd used it. Had his life been so frivolous before this moment?

Dearest Cora,
Phone talk has been difficult with us, so I am writing you a letter and maybe that will help bridge whatever problem we've been having. What is this problem? I don't know. I was wrong, whatever it was. I'm sorry. Let's not live apart anymore. You are my boat, the water beneath, the stars above to guide me and the very air that moves me forward. I think it's all been a misunderstanding due, no doubt, as you

*have so often said, to my total lack of communication skills.
We are so different in this regard. But isn't that why we are
attracted to one another? Loving opposites! I can see how
you might need a break from me but maybe you're ready to
have me back. I won't be morbid anymore. I will embrace
life. I will embrace more counseling! I will embrace you if
you will let me and I will embrace ...*

Then, just as he was about to write the words *our baby,* he stopped
with his pen in midair and put it down. He ran his fingertips across
the dry linen fibers, and for an instant the words became distant and
unreal. He rested his forehead on the linen paper and imagined he
could smell papyrus and see a basket hidden in the reeds. Was he
hesitant to bring another generation into the world shackled to the
business of dehydrated fish scraps? Was he subconsciously fighting
the transformation from son to father? Or was he just being a selfish,
self-absorbed jerk? Somewhere in all these questions he heard Cora's
voice. But above them all was the shrill warning in his brain that any
child of his would run the risk of madness.

Rather than commit to anything so specific as a baby, he finished
the sentence with an awkward ... *the future.* He stared at the paper.
So much empty space. He looked outside the window to focus but
could see nothing through the fog that now coated the harbor, and
he considered the water, how it could change its very nature, turning
into fog or ice with only the most delicate swings of temperature.
Yet underneath it was water, no matter the form it took. His mind
continued to stalk the essential nature of matter and meaning before
snapping him back to the task at hand: the letter.

The thing to do was to throw in words Cora liked to use.
Harmony. Peace. Openness. Adjustment disorder with mixed
emotional features.

No, no, that was all wrong. Truth be told, he'd rather not be using words at all. Cora had once said that their marriage would last forever because there was something in each other they couldn't reach, and it was that unknown quantity that fueled erotic tension. Over the years, his hands had traveled miles over her body, searching for that something. When they'd first met, they made love as if they were an endangered species, but then it all changed when it seemed as if that could very well be the case. When they had to act on precisely timed couplings meant for procreation, there was no more searching for anything other than the right fertile moment. Conscious action had been his undoing. He picked up the photo of her he kept on his desk. He had taken it a couple of years ago, in their backyard, a landscape she kept in a perfect balance of nature and cultivation, very much as she kept herself. Her dark hair flew around her oval face in delicate wisps, and she wore no makeup except for a little pink on her lips to make them more kissable. Her eyes were a soft, animal brown, so wide and alert she seemed like some beautiful creature of the forest. Sometimes she dabbed cover-up under her eyes because she hated what she considered bags, and what he thought of as depth.

He reread the words he'd written, and with elaborate precision he ripped up the page. He pulled out a fresh sheet and, starting at the upper left corner, he wrote "Cora, my sweets, I love you, I love you, I love you" down the page to the very bottom, turning it over and covering the back, until he reached the lower right corner, where he signed his name.

When he was done, he folded it up as carefully as a memorial flag and slipped it into its Florentine-lined envelope. He closed his eyes as he wet the flap with his tongue. He was oozing with warmth as he picked up his pen to address the envelope, but when he was done and saw his former street—his real home—written out in his own hand, he began to feel remote, even from himself. How was it possible that he could live in the same city with Cora and yet be so far away? What was keeping them from getting back together? He hoped it was not someone new.

"Duncan?"

Nod, wearing sailing shorts, a light windbreaker, and a baseball cap with the logo of a sailmaker on the front, stood at the door, looking down at his boat shoes. He left the house so infrequently these days, it was a shock to see him. With his bald head covered by the hat, he looked more like the Nod of their childhood—rounded cheeks and cherubic lips, a perennially burnt nose, and a shy but determined look about him. He would be thirty-seven in a few weeks. Who could have foreseen that this would be his life? Nod was the oldest son—why wasn't he sitting here, at their father's desk with all these worries, freeing Duncan to live his own life far away?

"Hey, Nod. Did you sail here?"

Nod shook his head and looked around the office. "I just came back from Portland. I went to buy a Duck."

"Duck?"

Nod inched slowly into the room, as if he were a lobster entering a trap. "You know, a Sea Duck, an amphibious vehicle. Army surplus."

They stared at each other for a minute, both unable to bring the topic to its next natural step. Duncan broke the spell. "Why?"

Nod smiled and cleared his throat. "I thought about, you know, the money thing. I was thinking, here Mom and I just drain the company of dividends, when I should be doing something to help."

"Really?"

He nodded. "The bank let me borrow against the house. Mom is all for it."

"The house? I couldn't borrow against it to save Seacrest's, but it's okay to do it for a boat?"

"Not a boat. A business. I'm going to run sea-land tours here in the summer, right off this beach. I'll do Kelp-in-the-Wild tours. That's why I'm here."

"Here?"

"I need more funding to get *Sea Turtle* off the ground. Bear is going to refit the engine to run on used cooking oil. I'm getting that from Slocum in exchange for an ad painted on her side. He says that if his ship comes in by next summer, he'll even invest in the business, but I wanted to offer it to you first. For a price, Seacrest's Ocean Products can be her main sponsor."

"Who knows if there'll be a Seacrest's next summer?" said Duncan. "If I don't come up with the money to pay the loan sharks back in a few months, they'll own it, not me."

"Maybe I should talk to them."

"If I lost the company to Osbert, you wouldn't do business with him, would you?"

"You know, Duncan," said Nod, looking out at the blank wall of fog outside the window, "in sailing, to change direction is a risk because if you're caught in the eye of the wind, you stop dead and go in irons. You have to have momentum to change." He turned to look at Duncan. "One of the benefits of the Duck is that it can adapt quickly to changing conditions, on land or sea. It might be our salvation. It might be yours."

"What is your point?"

Nod laughed in his peculiar way, a prolonged *haa* that sounded like the whiz of the wind. "No point."

Duncan stood up with his envelope. "I've got to go to the post office," he said. "I guess you'll just have to see who's sitting at this desk when you're ready to paint a sponsor's name on the Duck."

"Sounds like a deal," Nod said, not understanding that Duncan was being snarky. No matter. If Duncan lost Seacrest's, he would be out of this town in a heartbeat, so he wouldn't have to look at some treacherous ad on the Duck.

"Come see my baby," said Nod, turning to the door. "She's in the parking lot."

"She is? You own her already?"

Nod smiled. "I took my car to Portland and drove the Duck back. The dealer took the car as part of the down payment."

"You have no more car?"

"I won't need one anymore. I've got the Duck. Now I'm going to motor it home along the harbor."

Duncan had a hard time imagining Nod doing errands around town in a massive barge-like vehicle, whether he came by land or sea. But it was harder still to believe that Nod had the initiative to start a business, or that come next summer he would give up racing in order to run it. He wondered if his mother understood what changes lay ahead.

~

"Sea Turtle." Duncan said her name out loud as he walked around her metal hull. There were restaurant and ferry ads painted on her side, remnants of her former life running out of Portland. Under the scratches, he saw her old camouflage paint, and he wondered if she'd been at the D-Day landings. Osbert, with his Churchill fixation, would love that.

"I thought I'd have big, colorful turtles painted on her sides," said Nod, holding his arms out and wiggling them. "Have the paddled arms and shells available for sponsors' ads. Come on up—have a look at these controls." Nod arranged himself in the captain's seat while Duncan stood on the wheel bumper and watched him push a lever to change it from land to sea. The frame sank slightly as the wheels raised up. "It's not any harder than changing to four-wheel drive. Want to come along for her maiden voyage?"

"She's not exactly a maiden," said Duncan, jumping down to the pavement. "I think I'll let her show you the ropes first." He looked out at the fog. He heard the sea breaking on the opposite shore, and the bell buoy clanged a warning. "Are you sure you should be going home by way of water? Is your radio working in case something goes wrong?"

"Bear is going to install new electronics this winter. I'm going to hug the shore until I can beach her at the Boat Club landing. Then I can just drive around the corner to home."

"Do you have a mariner's license to drive her?"

"Don't need one," said Nod. "I have a driver's license, so I'm halfway there."

"Halfway there," mused Duncan, patting the side of the vehicle. "Maybe Mom'll go for a ride with you someday. Maybe this could get her back into the world."

Nod fiddled with some controls. "She's not out of this world now."

"Nod, her feet have barely touched earth since Dad died."

"Just because she doesn't want to leave the house? She's perfectly sane. Just cautious."

"Not cautious. Nuts."

Nod laughed his breezy laugh again and put *Sea Turtle* in gear. With that, he turned the heavy vehicle slowly around, her parts and panels creaking with the effort, and headed for the water, where she transformed into a seagoing vessel. She was not elegant, she was not graceful, but she moved forward, churning and bobbing happily into the harbor before disappearing into the great banks of fog.

"Good luck," Duncan whispered.

As he zippered his jacket, he looked up at Seacrest's. It was slab-sided and flat-topped, but in the softening mist, it seemed magisterial in its bulk, and as much as he resented the drain it took on his psyche, there were times when it had a pull on him that went beyond reason. He was glad he had risked doing business with Osbert to save it. It would have been much nicer if he could have avoided it, oh, say, by mortgaging the family home as Nod had just been allowed to do—Nod with no business experience and no work experience. But still. It was nice to know that Seacrest's was safe for the moment. He touched the envelope in his jacket. Now he had to secure his marriage.

As he left the parking lot, he waved to the men on the loading dock. The savory odor of marijuana cut through the motionless fog. It used to be that the smell of rotting fish parts covered up all other scents, but now that the new system contained all the vapors, pot smoke was the predominant note outside the factory. He ignored it. If he had to handle shipments of decaying chum all day, he'd want to hover a few inches above it, too. He wished he had such a simple chemical solution to all his problems.

Maybe he did. Pheromones. He took the envelope out of his pocket and slipped it under his shirt and against his skin, where his essence would rub off on his walk into town. Cora would vaguely wonder why she could not put his letter down. He hurried his step up the hill toward the post office. It had been unseasonably hot before the fog rolled in, so the damp pavement gave off an urban smell of cement and asphalt. He missed the city. He yearned for those years of anonymity again, when he could be anyone he wanted, as opposed to being here in Port Ellery, where it seemed the most intimate details of his daily life were played out in the open.

Duncan put his hood up and tried to disappear inside of it as he hurried through town, but he was stopped by every passing pedestrian to chat. He had a fresh appeal for the locals, as if being on YouTube had transformed him into a different person—familiar, yet totally strange. He found himself trying to avoid people he knew, but there was no place to hide, no alleys or streets where he would not bump into someone, so he just walked faster. He was practically running as he turned the corner to the post office. The collision with Syrie was sudden, loud, and dramatic. She dropped her armload of packages and squeaked in profound delight. Her dog, protected in a quilted shoulder bag, growled.

"Duncan!" she said, pushing back her golden sheet of hair. "I had so much in my arms I couldn't see where I was going."

"My bad," he said, already scrambling to pick up the boxes. "I'll get them." As he stacked them in his arms, he wondered at their lightness.

Syrie dug around in her bag for her keys, and the dog made irritable noises. "Do you mind?" she asked, swaying to the music of her own voice. "My car is only right there."

"Sure," said Duncan. He stood up with the packages and dropped two of them, which she retrieved herself, bending over from the waist, and as she did, her white raincoat slid up her back, exposing purple form-fitting slacks.

"This way," she said, standing up and gesturing with her bag of dog.

The fog was thick up on the hill, and the packages were piled so high in Duncan's arms they blocked what little vision he may have had, so he stuck as close as a barnacle behind her. She rippled when she walked, as if waves were passing through her body. He almost bumped right into her again as she stopped abruptly in front of an older lilac Jaguar.

"I know this car," he said. "It's my mother's. It's the one she drove before she ... before she didn't."

"I know," Syrie said as she opened the trunk. "Last summer Nod told me he needed room in the garage and did I want to buy it. It's been on blocks all these years, so it was in good shape for the years." She ran her hands down her raincoat. "So I bought it and had it restored. I love the older models, don't you? The cracked leather, the varnished wood. You know, when I was young, I always looked up to your mom. I wanted to be just like her."

"You don't mean that."

"I do. Or I did. She was so carefree, she didn't give a fuck what anyone thought of her or what she did. It was too bad she sort of buried herself in that house after your dad died. They must have loved one another very much."

"I suppose." Duncan let the packages fall out of his arms and into the trunk. "What are all the boxes?"

"Promotional gifts. Velvet masks to put over your eyes when you sleep, with my ad printed on them." She opened a box and removed a small plastic bag, through which Duncan could see the purple mask and the words WAKE UP SMILING, DIRTY TALK WAKE-UP SERVICE and a telephone number. She handed it to him. "Take one, and let me give you a ride back to the office." She slammed the trunk shut.

"Why not?" he said, and he slipped the mask into his pocket. The fog settled in sparkling drops on her face, and he saw her as through a white gauze—innocent, even angelic. She smiled at him as she unlocked her door, and he smiled back, but the moment he lowered himself in the soft leather he immediately regretted his decision. This was the car he'd learned to drive in. It was that very backseat where he'd lost his virginity. With Syrie. His shoulders stiffened to sharp points, and he began to feel a subliminal current pulling him to her side of the car.

"Buckle up," said Syrie as she turned on the ignition. "I had to have seatbelts installed, of course. Your mom didn't believe in them." She pulled down the reflector and freshened her lipstick in the vanity mirror until her lips shimmered like the underside of a shell. The dog sat in her lap and showed Duncan his mean little teeth.

In an effort to make himself busy, he put his jacket hood down, and rivulets of condensed fog ran down his shoulders. "I'm getting your seat all wet."

She gave him a sidelong smile. "I'll turn the blower on, but it'll take a couple of minutes for the windows to defog. The old girl needs to get up to speed."

"Can I ask you a personal question?" asked Duncan.

She turned to face him. "If I can ask you one."

"I'm curious. Why did you tell me your suspicions about Osbert, then turn around and start doing business with him yourself? And what did you need money from Osbert for, anyway? I thought business was booming."

"That's two questions," she said.

"I know, but still."

"If you paid more attention to Club gossip, you'd know all about it." She ran her palms over the dark, hand-whipped leather of the steering wheel and gazed at its center as she spoke. "When Lance and I were married, I was that oblivious, too. I didn't have anything to do with the bills. He took care of all that. Then one day I opened a phone bill looking for a number and found one—nine thousand four hundred dollars. You can imagine my surprise. It wasn't long before I found out we were in serious debt because of his phone-sex addiction. After the divorce, we were both broke. And I thought, if phone sex is that good, maybe I can get my money back from it. I called some of the nine-hundred numbers and learned a few tricks. But I didn't want to work nights, and I didn't want to actually talk to those perverts. That's when I came up with Dirty Talk Wake-Up and started advertising on Craigslist. I record a new message every day, but recently I've had to start hiring other voices. Men like variety." She gave Duncan a wry smile before continuing. "The business just grew and grew, and I needed to update the system, but none of the banks would listen to me. When I heard you and Osbert on the Club porch that day, I realized he was the answer to my prayers. You and I were in the same boat, Duncan. The banks wouldn't give us any more money and Osbert would. But unlike you, I rather like the danger involved in dealing with him. But you—you're so easily frightened."

"I am not," Duncan said. "Of Osbert or anything."

Syrie looked down at her teeny dog and scratched its head. "I remember when you were a kid, and you'd stand on the rocks as storms came in, letting the waves hit you, and you wouldn't budge. You were absolutely fearless. Now you're even afraid of me, and I'm rather a mild danger compared to Osbert." She raised her hand to the top button of her blouse and peeked over at him.

Duncan smiled and looked down at his hands. "I remember standing in the waves. When my father caught me, he said I was thicker than a sea slug. And he was right. It was a stupid thing to do. I'd never let a kid of mine … " He trailed off into an awkward silence.

"You were so fearless, you actually left Port Ellery."

He felt his face get warm. "Are you still mad at me for going?"

"That's three questions. No, I'm mad at you for coming back with someone else."

He shrugged. "I fell in love."

"I thought we were in love."

"No, we were just young and … "

"And horny?"

"I was going to say hormonal."

"Hormonal? You make it sound as if we were in the grips of PMS. I think it's time I asked my question before you have a mood swing." She stared at Duncan until he was looking right at her. "Would you still be in New York if your father hadn't gotten lost at sea?"

"Yes."

Her eyes turned sharp. "You might have taken me with you."

He shook his head. "Once I got away, I felt I needed to be with someone from 'not here.' And then, when I had to come back, I wanted to bring some 'out there' with me. Cora loved it from the beginning. She let me see Port Ellery in a whole new light. It wasn't the dismal brick town of my childhood anymore. It was full of character and depth and natural wonders. She said it was the perfect place to raise … " He was unable to finish the sentence.

"Raise what? Chickens?" She laughed as she clicked off the blower, being protective of her long nails.

They sat quietly for a minute, listening to a freighter groan out in the harbor. The fog seemed to wrap them up in a distant land and time, and his thoughts wandered out past the harbor and onto the cold dark sea. He was awash in emotions he could not name, and when he spoke his voice was cracked.

"At any rate, we're just going through a little rough water right now."

"Over a month of rough water. Tell me what's going on."

He focused his eyes on the intermittent wipers. "I don't know. I just don't know."

"Duncan, in every marriage there's one who's anchored and one who floats. Not only have you been cut loose, but you're in serious danger of washing out to sea." She turned off the wipers. "Now, you got two questions, so do I. Tit for tat."

"Shoot," he said.

"Not to put too fine a point on it, Duncan, what I want to know is, are you two getting back together?"

He looked outside. "I think the fog is breaking up," he said, with some false amazement.

She smiled at his conventional evasion, then she trotted her fingers along his leg.

"Syrie." He looked at her and wondered whether this was what Cora would call a "pseudo-sexual invitation," done to reaffirm Syrie's femininity for him, or something else. He felt his insides flop, and yet … and yet he was intrigued by the promise of some wilder shore of sexuality, especially when he could see no shore at all anymore.

He offered the most feeble of protests. "I'm a married man."

"That's okay," she said. "I'm not a jealous woman." She leaned toward him and tapped his headrest with the tips of her fingers. "We used to have a lot of good times in this car."

He felt her closing in on him and moved her hand from behind his head. "Syrie, we're in the middle of town."

She sat up straight. "We can go to my place."

"No. That isn't what I mean."

"What do you mean, Duncan? What do you *ever* mean?"

He leaned back in his seat, feeling as if he just might faint. He was sweating. He unzipped the top few inches of his jacket and felt something stiff. He pulled out the envelope to Cora and looked at it in horror.

"I've got to go," he said, and with a sudden burst of air, he was out of the car, leaving the door open in his rush to get back to the post office. His errand of love had almost turned into a quickie divorce. Cora would point to this as an example of his ambivalence about their marriage. And then she would leave him. As he ran, hard slashes of rain started to fall, as if the air were being wrung out like a towel. He heard Syrie give a little three-note song of good-bye, then slam the door shut.

eleven

A few days later, Duncan bounced up the stairs to Slocum's apartment to share some good news from the lab: Trevor had wrangled money from the university for further study of the soup. The jellyfish concoction, which had nearly killed Osbert, was continuing to show promise as plastic. Boiling water, brine, acid rain, and dozens of other likely elements had failed to change its shape, making it commercially viable, and yet, because it was made of jellyfish, environmentally sound. Most so-called biodegradable plastic was still made from petroleum that lurked in the environment forever, making it questionable at best, and true biodegradables, made from corn, were fertilized with petroleum products and used up valuable farming land. Jellyfish, however, were the cockroaches of the sea, plentiful and free for the taking.

"I knew it," said Slocum, slapping his hands together, his body still wrapped in a white linen apron from work. "My jellyfish might have failed at soup, but they'll rule the world as bags." The kitchen walls, the color of lard, were tinted orange by the oblique light of the setting sun coming in through the window and cast Slocum in a Renaissance glow. Ancient utensils hung from the rafters, along with bundles of herbs, various scales, and a smoked ham. For someone who espoused a modern, molecular approach to cooking, Slocum's kitchen was practically medieval.

"You can't patent a jellyfish," said Duncan as he took his windbreaker off. "But you can patent the process. And if it turns out you're the one responsible for creating the plastic, and not nature, you'll be a wealthy man. Now we wait and see what it does in time-simulated experiments. A lot depends on how and when it finally breaks down into its molecules."

Slocum leaned against the kitchen sink to take this news in, and a faraway look crossed his face. "Ashes to ashes, dust to dust, molecule to molecule," he mused. "We're all from the same basic material, aren't we?"

"Speak for yourself," said Duncan, grabbing a beer from the refrigerator. "I'd like to think I'm different from a jellyfish."

"That's where you're wrong," said Slocum, giving his mustache a little twist. "All living things—us, the eel, the bird on the wing—we live and die at the cellular level."

"Well, your soup had better not break up into its cells too soon, or else we won't have a product. Besides, we're getting ahead of ourselves. Most research ends at a dead end."

"The Stone Age didn't end because they ran out of stones, my friend, it ended because something better came along. We're standing on the edge of the Petroleum Age and the beginning of the Jellyfish Era. One day, they'll put a plaque on the restaurant door."

"Trevor has to first determine if it's really a workable plastic substance, and that's a big if. But if it is, you'll be first in line for a slice of the pie."

"If that's the case," Slocum said, wrapping the crook of his arm around Duncan's head and drawing him near, "I'll make sure you're awarded the exclusive contract to process the jellyfish and you'll never have to borrow from shady characters again. Let's celebrate. We'll throw a big bash next weekend. I've been mulling over a new high-concept lobster dish, and I can use the party to launch it. As for tonight, I'll whip up a special dinner here for just the two of us. Then off to Ten Bells to share our joy!"

"Here?" Duncan said, untangling himself from Slocum's hug. "How about I grab a calzone from downstairs and then we go to Ten Bells after you've finished work?"

"Rheya's cooking tonight. She needed money so I gave her a few shifts a week. Poor kid. Here she's got a baby coming in a few months and a husband who keeps drifting up on shore. At least now she can gather up the pieces of that bastard and hold the funeral so she can go on with her life." Slocum opened the refrigerator, which washed him in a white light.

Duncan wanted to suggest they eat downstairs for Rheya's cooking, but that would hurt Slocum's culinary pride. There were some lines that couldn't be crossed in friendship.

"Have the police figured out why he's in pieces yet?"

Slocum couldn't hear with his head deep in the refrigerator. "A diver brought in a box of europeans this morning to pay his tab, and I've got a bag of bait lying around. Wade has been pushing all this whiting on me lately. He wants me to make something of them and put them on the regular menu."

Duncan smiled the smile of the damned and sat slumped at the counter to watch Slocum work his peculiar magic. Harley, Clover's kid, was in the apartment, too, but he had locked himself in the bathroom to work on a school project, and whatever that involved was scenting the air with sulfur. They heard him laughing.

"My budding scientist," Slocum said as he placed a waxy box on the counter and opened it to reveal a dozen or more rubber-banded Belon oysters—the europeans—carefully laid out on a bed of seaweed, like jewels. He turned back to the refrigerator and produced a dripping plastic bag of small dark fish and dumped the whiting in the sink to drain. "When he graduates from high school in a few years, I want him to move here and work by my side in the restaurant. Who knows what we could do with his knowledge and my daring?" He rooted through the freezer. "I know I have a bottle of lemon vodka here somewhere."

"You're such a good dad," Duncan said, and surprised himself with a twinge of jealousy. "And he's not even your kid."

"It's not all about the genes," said Slocum, holding the frosty blue bottle over his head like a trophy. "It's the connection between two souls. Nature, nurture, fuck it. Clover loves Harley, but it's just not in her nature to mother anyone. In spite of that, she still figured it out by finding me for her boy to shelter by. If she can do it—somehow manage to produce a normal kid—by God, man, you can, too."

From the bathroom came the sound of breaking glass and an "oops," after which floor-hugging vapors came creeping down the hall. Slocum didn't even look up as he studied the lineup of condiment jars stored inside the refrigerator door. "Here she is," he said, tossing a small jar of black caviar into the air and catching it.

"I don't think Cora wants me around to nature *or* nurture," said Duncan. "I have a feeling she heard about Syrie kissing me on the lips at Manavilins. For all I know, someone sent her a video." He thought chillingly of the scene of the two of them in the car the week before. What had possessed him?

"Syrie's a spicy number," said Slocum. "But Cora doesn't care about her; she cares about you. Your feelings are no thicker than a pudding skin. Toughen up and forge ahead. Call Cora and go home. She needs you."

Duncan ran both hands through his hair and took off his glasses. "She doesn't want me back. I think she wants me to sort the kid thing out in my head, but I haven't and I can't. I can't justify a kid when I can't even justify me. I mean, what am I doing here? What am I even *supposed* to be doing here?"

Slocum took an oyster out of the box. "What is the meaning of this oyster? It just is, you just is, we just is. You worry too much about irrelevant things. You've got to face the world fresh off the half shell every morning!"

"Cora said that, too. Not about the half shell, but she said I was avoiding myself with worry." He put his glasses back on. "I just don't see how self-knowledge serves any purpose."

"Worry has made a hash of your life, my friend. You've scrambled your nest egg and gotten yourself involved in unsavory business practices. Worse, you continue to live in your childhood home, where you go to bed at night hugging your misery instead of your wife." He picked up a rusty oyster knife and pried the shell apart, holding it expertly with his three fingers and a thumb as he recited Lewis Carroll:

"O Oysters," said the Carpenter,
"You've had a pleasant run!
Shall we be trotting home again?"
But answer came there none—

And this was scarcely odd, because
They'd eaten every one.

With this, Slocum lifted the shell to his lips and swallowed its contents. "Like drinking a mermaid." He was still humming with pleasure as he opened the next oyster. When he pried the top off, he brought it close to his eyes, using the blade to lift the meat and inspect the grayish-pink underbelly. "Annuncia says that plastics have been messing with the gonads of the oyster, turning them into hermaphrodites. That can't be good." He placed the oyster in front of Duncan. "Here, eat while I make us some cocktails."

Duncan picked it up. "Oysters are born hermaphrodites, switching from male to female and back at whim."

"Yes, but now they're getting stalled in the middle. Can't decide! Don't have enough *push* one way or another from their hormones."

Duncan inspected the oyster more closely, not for gonads but for hidden ingredients. Satisfied that it was an oyster as nature intended, he tilted his head and let the contents spend a brief but enjoyable moment in his mouth before sliding down his throat. The little bivalve was so fresh and full of the sea that it tasted like tears, which brought on a new wave of sadness. It was Cora's favorite food, one they had shared so often it had become a bond between them. To celebrate their first morning in their new home—so long ago, it seemed—they had made oyster stew, opening the shells directly over heated cream on the stove. He remembered thinking: How perfect. How perfect the stew, the morning, the marriage, and their life together. But that life was fading into something vague and watery, until now, the oyster, once an emblem of their joy, was just a couple of empty shells.

Slocum set up two pony glasses and shucked an oyster into each one, then spooned a dab of caviar over both. When he poured the vodka over the combination, the caviar ran like squid ink and turned the drink the color of bilge water. He put his hands on his hips and studied the herbs hanging from the rafters. "Just what we need," he said and pinched a desiccated leaf from a branch. "Sassafras." He rubbed it between his large hands until it was dust, then sprinkled it on the drinks, which began to turn even cloudier, then thicken. "Cora's counting on you to pull yourself out of your funk soon, buddy." He pushed the oyster shooter in front of Duncan and raised his glass. "To jellyfish!"

Slocum took a loud sip, savoring the dark, alcoholic brine, but Duncan drank too much of it on the first swallow and felt a little knocked back. But it didn't taste as bad as it looked.

Slocum pointed out the window, where the sun teetered on the edge of night, toward the golden water. "Consider the tides, my friend. Ebb and flow, ebb and flow! The same old, twice a day? No! Each tide leaves the new behind and takes the old with it when it goes, and, if we're lucky, it exposes something miraculous like an oyster. And if we look deep into that, maybe even a pearl."

"Life is not feeling like gentle, regular tides these days—it feels more like waves. Big, relentless, monster waves."

Slocum nodded. "True. Monsters are part of the cycle, but even they recede in time. They're not going to change, but you can. You just have to tweak your attitude until they pass."

Duncan stared at his shooter. "If change was that easy I'd have done it long ago."

"You know what the French say," said Slocum, turning back to the refrigerator. "Only idiots don't change."

Duncan did not rise to the bait; instead he drank and watched Slocum, who removed bag after bag from the produce bin, then, in a flurry of chopping and ripping, filled a wooden bowl with vegetation and dressed it. At the stove, he lifted a lid and brought his nose so close to the action that his mustache grazed the surface of the parsley sauce. He wet his finger with his tongue and dabbed at the bubbling liquid. After a moment's consideration, he added a dollop of blueberry jam, more cream, and a pat of butter. "You can't have too much fat."

"You can have too much fat," said Duncan. "It'll kill you."

"Rubbish. Species with bigger brains need to sup on richer food."

"You just said I was an idiot," said Duncan. "I can't have that big a brain."

"You have missed my point entirely. You're not an idiot, hence, you *can* change." He pushed the bowl toward Duncan as he sat down. "Here, serve yourself some salad."

Duncan put a small helping on his plate and picked at the soggy lettuce leaves, which tasted as if they were dressed from a crankcase.

"What did you use in this?" asked Duncan.

"Flax oil," said Slocum, taking a mouthful, "for the bowels."

Slocum finished his greens in a few bites, then turned his attention to the main course. As pans sizzled and pots boiled, Duncan held his drink up to the light and through the murky liquid considered the frilly oyster at the bottom of the glass. It was beginning to pickle and tighten up in a fetal position, the sight of which made him so depressed he downed the glass so he wouldn't have to look at it anymore. The metallic bite of caviar and its sudden release of brine in his mouth was surprising but not unpleasant. Only the color was truly unpleasant. "Nice crunch," he said, and this encouraged Slocum to make them both another, accompanied by more beer.

Slocum emptied his shooter in a single gulp this time, then sucked on the oyster like an ice cube, rolling it around in his mouth. "It'll cure what ails you."

Duncan sipped his more slowly this time. "I didn't know I needed curing."

"Neither did this pig," Slocum said as he patted the ham over his head. "But I cured him myself in the smoker right out back."

Duncan had no answer to this, and Slocum was laughing as he returned to his stove. In no time, pots were spilling over and dark smoke began to billow out from the oven, causing Slocum to release a steady string of swear words like magic incantations. Duncan kept his head down as hot oil spattered across the room. Finally, flush with sweat and glowing with high blood pressure, Slocum turned back to face Duncan, holding aloft a platter of fried whiting.

"Ta da!" The little fish were served upright, pretending to leap out of the sea, held in place with an ocean of Tater Tots and a drizzle of the blue-green sauce. Their eyes were open in fright, as if they were being pursued by a school of snappers. "All ye fishes in the sea, all ye children of men," Slocum said as he placed the platter on the counter. He pressed his hands together and put his fingers to his lips in admiration of his creation.

"Is that coconut?" asked Duncan, pointing to white sprinkles on the Tater Tots.

Slocum nodded. "Whitecaps. Look at this little dude." Slocum pointed to a whiting that had been harvested in the act of eating a smaller whiting, so that a head stuck out of its mouth. "That's how I found him. I love when that happens." He put the fish on Duncan's plate, along with a half dozen others.

"Isn't Harley eating?" Duncan asked, hoping to share the wealth.

"I don't want to interrupt his work." They heard the tinkle of glass hitting the floor. "He'll eat later. He prefers his food after it's been thoroughly nuked in the microwave anyway."

Duncan pulled bits of flesh off the bones of the double fish. It did not taste any different from any other fried fish: crunchy on the outside, moist on the inside, with an elusive ocean flavor. It was the two-headed skeleton that remained on his plate that was so disturbing. He put his fork down. Slocum, however, attacked his meal like a feeding shark, popping the little fish whole into his mouth. "Eat," he said. "We need to fill the hatches as ballast for the drinking we intend to do later." To augment the coconut-crusted Tater Tots, he shook some ketchup on his plate like a pool of blood, and when he put the plastic bottle down, it gurgled as if it were alive.

"I can't." Duncan poked at the skeleton. "It's too … dog-eat-dog."

"Did you hear about the cannibal who made superb finger sandwiches?" Slocum asked as he dipped a fish head, cut side down, into the ketchup. Duncan blinked in response.

"Come on, Dunc, laugh, we're supposed to be celebrating!"

"I am what I am." Duncan pushed away his plate.

"What? Popeye?"

"I mean, I can't change the way I feel. You can't make anything out of cookie dough except cookies." But as the words fell out of his mouth he knew he was talking to the wrong person.

"I once stuffed a turkey with mint-chocolate-chip cookie dough," said Slocum, as he belched in three keys. "Added rosemary, whipped it in a blender with egg whites, and pumped the foam into the cavity. It gave the bird a rare and fetching flavor and was a great success. The guests were surprised and delighted because their minds were open to the possibilities. You can make something out of anything, my friend, if you put your whole heart into it."

~

After dinner, of which Duncan had eaten not much more than the double whiting, they walked down the street to Ten Bells and put their whole hearts into drinking. Ten Bells was the seediest bar in a town belly-deep in seedy bars. Three stained and threadbare pool tables provided entertainment, hard-boiled eggs from a jar of cloudy liquid gave sustenance, and the price-per-shot of liquor was written in Magic Marker on each bottle of booze on the shelves. They sold no wine, at any price. In the back room were two old-school pinball machines and a glass tank of lobsters, where for five dollars patrons got a chance at catching one with a small crane, like an arcade game. Ten Bells' doors opened at 5:30 a.m. so that dock workers could get a quick snort before work, or to offer amber consolation if there was none. In the past, and perhaps even into the present, the bar was known as a place where captains, short of men for some dangerous journey or another, would troll for crew, make them paralytic with drink, then carry them on board on stretchers and lay them out like corpses in the hold. And that was exactly how Duncan felt the next morning.

"*Sassafras,*" he croaked without opening his eyes. Thanks to several more oyster shooters after dinner, Duncan had already reached his waterline by the time they left Slocum's apartment, then he took more on board at Ten Bells. Bottom-shelf bourbon, $3.05 a shot. He'd ended up, somehow, fully clothed on the sofa in his office and woke to the sound of a rally outside his window. Annuncia's basso profundo blared through a loudspeaker. "A clean sea is a profitable sea!" she shouted. It was 10 a.m.

He curled tighter into the ball he was already in and pulled his windbreaker over his head. He'd forgotten that he'd told her she could launch her Boat Garbage Project from Seacrest's loading dock today, but it was coming back to him loud and clear now. He had assumed she meant at the end of the workday, but of course, she would want to do it early enough to catch that evening's news cycle.

The crowd started to chant, and the steady noise bore through his eardrums like sea worms. "Bring the garbage back to shore! Bring the garbage back to shore!"

Annuncia quieted them down and continued speaking. "We

complain about the crap from outfall pipes and pollution on our fish, and then we throw our own garbage overboard. What's up with that?"

The crowd emitted a low boo, and he could hear Wade's voice leading the pack. Even though Annuncia was at the microphone, this project was really his baby. On Earth Day that spring, instead of cleaning beaches with the other volunteers, Wade decided to motor from boat to boat asking for garbage. When they saw how successful he'd been, a group of kids started making the rounds every weekend in a pedal-driven barge built from plastic water bottles, and it wasn't long before some of the fishermen and pleasure boaters started to bring it in on their own. The problem, as always, was that there was no place to put it. Often the bags were just left on the docks at the mercy of the gulls and crows, and that meant debris scattered everywhere, on land and water. Annuncia hadn't realized the extent to which everyone had been throwing their trash overboard before that. It was against the law, but they had to catch you first, and the ocean was a mighty big place. The only people who ever got caught were people like Duncan. Two summers before, he and Cora had motored outside the harbor in a borrowed Whaler, a rare water adventure for them both. Cora had always complained about the shortage of the color blue in sea glass, so she collected the empty Skyy vodka bottles from the Boat Club for a few weeks then asked Duncan to take her out to sea to dump them so they could begin their long transformational journey. Cora was a woman who liked to plan for the future. Unfortunately, Duncan was out on the water so infrequently that he failed to recognize the dark green boat of the Environmental Police coming up behind them as they were tossing vodka bottles into the sea. They got a $500 citation and lots of laughs back at the Club.

Annuncia raised her voice. "Our fish and lobsters need a clean home, so from now on I want you to bring your garbage back to shore, all of it—the soda cans, the plastic wrap, crumpled tin foil, coolant jugs, even dental floss. Always, always, always bring back old fishing line. This isn't to keep the beaches clean for tourists; it's so our children won't have to fish from a garbage dump. So we can have children at all. Fish eat the plastic, and if it doesn't kill them by blocking the guts, it messes with their hormones. Any more plastic in the sea and our own systems will be so twisted we won't be able to reproduce anymore, never mind the fish."

There was some sniggering from the audience, probably single men, for whom this might be a very good thing. Duncan thought of his own reproductive failure and wondered, but wondering put too much stress on a brain so riddled with oyster shooters. "If we want the rest of the world to stop trashing the water," she continued, "we have to set the example. And you commercial boats, before we unload your gurry, I want to see full bags at the end of every trip."

"Annuncia," said Duncan, as if she could hear him. He struggled to sit upright. "Don't threaten our clients."

"We believe in this project so much that we planned to take your garbage for you," she announced. "Right here, in the parking lot." There was loud applause and whistles.

"*We?*" Duncan asked. He patted the floor for his glasses and pulled himself up, inch by painful inch, until he was standing, then somehow hobbled over to the window without falling.

Annuncia continued. "But, instead, the mayor has agreed to install Dumpsters and recycling bins on the docks in support of a cleaner city and sea."

There was more applause, and Duncan peeked through the window blinds. It was an overcast day, but sheaves of light fell through the cracks in the sky. The mayor stood next to Annuncia, waving at the crowd and proclamating as mayors do. "What's good for the sea life is good for our life!"

There was a polite smattering of applause. He was not a popular man with the local fish movement because he was always courting foreign boats to land in Port Ellery, but he must have learned by now that saying no to Annuncia would only double her efforts. Duncan had learned that lesson long ago, and so he was relieved that she'd decided the Dumpsters should go on the docks and not Seacrest's parking lot. If the garbage was here, she would have wanted to process the trash, too, and he was processing quite enough garbage as it was. Annuncia held up a large green plastic bag emblazoned with Seacrest's logo to the cheers of the crowd.

"Seacrest's?" he said, once again to no one. He did not remember telling her the company would finance the project—in fact, he knew he hadn't. He scanned the crowd, a bunch of scruffy harbor denizens of lumpers and lobstermen, along with some pierced environmental kids and the recently unemployed of all ages, for whom any event in the middle of the day was a welcome distraction. He recognized many faces, including a few well-dressed members from the Boat Club. Signs bobbed above all the heads: To SAVE THE PLANET, SAVE THE SEAS and BRING IT BACK TO SHORE. Marney, the waitress from Manavilins, waved a sign that read SEACREST'S KILLS SEA ANIMALS. SUPPORT SEA ANIMAL RIGHTS.

Why was she picking on his company, which only processed waste and had never killed so much as a clam? That's what he got for sponsoring a program to help her "sea animals," by which she must mean fish. He continued to scan the crowd and noticed a sign so beautifully written in archaic script it took him a moment to digest the words: RECYCLE OR DIE. It was nailed onto a sheleighly.

Osbert. He stood out not just by his sign but his dress. He wore a suit fit for an undertaker in a crowd of Carhartt and L. L. Bean. The light reflected off his sunglasses, flashing with his every move. Duncan had not seen Osbert since their lunch at Manavilins three weeks before. "Strange," Duncan said, but once again, the exertion of thinking hurt his brain, so he put all complex thoughts on hold.

Annuncia waved a bag over her head like a flag. "You've got the tools—now get the will! Let peer pressure and public opinion do its magic." She looked pointedly at the TV camera, and then Duncan thought he saw a look exchanged between her and Osbert.

~

After he restored his body's ability to function, somewhat, with aspirin from the first-aid kit in the front office, Duncan snuck out of Seacrest's, not by the fire escape in full view of everyone but through the empty factory. Empty during prime working hours. He rubbed his temples. He felt Osbert tightening the net around him, slowly taking charge of one thing, then another, and using Annuncia to do it. Ducking below the windows, Duncan let himself out of the side door into the alley and wondered which way to turn. He did not have many options. He wanted Manavilins coffee, which was black and brutal, but he could not get there without being seen by the crowd, and he could not bear to talk to anyone right now, least of all Annuncia. He needed to have his head on straight for the conversation they had to have.

Where could he go for coffee? What else was guaranteed to wake him up?

Then he remembered, with increasing queasiness, that he'd woken Cora up at 3:00 a.m., calling her on the phone with sentimentally drunk declarations of his feelings. He could not remember his words, but he was afraid they might have had more to do with his loins than his heart. He believed he'd made the fatal error of saying that Syrie meant nothing to him, which begged the question.

Whatever it was, it had caused her to respond with, "Duncan, go stick your head in a bucket," before hanging up on him. He remembered that much. She was probably calling a divorce lawyer at that very moment or, at the least, was on the phone to their marriage counselor to process this new bit of self-defeating behavior.

"On we go," he said out loud, startling a tailless harbor cat out of the Dumpster. "It's time to act."

He looked for the ripped section of the chain-link fence that led to Petersen's Marina. Instead of pushing his troubled marriage out of his head as he'd been doing, he would listen, really listen to what Cora had to say. For starters, he would do as she suggested and go stick his head in a bucket. She wouldn't have known it at 3:00 a.m., but a bracing wake-up was exactly what he needed right now. He would go one better. Instead of a bucket, he would dunk his head in the immense, life-giving ocean to clear his mind for everything that lay before him. It was time to get back to some kind of normal.

He found the hole in the fence and slipped through it, catching his windbreaker at the shoulder and tearing the nylon shell. It was one of his blue promotional jackets, with the Seacrest's logo on the back, so it wasn't much of a loss. He had an unlimited supply of those, thanks to a cousin of Wade's who got them printed cheap from somewhere far away. As he walked down to the end of the dock, seagulls flapped away at his approach, then settled back down after he passed. Most of the floats attached to either side of the dock had a boat or two attached, and he kept going until he found one that had none. It was low tide, so the metal ramp down to the water was steep, and he experienced a bit of hangover vertigo, but he held on and made it to the relative safety of the wood. He got down on his stomach, but before he made the plunge, he checked underneath the float for harbor seals, who were already moving in. They were winter residents, migrants from farther north coming to live in the relatively gentler climate of Port Ellery for a few months, a reminder that no matter how bad the winters were, there was always someplace worse off. There were no seals beneath the float, but there was plenty of trash pushing up against the foam flotation. Aside from a few Styrofoam Dunkin Donuts cups, he saw a plastic cone used to trap slime eels and some spent chemical glow sticks for attracting swordfish, all of which must have come from some distance at sea, and yet here they were, back forever. "Perfect applications for the jellyfish plastic," he said, feeling a rush of optimism for the future.

He used his hand to swoosh away a slick of pogy oil on the surface so that he would not reek of fish for the rest of the day. "On we go." He took off his glasses and inhaled deeply before sticking his head in the water. The cold shocked him right back up again, and he gasped. Salt water dripped down the back of his neck to his spine, sending an alarm through his entire nervous system. He wiped his eyes and saw Bear Petersen at the open door of the marina shed. He had a cigarette cupped in his hand and held close to his thigh. They waved at each other. No questions. Apparently satisfied that Duncan wasn't going to do himself in on his property, Bear disappeared into the darkness of his office, and Duncan watched until the little flicker of light was gone.

"Okay then." He took another deep breath and plunged his head in again, but this time he fought the urge to come right back up. He just held his breath and waited. The float moved up and down with the gentle movement of the harbor, and the water pressing against his face became a calming, enfolding presence, sharpening all his senses. He felt his heart slowing. It seemed as if he could hear salt settling to the bottom of the sea. Brine seeped in at the edges of his mouth, and he opened his eyes. The tide was so low he could see through the muddy transparency of the water to the bottom a few feet away, where teeny clouds kicked up as crawly creatures dashed into hiding, and crabs inched sideways over silt-coated debris. Life was becoming suddenly clear.

Just when he felt he could reach out and touch all the answers, he ran out of breath and popped back up for air. He exhaled and wiped his face on his sleeve. As he adjusted his lungs to oxygen again, he sensed a shadow fall upon him.

"Must you?" Annuncia said as she handed him a towel. "Must you go running off just at the moment you're needed? You were supposed to speak at the rally."

Duncan rubbed his face and put his glasses back on, making the world sharp-edged and mean again. "I was there long enough to hear you bully our clients. Why do you always have to be so extreme?"

"You have to know the extremes before you can find the middle," she said. "Besides, I consider myself fairly moderate." She looked in the water. "Did you just dunk your head in that mess of pogy oil?"

"I cleared it away first." He rubbed his hands on the towel.

"Hmm," she said but did not comment. "Anyways, if you want to see extreme, you should get a load of what Marney did when she got to work this morning. Slocum was sleeping in, so she emptied his tanks of lobsters and eels and released them into the harbor."

"You're kidding. Did he fire her?"

"No. She'd called a reporter to cover the story, and then she had Densch film it for YouTube. Slocum figures it'll be good for business. Besides, he respects her right to free speech. Why can't you respect mine?"

"Free speech doesn't apply at work, not when it hurts business."

"You have to think of the future," she said. She used two hands to slam a mosquito midair.

He tasted salt on his lips, like blood. "It was all that thinking about the future when we revamped the factory at great expense and debt that's gotten me in all this trouble in the first place."

She raised a hand and waved his words away. "It's to your benefit to have a cleaner ocean and cleaner fish frames to process. I've been thinking how Seacrest's products could be contaminated with all sorts of crap in the fish bodies, and here we are, sending it all over the country to enter distant water supplies. It's time to insure the safety of the powder."

"We can't do everything."

"No, but we can do something. Come on now, we can't laze all day on the docks. We've got work to do, even if you've got a hangover."

"How do you know I have a hangover?" he said, refusing the hand she offered to help him stand up.

"Funny YouTube video going around of you at Ten Bells on a pool table flapping your wings like a gull. Posted by Slocum. I figured your anchor chains must be pretty rusty this morning."

Duncan groaned. It was all coming back to him. He'd been playing pool all night, badly, and at last call owed Slocum $100. But Slocum said he would wipe the slate clean in exchange for a reenactment of the rescue of Kelp, and Duncan was so drunk he thought that was a good idea, what with money being so tight. Who would have thought that Slocum would stoop so low as to film it?

"What a pal," he said, following Annuncia back up the ramp, which swayed like a ship's gangway from their combined weight. "We were out celebrating. I'm guessing you heard about the jellyfish grant. It could be our long-term salvation."

"I heard, and I've been thinking. If we end up processing the jellyfish, I want it to be green." She pointed at the factory. "Instead of generators powered by oil, we use the water. Osbert thinks wave energy is the wave of the future. We tap into the ocean with buoys that generate energy with a souped-up rubber band. The buoys could be anchored just beneath the water where they won't obstruct the ocean view."

"How much is *that* going to cost?"

"Osbert will take care of it."

"It's not his company to take care of. It's mine. In fact, why is our logo on the new garbage bags? I didn't say Seacrest's would pay for them. We don't have the money."

"Osbert does. And what do we care who pays for it? It's a win-win for all of us."

"What's in it for him?"

Annuncia paused. "Let's call it his long-term business plan."

"Where do I fit into this plan?"

Annuncia smiled. She never smiled, and it made him think the world was turning upside down.

"The tide is still out on that one," she said as she began walking back up the dock, unsettling seagulls with every step.

Duncan followed, and not for the first time wondered whose side she was on. If she was actively working to get the factory from his hands and into Osbert's, he would have to do something about it. Could he fire her?

She stopped suddenly to let him catch up and touched his jacket. "You ripped the back, Dun'n."

"I know. But there's plenty more where it came from."

"Don't be so sure," she said and continued walking. "It's that sort of attitude that's gotten us in trouble in the first place. There's not plenty more of anything anymore."

twelve

Duncan was back in his Brooks Brothers suit again, and it wasn't, as he had predicted, for his funeral. Josefa had asked him to appear in a live TV morning news segment, with whatever gull was posing as Kelp at the moment, to help the local station promote their coverage of Kelp Day in a couple of weeks. She wanted a full-scale reenactment, with him cornering the bird using fancy footwork and his jacket as a net, but he drew the line in the sand. "If I have to play the fool for your cause, I'll do it, but I'm not doing the dance again."

"Don't see why not," said Josefa. "Annuncia tells me that the Ten Bells video has drummed up all sorts of good will and orders."

Duncan was reluctant to admit this was true. After Nod had linked Slocum's video to Seacrest's website, they got a flush of orders for spring delivery of Go Kelp! If he wanted to make a career out of the Kelp dance, he might be able to return Osbert's money in no time, but his pride was still worth something. Not much, but something. In the end, he agreed to wear the original outfit for the television interview while he held the gull under his arm. His pants were tucked into his black boots, just as they'd been before, but this time he could feel October's early chill seeping through the rubber soles. As the TV crew was setting up, he stared at the dozens of seagulls standing in conference at the low-tide line, eyeing him and waiting to reclaim their beach. He turned to make sure he had Seacrest's name directly behind him and that the lettering was clearly visible to viewers. Unfortunately, the cameraman had asked him to take off his glasses because they were reflecting too much sunlight, so the words on the building were out of focus. He had to squint to make out the cluster of humans gathering in the parking lot, lured there by the sight of the TV truck. Many of them probably didn't even know why they were there, only that it must be something if TV was interested.

It was definitely something. For one thing, it was windy, so it took a while for Josefa to transfer "Kelp" from her arms to Duncan's without its wings hitting his face or without losing the bird entirely. In the meantime, a station assistant was drawing *Go Kelp!* in the sand in front of them. When the gull was set to rights, Josefa left. At the end of the shot they were going to pan from Duncan to her as she pulled into the parking lot with a shiny new white van fitted out for rescue, with Kelp's picture painted on the side, the rich spoils of YouTube fame.

The camera light went on, and the interview began. It was at this moment that Annuncia and Wade lowered banners down from the factory—SAVE FAMILY BOATS and EAT GREEN FISH—effectively covering the SEACREST'S OCEAN PRODUCTS, LTD. sign. The blonde newscaster asked him to confirm that he had saved Kelp right there in front of his office.

"When did you first notice there was something wrong with the seagull?" she asked.

"I guess when his buddies flew off and he was left behind. He had a six-pack holder stuck in his beak, and his wing was dragging. They get hurt trying to free themselves."

"You'd never know it from looking at Kelp now, would you?"

"Now you wouldn't know it." Duncan smiled. "I was happy I could help."

"What do you have to say about that, Kelp?" She put the microphone to the seagull's beak, and the gull turned its head to Duncan, which made the interviewer laugh because it seemed as if the bird was looking to him for guidance. Duncan knew the look for what it was: a mute indictment of his part in this charade. The bird in his arms was not even Kelp the Second. That one, too, had met its maker. This one was Kelp the Third, a perfect seagull in robust health that Josefa had trapped for the very purpose of releasing on Kelp Day. The gull was so recently captured that it still had sea salt running out of its nostrils and down its bill, like tears. The interviewer turned back to the camera to tell the listeners about the station's full coverage of the release in two weeks' time. As previously instructed, Duncan picked up the "healed" wing and waved it in the direction of the camera. Then Josefa pulled up into the parking lot and honked her horn, and the shot was over.

The interviewer dropped her smile and hobbled back to the camera in her heels, anxious to see how she looked in the playback, what with the wind blowing her hair around. Duncan already knew how he looked: squinty and guilty. He put on his glasses and carried the gull back to its crate—not the banged-up dog carrier Josefa had always used but a clean, airy cage built specifically for large birds. Before putting the gull back in he held it close to his body. Birds were not by nature cuddly creatures, especially ones so recently abducted from the wild, but this one did not put up a fuss. Duncan bent his head and smelled the sea upon him, then gave it a squeeze.

"I'm sorry," he said, kneeling down to open the door. "Maybe you have to do a little prison time before you can appreciate your freedom again." The bird did not look convinced as Duncan eased him back in. "Soon, very soon," Duncan said as he stood up and brushed some feathers off his clothes.

He walked to the office along an unnaturally clean sweep of beach. The TV crew had tidied it up before the shot, so there were no bleach bottles, no plastic bags, no seaweed tangled with fishing line and gull feathers. It was all raked off to the side in a pile, waiting for nature's garbage collector—the outgoing tide—to take it away. He stepped onto the words *Go Kelp!* and stopped. Marketing had still not come up with a label. Maybe they could just photograph the letters in the sand. He stood pondering, then sensed someone standing next to him.

"Hello, Mr. Leland," said Beaky Harrow. Beaky's tie had come unmoored from his jacket and was fluttering in the wind. On his shoulder sat Fingers. "You've become quite the seagull celebrity, haven't you?"

Duncan shrugged. He hadn't seen or heard from Beaky since the day he delivered the contract from Osbert, weeks ago. It was not a good sign that he was circling Seacrest's again. "It's good for business, I guess."

"That's important, isn't it?" Beaky smiled, exposing a gap-toothed grin as he tucked his tie back into his jacket. "Keeping things good for business. Especially now that Osbert is so concerned about yours. What's good for Seacrest's is good for him."

Duncan pointed to the factory. "Speaking of which, I should go back there and get some work done."

"Yes, they rely on you, don't they?"

Duncan felt he was being made fun of, and he turned to go.

Beaky touched him on the elbow. "'Kites rise highest against the wind—not with it,' as our friend Osbert would say."

"Osbert didn't say that. Churchill did. What's with you two and Churchill?"

Beaky grabbed Fingers, who'd run down his arm, and put him back on his shoulder. "Churchill, Osbert, whoever. Identity is such a fragile construct." Then he turned and tromped up the beach like a Breugel peasant. At the edge of the parking lot he stopped and twisted his body back toward Duncan. "Check your pocket, Leland." He smiled before disappearing into the crowd.

Duncan put his hand in his jacket pocket and felt an envelope, cold to the touch. When he brought it close to his face, it smelled vaguely musky. He was afraid to open it, but the envelope was unsealed, so he let the contents fall into his hand.

It was a picture of him emptying the garbage bag of two dead gulls into the chute.

"No." He'd been so careful. It had been dark, and there'd been no one around. He studied the angle of the photo, and it seemed to have been taken with a night-vision camera from a distant corner of the parking lot. Who would have a camera like that but a criminal? A criminal like Osbert. Duncan emptied the envelope, but there was no letter with demands. Osbert would have no interest in letting Duncan bail himself out of this compromising photo with money—as if he had any. Osbert was out to destroy him with it, ruining his name and making it impossible for him to pay back the loan. When Duncan defaulted, Seacrest's would fall into Osbert's hands.

Duncan looked over at the parking lot, where Josefa was showing off the van. Poor Josefa. Her plans were doomed. The general public would never understand that rescue did not always mean to protect from death. They would never get how very few actually got saved. Her contribution was in giving them a quiet, dignified death, with maybe just a smidgen of hope.

He should have trusted his instincts and refused the birds. Josefa did not experience the world as he did, how unforgiving it was. He wrinkled the photo up in his hand and crammed it into his jacket pocket. He stood like that for an empty length of time, not moving, not thinking, not feeling. With a start, he felt his phone vibrate under his hand, which shook off the silence in his head. He wondered if there would come a day when he would be unable to shake reveries off so easily. The silent interludes were happening more frequently, perhaps the first sign of impending insanity.

"Hey, it's the TV star."

"Cora?" Duncan's voice caught in his throat. He had not talked to her since the drunken phone call at the beginning of the week, which must have negated any positive effects he might have gained from the love letter the week before. The letter itself hadn't turned out as well as he'd planned either, and not just because he got waylaid by Syrie. After his close call in the car with her, he'd run back to the post office, and when he pulled the envelope out from under his shirt, it was damp with sweat. The address was smeared and barely legible. He'd had to borrow a pen from a stranger and write over the words on the envelope, making it look like the deranged script of a lost explorer. "You were watching the news?"

"Annuncia called to make sure I was."

Duncan looked up at the plant and saw his staff at the windows, rolling up the banners that had obstructed his free advertising. They waved and gave him a thumbs-up, including Annuncia. If only they knew how thin a thread their jobs were hanging on at that moment.

He had to talk to Annuncia about her relationship to Osbert. If they were not too enmeshed by now with all their plans, maybe he could play on her sympathies to get her to help him instead of Osbert. She would be shocked to hear about the blackmail. He hoped.

"I did it as a favor for Josefa," said Duncan. "And I thought I'd get free advertising, but then Annuncia draped the building with banners."

"The banners were a nice touch. They showed how much Seacrest's cares about the environment."

"It would have been nicer if my employees could have shown how much they care about Seacrest's. But I don't want to talk about the company. I want to talk about us. Did you get my letter?"

"I got it. It was wrinkled and oddly rank, but I loved it in spite of its faults."

Duncan ran his fingers through his hair. He hadn't wanted her to dwell on faults. Josefa came up behind him to get the crate.

"Hello, Cora!" she shouted.

He held the phone away from his mouth. "How did you know that was Cora?"

"The look on your face," she said, and she walked away, lugging the cage with two hands. The crowd in the parking lot clapped as she approached with Kelp the Pretender.

"Did she say 'the look on your face'?" asked Cora. "Do you look that tense?"

"Maybe the look she saw on my face was love. Have you ever thought of that?"

"I guess I'll have a chance to see that look on Sunday, at the party."

"Party?"

"At your house? Your mother invited me to a party Slocum is throwing there. I thought you knew all about it."

"I knew Slocum wanted to throw a party. I didn't know it was at the house."

"I guess he was expecting your mom to tell you. She insisted on having it at home, seeing as how she is unable to leave it. I guess she thought you'd find out one way or another, since you live there."

She said the last three words with such pain in her voice he could barely respond.

"I don't have to live there," he said at last.

"Maybe you do, for a while at least."

"I'm not sure what the rules are. Can I call you?"

"Sure, during normal hours."

He cringed. "I'm sorry about the call in the middle of the night last week. That was pretty thoughtless of me."

"It was. I need my sleep." She stopped. "I think we can just both agree you were drunk and try to move on from there. But it did seem to me you wanted to ask me something important, in between the rather lucid descriptions of your sexual fantasies."

"Yes. There is something important." He was afraid to say it, but he might as well get it out in the open while he had her. "It's silly. I have no reason for even thinking it, but I have to ask."

"Go ahead," she said, sounding a little giggly.

"Cora, I have to know if there's someone else in your life."

She made a little gasp. "Yes, as a matter of fact, there is. What are you going to do about it?"

"I'm coming over right now."

"No, you can't. I'm in Portland. I watched you on a reception area TV." The wind came in off the water, making it hard to hear her. It was as if his head was in a shell and the only sound was the ocean.

"Reception area? Like in a hotel?"

"I'll come early on Sunday," she said. "We'll thrash it out then."

A blast of wind scudded in off the water and whistled into the phone, and in that moment he lost her. She was gone. He clicked the phone closed and put it in his pocket.

His felt himself growing numb from the feet up, but he was not ready to go inside. He looked at the water, and he noticed a small sand castle sitting right on the waterline, built by some restless child while his parents had been mesmerized by the filming. He watched as the wind pushed a strong tide up the beach, undermining the foundation. Two more waves followed, taking first one wall, then another, until there was nothing left standing.

He studied the words *Go Kelp!* at his feet, then picked up a gaffing hook left by an earlier tide and, with careful lettering, returned them to their original intention. *God Help Us.*

thirteen

As Duncan carried a box of lobsters to his mother's porch, he could hear the crustaceans inside, tap, tap, tapping on their waxed cardboard enclosure, shell rattling against shell as they clambered over one another, dragging strands of seaweed on banded claws. They weren't happy to find themselves in a box, but even more than that, they, like everyone else, seemed to be on edge over the uneasy weather. After a week of increasing winds, the day had arrived preternaturally calm and charged with unspent energy. The atmosphere was pressing down hard, condensing the air and draining it of oxygen. By noon, the wind had come back, this time blowing in from the ocean like a curved arm, flexing its muscles. The sun seemed somehow closer than it should have been, turning the sky yellow. Waves rose up and started slamming against the beach—spray was being blown up on the lawn. Hurricanes were infrequent visitors to Maine, especially in October, but he was not so sure that this one would give them a pass.

He smiled as he put the box down by the door. An act of nature was just what was needed to prevent Cora from returning home after the party. High tide and its evil twin, flooding, were due to arrive just after the guests. If he was lucky the causeway would wash out as so often happened, trapping the Batten Cove residents in until the water went out. By his reckoning, they would be free at dawn, with a rising sun showing him and Cora the way back to their life and their home, together, hand in hand, wading through the warm tropical waters of marital bliss.

"Run!" A man's voice sounded from deep inside the house, and Duncan could guess what that was all about. A black sedan was parked in the driveway, its rear window spotted with parking permits from a Boston museum. Poor bastards, they'd driven all this way one step ahead of a storm, and he bet his mother didn't even let them see the Dodge floor, never mind listen to a lucrative proposal for its removal. He gave the door a shove to get it unstuck, then opened it in time to step back and let the two museum representatives escape. Behind them he saw his mother coming down the stairs with a spinnaker pole, and he closed the door.

"Sorry," Duncan called after them as they headed to their car. The woman was expertly running in heels, which made him think she'd been down similar roads before. The car doors slammed, and they spun out of the driveway, flinging a storm of marble gravel into the air.

Chandu, who'd been sleeping on a pile of sails under the jumble of lawn furniture on the porch, pulled himself up to a sitting position when a pebble landed on his nose. He was not much of a guard dog. His was of an ancient line meant to pull family members from the sea, not to protect them from museum curators or crooks, all one and the same in his mother's lights. She yanked open the door and stood on the threshold holding her pole upright by her side. Her eyes had that mean and distant look usually found in sailors too long at sea.

"The nerve." Her braid flopped in the wind, almost hitting Duncan in the face. "The scavengers snuck in through the living room window."

The "window" was one of the slender French doors spaced around the many faces of the house. Only entrenched habit brought the family to this boat-hatch of a front door that was so difficult to open, when other alternatives lay unused all around them.

"Mom," he said. "You have got to stop treating museums like this. We don't know if someday we might want to call on them about the floor. It's gotten so valuable, I'm not sure it's even fair to keep it in private hands anymore." Left unsaid, but much on his mind, was the incriminating photo that had been hanging over his head all week. He would need pots of money to pay a PR firm for damage control if he had any hope of keeping the business out of Osbert's hands. If he had to start throwing cargo overboard to stay afloat, it would be nice to know the floor was an option.

"Call them?" His mother bent down to rub Chandu's head. "Whatever for? It's not leaving this house any more than I am."

Duncan was surprised that she was actually acknowledging that fact of her existence. Cora, who so often wondered at his ability to go along with his mother's self-imposed house arrest as if nothing were the matter—"An untreated mental illness soon becomes a family disease," as she so often said—would interpret this admission as a call for help. Maybe it was time to start waving his mother in.

"Mom, forget the floor for now. Why don't we go into town for lunch and leave the cleaning to Mrs. McNordfy?"

"This is no time, Duncan, dear, there's work to be done." And with that she turned back inside to continue her pantomime of housekeeping. Chandu followed close at her heel, shaking debris from his thick coat as he swayed along. "It's a wonderful thing to have company," she told Chandu. "Forces you to do all those little things."

"All those little things," Duncan said to the lobsters. The fall racing season was over, and frostbiting would not begin for a few weeks, so in theory this was repair season for the house, when his mother would draw up elaborate lists of neglected domestic matters, such as caulking cracks and seams with tar, replacing broken panes of glass, and banking the foundation of the house with seaweed for winter insulation. Much was made of the lists, but the chores themselves usually remained words on paper. As far as today's business of tidying up for the party, there was some progress being made, but not by her, whose idea it was to have it there in the first place. Mrs. McNordfy had been called in and was already doing her job of pushing sand from one room to another with her broom.

Duncan wiped his feet on the sea-grass mat, and the wind lifted the sand into the house as it blew from his shoes. "Good-bye, lobsters," he said, checking that their box was firmly closed before leaving them on the porch. "See you for dinner."

Since there was no helping his mother, he wound his way through the house to the kitchen to ask Slocum what needed to be done next. He passed the living room where his mother and Mrs. McNordfy were settling down for a mug-up to hash over the scintillating events of Port Ellery. Duncan stopped at the door of the library and watched Nod, his eyes transfixed on the cool glow of the computer screen, as always. No one was concerned about the party. The house would remain a mess, but Slocum's friends would probably be too full of rum to notice, and Cora, he hoped, would be too fully absorbed in their reunion.

At the kitchen door, he stalled for a moment to watch Slocum arrange his materials along the butcher-block table, muttering to himself as he caressed the eggplants and patted the grapefruit. He removed a poorly wrapped hunk of meat from a cooler and put it in the refrigerator, leaving a trail of watery blood. No matter. The floor, patterned after decks on a British warship, was painted red to mask spilled blood. It was too dark to see much of anything anyway. The skylight was broken and covered in seagull droppings, and the one window in the room was fitted with a metal grill like a confessional, looking out onto the neighbor's privacy hedge. The alley in between it and the house created a wind tunnel, the force of which jiggled the glass in its frame.

Against the gray-stuccoed wall was a mead bench from the dark ages—or so said his mother's cousin Belinda when she'd dragged the weathered arrangement of planks up from the beach many years ago. Duncan sat heavily upon it, suddenly weak from thinking about his meeting with Cora in just a few hours. Mental exhaustion caused him to sink further down until he was stretched out along its length, staring up at the flypaper that swung from the raftered ceiling above.

"You look like a marble knight on a slab, my friend," said Slocum. He tossed a red grape at him, and Duncan let it roll to the floor. Chandu shuffled over to sniff at it, then declined. "I marinated a green grape in beet juice," said Slocum. "Great color, huh?"

"Tell me again, Slocum," said Duncan, thinking of the safe and familiar fryolater meals at Manavilins, "why are we having the party here and not at the restaurant?"

"Romance! Adventure! And now a storm! Couldn't be better. The dinner will bring you and Cora together, or my name's not

Slocum Statler!"

"You know, you might have asked if it was okay with me to have it here."

"Wasn't my idea. The problem started when I called the land line instead of your cell by mistake. For that I blame the jellyfish fumes. The rest, I don't know. Your mum picked up, and one thing led to another. By the end of our talk, the party was here and she was calling Cora. I guess I thought she'd tell you our plans."

"I'm nervous, Slocum. It's been more than six weeks since I've seen Cora. She's angry with me, and I just can't figure out why or how to fix it."

"Don't worry. Nothing that food can't cure. Every dish is designed to delight the relationship senses. First, the *bêche de mer*."

"Sea slug?"

"A proven aphrodisiac." And with this, Slocum lifted a tray out of the cooler and put it on the table. "The recipe called for a filling of pork, cornstarch, and chopped, fried, dried fish, but I ground up my fried calamari instead. It's dangerous good."

Duncan sat up to take a look at this monstrosity. On the platter sat a large pale sausage that seemed to slither across the porcelain. "You have to remember," Duncan said, "Cora is keenly aware of Freudian representations. You won't be able to sneak anything past her subconscious."

"Sympathetic magic, my friend," said Slocum as he tucked the plastic wrap tighter around the phallic object and put it back in the cooler. "I'll slice it as thin as bible leaves and serve it with my tomato-anchovy butter. You could eat your foot with that sauce. Now look at this." Out of the same cooler he produced a tray and set it down with elaborate ceremony.

Duncan couldn't tell what was under the thick layer of gelatin. "This doesn't look very sympathetic."

"But it is! The famous *cuisses de nymphes à l'aurore*—the thighs of nymphs at dawn. Little white frog thighs. Traditionally, they're poached in a wine-and-cream sauce and covered with a champagne aspic. What a bore! So I played with those ingredients a bit, and I think you'll be very surprised."

The little legs seemed to tremble under the weight of a dark aspic, and Duncan would indeed be very surprised if they helped to win Cora back. "Does it taste like chicken?"

"Interesting question." Slocum massaged his stubbly face. "You know, if you fed fish waste to a chicken, the butchered chicken would taste just like frog legs. We should work on it. Faux frog could be a lucrative sideline for Seacrest's. You know, like fake crab?"

"What's that?" Duncan stood up and approached a surgical-looking tool on the table.

"My new Crustastun," said Slocum, picking it up and wielding it like a sword. "It applies a current to the lobster, which anesthetizes and kills it in seconds. Not only is it humane, but it reduces stress and enhances flavor. Did you know that you can taste the emotional state of an animal at the moment of its death?"

"I didn't know lobster had an emotional state even alive," said Duncan.

"You need to get out on the water more, my friend. Gérard de Nerval, a famous French lunatic, used to walk his lobster down the boulevard with a pink ribbon for a leash. He claimed they were peaceful, serious creatures who knew the secrets of the sea and didn't bark. Therefore, we should treat them with the utmost respect when we off them." Slocum put the Crustastun down and rubbed his hands together. "I was going to keep it a surprise, but I can't hold it in anymore." He started rummaging through the boxes on the table and pulled out a plastic bag filled with cherry-red lollypops. "This! This will be my signature dish in the underwater restaurant

I'm going to open when the jellyfish money starts rolling in. Baked lobster enrobed in a red lollipop glaze."

Duncan stared at him. He might have waited too long to recognize his mother's insanity, but maybe it was not too late for Slocum.

"Listen, Slocum," Duncan ventured. "I think you should get some help."

"Don't worry about that. I've got Marney coming over in about an hour to prep. Think of it, Duncan, the baked lobster spread open, the insides glistening and dark pink, the outside the red of human blood and sweet desire. I call it … the Lovester!"

Duncan was suddenly overwhelmed by acute nostalgia for the austere Sunday meals of his youth. New England Puritan tradition held that you ate only milk and crackers on Sunday because it was a sin to fill your stomach on a holy day, and even though the Lelands were lawless Unitarians, they had to follow suit because it was the cook's day off. But instead of crackers, they ate popcorn. The kids had it with milk like cereal, his father ate it with beer in a bowl, and his mother floated some in her mulberry wine.

"Won't Marney release your Lovesters back to the sea?"

"We made a deal. For every lobster I serve at the restaurant, I donate twenty-five cents to a lobster sanctuary up north. It's like a carbon offset." Slocum opened the freezer to reveal a small pagan statue. "Meet dessert! Aphrodite, the goddess of sex, carved of chocolate-oyster mousse and surrounded by waves of salty whipped cream."

"I thought the Lovesters were dessert."

"Whoever heard of lobster for dessert? That's crazy talk." Slocum closed the freezer and led Duncan to the door. "The Lovester is a deluxe entree. It'll be a hit in my new restaurant."

"We shouldn't be counting our chickens before they're hatched, Slocum. While jellyfish plastic is very promising, it's a long haul to the market. It might be years before we're making money."

Slocum dropped his arm. "Duncan, friend, I've been meaning to tell you about that."

"About what?"

"About the 'we' part." He paused and twisted his apron with his hands. "I had to sign over the exclusive rights to process the jellyfish to Osbert so he wouldn't sue me over the soup. You're such a pal, I knew you wouldn't mind if I did it to save my ass."

"What do you mean 'Osbert'? He doesn't own a processing plant."

"No … " said Slocum, and he averted his eyes. In the air hung the words *not yet*. "That's the good news. Osbert will probably pay Seacrest's to do it, so you'll still make your packet."

"He'll go through Seacrest's, all right, right over me. Our contract says that if I die before I pay off the loan, he gets the factory. You've made *it* more valuable to him and *me* more expendable."

Slocum stroked his mustache as he chewed on this information. "Well, that was a silly thing to sign, wasn't it?"

"I was a desperate man."

"And you're not now?"

Duncan turned to go, and Slocum grabbed him by the arm.

"Duncan, I'm sorry. Osbert was going to either sue me or kill me over the jellyfish soup until Annuncia convinced him he could profit by it instead. Wouldn't you rather have me alive? Duncan? Buddy?"

"*Annuncia,*" whispered Duncan. He had showed her the photo that Beaky had slipped into his pocket a few days ago in the hopes that she would stop working with Osbert, that she'd see him for what he was, a thug. But no. She just told Duncan to be more careful about disposing of birds in the future and walked away. This could not go on any longer. If she insisted on handing Seacrest's to Osbert, she would have to find a way to do it outside of the company, not in. He'd waited too long as it was. He'd waited too long for a great many things.

fourteen

Duncan stood motionless in the darkened dining room where he'd gone to escape the rising flood of Slocum's apologies. He was in no mood, and—as his mother liked to say—this wasn't the time. Slocum's culinary blowout was due to take place in just a few hours. He dialed Annuncia's number and left a message for her to call him. He wondered if she and Osbert were having an affair, love being the only force he could think of that would make Annuncia betray Duncan as she had. She'd been like a mother to him all these years, and it had come to this. She'd become as unpredictable as his own mother.

He looked around. He still had to get the place presentable for Cora. It was time to win her over, especially if he had a competitor for her affections out there. What with Annuncia and Slocum conspiring to make him vulnerable for extinction, it was time to set one thing right in his life before it *was* over.

Using a saddle-seated captain's chair, he propped open a hall door to air the room out. His family usually ate standing up wherever hunger struck them, so the dining room was rarely used and smelled stale, like a ship's hold. It was at the exact center of the house, a room left over from the badly conceived octagonal design, and because of this it had no windows. But what could have been a dungeon had been transformed into a fantasy when one relative or another had the walls paneled to bow out like a ship, then had a row of small, round recessed fixtures installed to mimic daylight coming in through oar-holes in a galley. He took off his shoes and, taking care to not pop out too much more of the inlaid wood on the marquetry, he climbed up on the tabletop to turn on the Venetian chandelier. Every crease and curl of the blown-glass light was filled with dust, and half the bulbs were out, but when he pulled the cord, the shells and coral arms glittered like phosphorescence on the evening tide.

Also reminiscent of the sea, in the worst possible way, was the seaweed collection that hung below the oar lights, dozens of framed and mounted specimens, labeled, dated, and signed by generations of Tarbells, like a family album. He was familiar with a great-great-aunt he might not otherwise had heard of because she had left behind *Toothed wrack (fucus serratus) Binny Tarbell, August 12, 1890.* He knew Cousin Tat by *Brown Algae (Padina pavonia), Tatiana Tarbell, September 2, 1948,* and long-haired Uncle Fergot, who was only briefly married into the family before disappearing into Canada, immortalized with *Green laver (Ulva latissima) Fergot P. Decker, April 29, 1967.* He removed the souvenir of his own youth from the wall, *Bladderwrack (fucus vesiculosus) Duncan Leland, July 1, 1987.* He'd been thirteen years old, soon to leave for boarding school, when he'd collected that seaweed off the beach with his father. He remembered the day. The two of them side by side, looking for just the right piece of seaweed to frame. Duncan had slipped on a wet rock and gashed his knee. Rather than tend to the wound, his father just sent him to rinse it off with seawater, which healed most any injury but stung like a serpent. "The joy you get out of life is tied to the amount of pain you're willing to bear," his father had said in response to his son's unchecked cries. Duncan had been painfully aware of his childhood coming to an end that day.

As Duncan held the frame in his hands, he became wistful to have a child to call his own. And yet, how in all good conscience could he perpetuate his family's mental infirmities? Cora accused him of being paranoid, but didn't his paranoia just prove his point? He wondered if she would agree to an anonymous sperm donor. Then they could have their baby and their marriage, and if he was offed by Osbert, oh, well, only Cora and the fertility clinic would know it wasn't his biological child.

First things first. The entire herbarium had to go. "Out to the porch, the stinky lot of you," he announced. He'd ask his mother if he could give them a permanent home in Seacrest's lobby—while he still had a lobby—where displaying seaweed varieties made at least a little sense. He gathered the pictures in a box and carried them out along a groined corridor to the porch, where the wind almost knocked them out of his arms. He stowed the frames securely behind a garden bench and hose, then braced himself against the wall to watch the storm coming in. The sea was troubled and noisy as the tide fought the wind, creating crests that shimmered white against the iron-green water. Seahorses, his father used to call them. Hundreds of gulls struggled to make land with wings outstretched, suspended in the wind as upright as angels. There were still a few restless yachts in the Boat Club basin, bows facing the wind and yanking at their mooring lines like nervous fillies, halyards slapping against the rigging, the wind whistling through their metal masts. *L'ark*, with her solid mast of wood, was still out there, too. If Judson couldn't get her pulled that afternoon, he'd better motor her out of the harbor and let her ride out the storm in the relative safety of the open water. It would take guts to do it, but if he loved her, it was what had to be done.

Duncan tested the ropes holding down the lawn furniture so that the chairs wouldn't go flying around like wooden missiles. Attached to the porch rails out back was a sun-bleached ship's wheel, where his mother often stood pretending to steer a yacht, but it was now spinning dangerously in the wind. He hadn't put his shoes back on from standing on the table, so he didn't want to climb over the splintery furniture in his bare feet to lash the wheel to the rail. He'd wait. The wheel was right outside the library window, and since he had to go there for the guest book anyway, he'd secure it then. As he turned to go back inside, he thought he saw a small boat, like a dory, rise in the waves, then drop out of sight. He stood still for a minute to see if it would reappear, then decided it was a trick of the eye.

~

Nod sat in the green-leather wing chair in the library, hunched over the laptop on the desk in front of him, and did not look up when Duncan entered.

"Do you know where the guest book is?" Duncan asked as he looked around the cluttered mess, seeing the room through Cora's eyes. It was clearly the home of deeply troubled souls, but as long as he lived there, too, he could not point fingers.

"It's right there," said Nod, still not looking up or indicating in any way what *right there* could possibly mean. Duncan began to sort through stacks of withered books in red morocco bindings and titles of gold. With a smile, he ran his hand across Great-Uncle Abington's "curious" books, as the family called his collection of nineteenth-century European pornography, chaste etchings of *grandes horizontales.* The books had probably not been touched since he and Nod were boys, and Duncan would not have been surprised to find mice nests instead of pages in between the covers after all this time. But he could not afford to linger in a happier past. Failing to find the guest book where it should be, he began to rummage through the shelves and counters, where crystal decanters of mulberry wine hid behind dusty volumes and broken knickknacks. He opened a drawer and found sheaves of documents going back to colonial land grants, all bearing the round red stains of glasses. On a side table, hidden among sea fans brought back as souvenirs by old family mariners, was the cast of a coelacanth he'd bought at a seafood conference. The coelacanth was a prehistoric fish once thought to be extinct but discovered to be still living in the modern ocean. It seemed somehow emblematic of his family, and he'd given it to his mother at Christmas.

As he worked his way around the room, he paused at a framed photo of his father at the tiller. He realized he did not even own a picture of his father and wondered why that was. Maybe he was still angry with him for dying.

"Where'd *that* thought come from?" he said, though he had not meant to say it out loud.

"What?" asked Nod.

"Nothing." Duncan slipped the photo into his pocket to have it copied.

"We'd better cancel the party," Nod said as he cleared his throat.

"Have a look at this NOAA weather map. Mom's gone upstairs to double-check all the instruments."

"We're not canceling anything," said Duncan. "I need to see Cora."

Nod looked up at him and blinked rapidly. "You need a party to see her? Just get in the car and go."

Duncan was annoyed at the question. It was his job to point out irrational behavior to his family, not the other way around. "I'm giving us time to process."

"Process?" Nod turned back to his computer screen. "Sounds like working a load of fish through a conveyor belt."

"I didn't know you were such an expert on relationships," Duncan said, intending a sharp poke at Nod's isolated life. But if Nod perceived any insult, he didn't show it. He looked up at the coffered ceiling in deep thought and then put his hands in his lap and spoke.

"I am an expert. There are many relationships to consider on the water, all more elemental than some silly marriage. In a boat, I'm not in a struggle with a mere mortal like a wife, but with Nature herself. Unlike marriage, a relationship with the water expands your horizons instead of shrinking it. It's both unknowable and changing, simultaneously. The trouble with you, dear brother, is that you are impatient with the unknown, when that's the most exciting thing there is."

"I hope all that excitement compensates for never winning a race," said Duncan, surprised not just by Nod's strange outburst but by his own nastiness.

Nod smiled his odd one-sided smile. "I'm not racing against the others, I'm racing against myself, so I always win. Every race takes me one step closer to understanding the mystery of my soul, making me feel whole. It cultivates patience and endurance under adversity and keeps alive my fires of hope, just like any good religion. More important, it's taught me how to steer around all the useless garbage life throws at me." Nod looked right at him. "It wouldn't kill you to try it. As far as I can tell, you've been clinging to an anchor in the middle of the sea."

Duncan was stunned to silence. He'd never heard so many words from Nod in his life, and certainly never ones pulled up from such depth. He softened his voice. "I don't know what you're talking about. What anchor?"

"Your ego. You want to win this fight you've been having with Cora, at any cost. Even if it means living here again." He looked around him and laughed. "Are you *insane?* Winning means nothing. You've got to love just being out there, or pull in your sails and call it a day."

"I'm not trying to win any fight, I'm trying to win Cora back."

Nod shrugged. "Win, win, one way or another," he said, then turned his attention back to the computer screen. Before Duncan could organize some sort of defense, their mother sailed through the door with a sextant under her arm.

"The blow's a bad one, my hearties," she said. "But the good news is that it will miss us entirely."

Nod clicked a few buttons. "It says here that Port Ellery is right in the way of the storm."

"By 'us' I didn't mean the town," said his mother in an exasperated voice. "I meant 'us' the house. There's no reason to call off the plans for tonight. After all, Cora is coming, and we have much to celebrate. But first, Nod, you go and tow the float back from the Boat Club before it washes away again and gets destroyed in the storm."

Duncan looked at Nod. "You haven't gotten the float back yet? They asked you to move it weeks ago."

Nod stood up. "I only got the gas can filled this morning.

Contrary to what you may think, my life is very full."

"If you want to keep that life you'd better stay on shore," said Duncan, pointing outside the French window. "Look at the waves."

"A smooth sea never made a skilled mariner," their mother said, tucking the sextant under her arm like a baton before walking out of the room.

Nod turned to the window and smiled at the raging sea. Trees were being quickly stripped of their leaves, and the sun had disappeared completely behind black fists of clouds. It was three in the afternoon, and it was already dark.

"Nod. You don't have to do this just because Mom told you to."

"I'm not. I'm doing it because I must. As Dad always said, never turn down a challenge."

"Don't go. It's suicide to sail during a hurricane, not a challenge."

Nod laughed. "I'm not *sailing. That* would be crazy." He clicked off the computer. "I'm motoring over in the inflatable." He continued to snorfle to himself as he unplugged his cell phone from its charger.

Duncan let it rest. No one could quarrel with a man who laughed like an idiot. Nod would go down to the dock and discover for himself that it was impossible to go anywhere, under any power. Duncan was turning away to go about his business when from the bottom of his bare feet he felt the house tremble, like a ship under way. There was a roar outside, and he turned to look. The cedars bent as if being held down by two heavy hands, and the air filled with dry leaves being sucked up into an invisible vortex. He saw, too late, that the ship's wheel on the porch was whipping around so fast it was gyrating its screws out of the wood. In one wild turning frenzy, it freed itself from the railing and in the same moment crashed right at them through the glass door, which burst into a galaxy of shards.

fifteen

Duncan hammered plywood over the shattered window while Mrs.
McNordfy swept up the glass. Nod was gone. While Duncan had
been running around trying to find nails, hammer, wood, and ladder,
all stored separately in far-reaching parts of the house, garage, and
boat shed, Nod had donned his raingear and left for the dock. By
the time Duncan returned to the library with tools, Nod was already
shouldering his way across the darkening lawn, listing to the right
with a full can of gas. He raised his hand without looking back when
Duncan screamed, "Come back!" over the wind. Since he would not
listen to reason, Duncan could only hope that the wind would keep

pushing him back until he gave up. While all this was going on, his mother rummaged through the library shelves looking for a book of party games.

"We haven't had a party in so long." She sighed. "I've forgotten the rules to 'Two on the Tower.'"

"It's like Truth, ain't it?" said Mrs. McNordfy.

"Oh, much better than Truth. You make believe you're on top of a tower with a friend on either side, and confess which of them you would push off first. Where could that book have gone?"

"Mom." Duncan put his hammer down just as the rain began to hit the plywood in heavy splats. "Why would you want to play something like that? It sets everyone up to get hurt."

"Speaking of hurt, my boy," said Mrs. McNordfy, leaning on her broom, "how's them feet of yours?"

His bare soles had gotten cut on the glass when he picked up the wheel. Blood stained the parquet, and this was not the kitchen floor, designed to hide such accidents. Duncan lifted a foot. Dirt seemed to have staunched the bleeding. "Just needs a good scrub." He looked meaningfully at the floor. "That could use a good scrub, too."

"Yesh, yesh, yesh," said Mrs. McNordfy, pushing her broom around.

"Half of them," his mother said, blowing dust off a gray volume.

"Half of what?" he asked.

"Only half the guests would get hurt playing the game. The other half would be very pleased." She opened the book and flattened a silverfish with her finger before closing it with evident satisfaction. "Time to hang the swordfish bait outside so everyone will know we're *en fête*. Duncan, dear, move the ladder to the porch."

"I'll hold it steady for you, Mrs. Leland," said Mrs. McNordfy. "Then I got to get out of here before my old Bob worries." She emptied her dustpan into the trash barrel she'd pulled in from the kitchen, making the room smell of garbage.

His mother stopped at the door. "I almost forgot, I brought your shoes in, Duncan, dear," she said, pointing to his loafers on the library table. "You left them in the dining room. Please try to be a little neater. We are expecting company, you know."

And then she left. Duncan looked around the room. The ship's wheel was leaning against a bookshelf. His blood was smeared on the floor. Leaves and papers had been blown all around the room and out into the hall, but his mother's priority was to decorate the outside of the house with glow sticks. Mrs. McNordfy didn't even take the trash barrel with her when she left.

He picked up his shoes and turned them over, knowing what he would find. Freshly painted white crosses on the soles, done with Wite-Out by his mother, who believed that they protected sailors from sea monsters and sharks. She periodically swept through the house marking all the shoes and boots, especially right before a storm. As for herself, she rarely wore anything on her feet at all.

~

Duncan knelt before the fireplace, lighting matches. He was getting his knees dirty with ash and wondered if he would have time to change. He'd been so nervous about Cora that he just couldn't decide what to wear and ended up being both too formal and too relaxed for the occasion. His tie wouldn't lie straight, his jacket collar kept popping up, and there was some sort of bleach stain on his chinos, but he didn't know what could be done about it all now. The guests were due any minute, those who were still coming. The storm was big and it was bad, and phone calls had been pouring in over the past hour with cancellations, but they would still have over a dozen adventurous souls. The wind roared as it swept over the top of the chimney, sucking out the matches as soon as he lit them. When he finally got a corner of a newspaper going, the driftwood caught all at once in a violent flash, throwing salty sparks of colors. Duncan looked at his watch. Nod had not come back yet. His mother said there was nothing to worry about—he was probably at the Boat Club biding his time inside one of the sheds until he saw an opening in the weather. Duncan was lost in distant thought when he heard a door creak open behind him.

"Still mad at me?" asked Slocum, his head peeking in.

"Mad? Why would I be mad?" asked Duncan, standing up and brushing debris off his pants. "Mad that you pulled a small fortune out from under my feet? Or mad that you've set me up to be disposed of?"

"*Amuse-bouches?*" Slocum held out a plate of food that couldn't be identified as fish, flesh, or good red herring, and Duncan hoped Cora would know enough to eat something before she came. "Day boat scallops with caper raisin emulsion," Slocum said helpfully. "A peace offering."

"No peace. I thought we were friends. I thought we were partners in jellyfish plastic."

"We are friends," said Slocum. "That's why I knew you'd want to sacrifice a few piddling potential profits for my life. And don't think I'm not grateful." He turned to look at Duncan's mother as she entered from the library with a tray. "Voilà! The *vino sacro* has arrived!"

The fireplace puffed back as the library door closed behind her and filled the air with smoke. She held up a black tin tray of jelly-jar glasses filled with mulberry wine.

"A sip with your snack, my hearties?" She wore damp white ducks and a striped jersey, and her braid was dripping water on the floor. A slicker had been no match for the driving rain when she hung her party lights. Duncan looked out the window, and against the complete darkness he saw the luminescent sticks strung out on a fishing line, draped from pillar to pillar and jerking madly in the wind.

Chandu, his thick coat heavy with water, collapsed with a sigh on the hearth, where the warmth of the fire released his doggie odors to the air. Duncan held up his hand, refusing the wine, then turned to the drinks table for a beer. Slocum cleared a spot for his platter.

"I'm worried about Nod," said Duncan, opening his Harpoon Ale. "Don't you think we should do something?"

"Nod is a grown man," said his mother. "You have to let him do what grown men do."

"Which is what?" asked Duncan.

"It's about time you found out," she said.

Slocum artfully whipped a glass from his mother's tray before she put it down on the coffee table. "Risk their lives in foolish escapades?"

"You see that painting?" His mother pointed to a paint-by-number replica of Rembrandt's *Storm on the Sea of Galilee*. "Christ yells at the wind in the face of a storm and prevents the boat from sinking. Cousin Biddle painted that for your father and me as a wedding present. There's much to be learned from art."

"Nod can shout at the wind all he wants," said Duncan. "But it's not going to save him."

"Notice how Christ stays calm in the midst of great turbulence. He floats above all the hubbub. Try to be more like that. Like Nod."

What is this? Duncan wondered. A Jesus complex by proxy? He would have loved to discuss this with Cora, but he had promised himself that he would not start talking about his mother while trying to win back his wife.

"My Sunday school teacher, Mrs. Havelock?" said Slocum. "She taught us that the Galilee storm was a metaphor for troubled souls."

"The point is," his mother continued, waving Slocum's words away, "you have to have faith."

"Faith," said Slocum. "Yes, indeed." They were quiet for a minute as they all continued to stare at the poorly executed painting. "Did your cousin stay in the arts?"

"Poor girl died of the chestnut blight before she made a name for herself."

"Mother, that's a horticultural disease, not a human one."

"Duncan." She sighed deeply. "You've always had such a limited mind. Even as a child."

Duncan stared at her. First Slocum turns on him, then Nod dumps on him, now his mother. He was about to say something about how it was better to have a limited mind than a snapped one when Slocum once again stepped in between them.

"Annabel," said Slocum, steering her attention to a figurehead on the wall, "tell me about your angel here."

The figurehead, hanging high up on a wall, had wormholed wooden curls and a distracted look. Her angel wings were long gone, and her white paint was worn away. "Great-Uncle Winnie on my mother's side," said his mother, "served as captain on the *U.S.S. Gabriella* in the Napoleonic wars. He died heroically in battle, so rather than commending him to the sea, they sent him home in a cask, preserved with alcohol. Years later, when the ship was decommissioned, the navy sent the family the figurehead. There's devotion for you."

"I didn't know America fought in the Napoleonic wars," said Duncan, knowing full well that the figurehead had washed up on the beach in Lucius's time. He wondered if his mother knew she was lying or was just straight-out delusional.

"This is no time, Duncan, dear." As she bent to pick up her

tray, the end of her braid knocked some scallops to the floor. "I hear guests! To your stations, men!"

And then she disappeared into the front hall, where Duncan heard torrents of water hitting the tile and shouts of greetings, with an unfamiliar voice saying, "The rain falls on the good and bad alike." There seemed to be a struggle to get the door closed against the wind.

Slocum was still admiring the figurehead. "Sailors used to believe that gales would subside if a naked woman appeared before them. That's why so many of these are bare-breasted. You don't often get to see the tits of an angel."

"My mother's driving me crazy," said Duncan.

Slocum slapped him on the back. "You know what Clover tells Harley: People are given the mom they need for a particular incarnation." He offered his glass to Duncan. "Here, this pungent little wine will give you a fast push out of the gate."

"I wouldn't use it to give a pig an enema, as my grandfather used to say," said Duncan. "Besides, it's only a gentle push out of the gate, low in alcohol."

"The fun isn't in the alcohol," said Slocum. "Mulberries are a known hallucinogen." He swallowed the drink and smacked his lips. "Your mom probably hasn't touched ground in years."

Duncan became so abruptly disoriented it seemed as if the floor had washed out from under his feet. He felt the too-familiar sensation of his skull emptying of sound, but this time he did not let his mind just drift out with the tide. He took off his glasses and rubbed his eyes. A hallucinogenic mother. His whole life suddenly started to make sense. He put his glasses back on and turned to the photo on the mantel with her posing with the marlin, and there was that look in her eyes. She'd probably been drinking the wine for days to celebrate her marriage, more so during the difficult landing of the marlin. Could an overdose have triggered a bummer trip, which prevented her from ever going out on the water again? The same with his father's funeral. She'd gotten pretty looped that day and hadn't left the house since. For that matter, his father was known to throw a few back now and again, especially at lunch, before he sailed back to work.

It could also explain a great deal about Nod. He was born nine months after the honeymoon, conceived during this binge. That couldn't be good.

Duncan felt the beer settle in his stomach like bilge water. "I thought it was the family genes."

"It was the family wine," said Slocum, refilling his glass. "Amazing that a few berries can be transformed into a mind-altering substance." He lifted his nose and sniffed, and they both looked toward the back hall, where a finger of black smoke beckoned from the kitchen. "Please, God, not the sea slug," said Slocum, and he was gone.

~

Outside, it was raining like all possessed. Duncan gazed at the fire. The chimney cap could not keep the water out, so it ran down the flue lining and popped into steam on contact with the fire. If it was true about the wine, he could not wait to tell Cora. His family was not particularly crazy; they were just drugged out of their minds. He and Cora could have normal kids as long as they kept them away from Grandma's jelly and decanters. To save what was left of his mother's mind, he would go down to the cellar and tap the casks, but he couldn't do anything about it now. Cora would be arriving in a few minutes, and he hadn't even programmed the music. The right songs would convey his joy and evoke the more romantic and forgiving aspects of Cora's psyche. He was thinking something moving and classical. Ravel. Beethoven. The Who.

But first he removed an open bottle of mulberry wine from the drinks table and hid it behind the sofa; then he knelt down at the stereo dock in the corner and fiddled with the iPod wheel. Guests continued to arrive. Newcomers entered brusquely, as if thrown in by a wave from the sea, filling the room, but Duncan was lost in thought. He had just clicked on "Pinball Wizard" when he heard a voice that made his barometer drop. He stood up too suddenly and, for the second time that night, felt himself with nothing to stand on.

"Syrie. What are you doing here?"

"What kind of a welcome is that?" Syrie wore an ice-green shantung silk dress so sheer it could have been threaded through a ring. Her earrings glittered like fishing lures, and milk-white pearls touched her collarbone. Her little dog was tucked into an evening bag she wore across her chest. She swiveled her attention to the stereo. "Have you ever noticed how great pieces of music follow the stages of sex? Desire, arousal, climax, and resolution?"

"Go!" Duncan hissed. He could see what was happening quite clearly now. Just as with the incriminating seagull pictures, Syrie was part of Osbert's elaborate plan to catch him in compromising positions. Or worse, she was an actual assassin. Now that he knew he was capable of producing normal children, he became very protective of his life. "Go home before Cora gets here."

"Why should Cora care if I'm here?" She smiled broadly. "Why do *you* care so much?"

The party was closing in around them. The guests, stripped of their wet gear, had come to anchor in front of the fireplace to burn off the damp, so Duncan had to pretend civility until he could usher her out of the house.

"Syrie, why don't you go to the kitchen and tell Slocum that people are arriving? Then you can leave by the back door."

"Oh, Duncan, you're too much." She laughed in such an intimate manner that some of the party turned and smiled knowingly.

"I have to go see to my guests. The *invited* guests."

"Your mother invited me," she said.

He took off his glasses, put them back on, and then left Syrie without a word. He busied himself at the drinks table, helping to dispense rum, open beers, and pass the strange scallops, and as he did, he wondered why his mother was out to destroy his marriage. What with sending Nod out to sea, it was as if she were trying to rid herself of her children altogether. The sooner she was weaned off the wine, the better.

The room went hush as the ancient timbers of the house creaked like a boat and wind whistled through the window sash. The roar of the waves could be heard in the living room as clearly as if they were standing in the middle of the sea, causing the chatter of the group to resume louder than before. He switched on the floodlights in the backyard so they could watch the Atlantic dash itself upon the lawn, flinging green tons of seaweed torn from the bottom of the ocean. Then he called Josefa and asked her to stop in at the Boat Club on her way to see if Nod was trapped there.

"These storms get sketchier and sketchier," said Marney. She wore an apron, as if she intended to go to the kitchen to help prep, but at the moment she was carrying around a drink with so much surface froth it looked polluted. "It's global warming. We'll all be underwater in a hundred years."

"I thought global warming was going to cause another Ice Age," said her boyfriend, Dirt, a local lumper on the docks.

"Nonsense," Duncan's mother said. "It's just the perigean tide coinciding with the northeast winds. There's a logical reason for everything."

Duncan looked at his watch. Where was Cora?

An older, rather distinguished-looking man wearing a white dinner jacket cleared his throat. He was tall and unstooped, with military-cropped gray hair and a large beak of a nose that hung over a cultivated mustache. The sac under his chin wobbled when he talked. "The Montauk lighthouse at the end of Long Island was built in 1796, three hundred feet from the cliff edge." He pressed out his bottom lip as he looked into his gin. "Today it is seventy-five. They don't know whether to reinforce the cliff or move the lighthouse."

"Who is that who just washed ashore?" Duncan whispered to Marney.

"Everard Blue," she whispered back. "An admiralty lawyer from New York who just retired here. Wandered into Manavilins looking for a men's room this morning, and Slocum invited him."

"Do we hold the line, or do we retreat?" asked Everard of no one as he looked out the window. "We'll all have to make that decision sooner or later."

Duncan's mother gave the man a sour look, then picked up her empty tray and walked over to Duncan. "What is that horrible man doing here? *Cet vieux carp.*"

"He's not an old trout," said Duncan, keeping his voice low. "Don't blame him for pointing out that the edge of the cliff is getting closer. All you have to do is look at the backyard to see it's true."

"We need more wine," she said, moving toward the library.

Duncan stopped her with a touch on her elbow. "No more wine. I think everyone is happy with what's out there."

"*I'm* not happy with what's out there." She turned to glare at Everard Blue, who, oddly, was staring back at her.

"Never mind him. I think it's time to call the Coast Guard about Nod."

do they know one another?

187

She closed her eyes, then talked slowly, as if explaining the obvious to the impaired. "The path one makes in the water is invisible, Duncan, dear. They can't find Nod there. Why, eighty-five percent of the planet is covered in salt water!" She turned to go, then stopped. "Did you try his cell phone?"

"Many times."

"Did it ring?"

"Yes."

"There. He's fine. It wouldn't ring if it was underwater. He probably blew a little off course and he's waiting the storm out in some sheltered place and just doesn't care to talk right now. I'm sure he's enjoying himself immensely." And then she continued to the library.

Duncan stepped into the empty dining room to look at his phone. He'd never heard back from Annuncia, and there was no message from Nod. He dialed the Coast Guard and listened to it ring. He heard Slocum in the kitchen, singing as he cooked. A soaking Densch walked through the room carrying the box of lobsters from the porch and nodded at him.

The Coast Guard dispatcher was calm in the face of what was obviously chaos out in the harbor. "Dozens of vessels broke loose from their moorings tonight, sir," he said. "You sure your brother just didn't take his vessel out to sea to ride it out?"

"It's not a yacht, it's an inflatable," said Duncan, feeling a flush of sweat under his clothes.

"An inflatable?"

"He was just going around the corner … " Duncan heard the crackle of ship-to-shore communications in the background. The officer cut him off.

"We'll alert the crews. They might already have him. We'll let you know when we know."

After the dispatcher hung up, Duncan tried Cora again. Nothing. He stood feeling a little lost. The chandelier swayed ever so slightly with the wind-blown house, making the room shimmer like a lagoon. The table was set for a buffet-style dinner, with stacks of porcelain plates and piles of silver utensils like pirate plunder, all faintly rattling. He wandered back into the living room to join the crowd gathered around the drinks table. Slocum put down a plate of slightly charred sliced sea slug, surrounded by other assorted nibbles. Clover, who was in Maine for the week for Harley's birthday, picked up a skewer of mango and periwinkle. "Dude, does a snail really need fruit?"

"Fruit is the centerpiece of the primate diet." Slocum spotted the bottle of wine behind the sofa and picked it up. "It's why we like wine! Nothing broadcasts the presence of ripe fruit better than the smell of fermentation." He poured a glass. "Water's a dangerous, nasty thing, full of cholera and bacteria. Ancestors who drank fermented and sterile liquids like this lived long enough to reproduce. Survival of the fittest!"

"I kind of like it," said Bear Petersen, slowly chewing the mango and periwinkle combo. "Different."

"Bear is sailing under false colors tonight," Syrie said softly, inching closer to Duncan.

Duncan looked at Bear, whose thin face and dry lips were chapped beyond repair by the salt and wind, but on his feet, peeking out from mustard Carhartt work pants, he wore pointy red heels.

"Bear," said Duncan. "I just talked to the Coast Guard. Boats are bouncing around all over the harbor. Not just the light-weight yachts but the fishing fleet, too."

"Damn," he said. "Thought the fun wouldn't start until high tide. Come on, boys, party's over. Got a head count to do."

Bear popped another periwinkle in his mouth and grabbed a

bottle of rum from the table, then turned in his heels toward the door. He was followed by his yard manager and crane operator, both raw men with deckhand knuckles and windburned faces, tough as iron but loyal to their boss no matter what he wore on his feet. Here they were, following him into the gnashing teeth of a storm, while Duncan doubted his own employees would follow him to the movies. Annuncia wouldn't even return his calls. Josefa arrived just then and helped the men gather their rain gear and got them out the door. Wind whipped through the living room until a few volunteers pushed the door shut again.

"No Nod," she told Duncan, after shedding her wet things. "The manager's there … hasn't seen him. Says it's a mess. Lots of boats gone. *L'ark* broke from her mooring hours ago, and no one can even find Judson to tell him."

Duncan groaned and looked out the window, as if the harbor could be seen through the wall of rain. *L'ark* would get tossed up on the beach or get swept against the submerged breakwater. Either way, she'd end up in splinters, if she wasn't already. He thought of Nod. If he wasn't at the Boat Club, where was he? There weren't many options left on the table.

"Doesn't surprise me about *L'ark*," said Estrella Campion, a close friend of Judson's ex-wife. "Judson has been carrying too much sail for his wind for a long time. He's in debt up to his gunwales and couldn't even afford the haul-out and winterizing for *L'Ark*. Not to mention that he's a year behind in Boat Club fees. I wouldn't be surprised if he left *L'ark* out there on purpose to collect the insurance."

"Insurance won't cover an act of God," said Josefa.

"It's all an act of God," said Everard. "Yacht insurance usually doesn't cover much more than liability—if a guest drowns on your boat, say."

They all looked out the windows at the raging storm and fell silent. There wasn't anyone in the room who hadn't lost a friend or family member to the sea.

"I keep a gun on the boat in case it sinks," said Clyde Harmon, owner of the *Mary Celeste*, a dragger in town. He had violet beard stubble and burst blood vessels in his eyes from thirty years of wind in his face. "I'll blow my head off before I drown."

Clover gave him a thumbs up. "Amen to that."

"Where's Leigh?" Josefa asked. Clyde was almost always with Leigh Higgens, his girlfriend and captain of another boat in the fleet.

"She exceeded the monkfish tails limit last week," said Clyde. "So she's in Portland for court tomorrow morning."

This news set off a loud grumble and cursing over regulations that were strangling the life out of the fishing industry. Over their noise, Syrie raised her voice as if singing an aria. "Speaking of court, late this afternoon the police went to arrest Slocum's sister, Rheya, for the murder of her husband, Marsilio. But she was gone. So was her dory."

"What?" Duncan looked around for Slocum, but he was back in the kitchen. He wondered if he knew. Then he wondered if he'd known for a long time.

Syrie smiled. "According to Chief Lovasco, that dog Marsilio had been anchoring in some other woman's harbor. They think Rheya cut him up like bait, then sank his boat in the last storm to make it look like an accident. Went out rowing every day and dropped a piece here and there for the bluefish until the police put it and him all together."

Duncan felt a strange sense of relief. Marsilio's body parts in the harbor had nothing to do with Osbert; it was just another marriage gone bad.

The crowd broke up into smaller clusters, all excitedly discussing the murder. Clover separated herself from them and came up to

Duncan. "Dude, your mom has such lovely skin."

"I suppose," said Duncan.

"She told me she adds a handful of seaweed to every bath," said Syrie, joining them. "When I was in Thailand, I went to a hot spring where little tropical fish nibbled away at my dead skin cells."

"Have you ever had a jellyfish facial?" asked Clover. "There's a salon in Oregon where they stretch sheets of jellyfish over the face. They pull them out of the tanks live, like sheet of phlegm."

"Where is Cora?" asked Duncan, looking toward the door. He felt the phone vibrate in his pocket and walked away from the two women to answer it. "Oh, no," he said when he saw the number. He flipped it open. "Where are you?"

"I had to turn back," said Cora. "It was too much. Trees are falling all over town."

"Stay where you are. I'll come get you."

"No, I'm almost home."

"Can I come to you? I don't want you to be alone on a night like this."

"You've got a party going on there."

"It's not my party. I don't have a single thing to celebrate unless I have you. And I have wonderful news."

"*You* have news? All news and no questions?" she said, and then there was more silence as the house pitched and yawed as if it were on anchor. "Come if you want. I'm curious to find out if you're as dense as you seem."

He hung up overjoyed. He was going to see Cora. Alone. Syrie took a step toward him, and the crowd seemed to step back to give them a little room, sensing something cooking.

"Duncan, did I hear you say you were leaving? I wonder if I can get a ride into town. The old Jaguar is too low to make it back out the causeway." She smoothed down her dress and clutched her bag of dog. "Besides, might be nice to get a little time alone in case Cora takes you back tonight."

"Syrie, I don't want to be alone with you. My mother was just trying to pull you into her strange plan to mess up my life."

"Are you still blaming your mother for everything? I don't recall that she made you get into my car a couple of weeks ago." She scratched her dog's head. "Regardless of your virtue, I still need a ride into town. I'm not spending the night here."

"No. I'm going, and I'm going alone."

He turned away, and at that moment the lights flickered and everyone held still. They seemed to be counting the seconds, then gasped as a single body when the lights went out altogether. The fireplace cast shadows across the room. Slocum, dressed in chef whites, appeared like an apparition at the dining room entrance. He was holding a flashlight and the Crustastun.

"I think I blew a fuse," he said.

"Everyone just stay put for a minute," said Duncan. "I'll go to the basement and fix it."

The crowd edged closer to the fireplace, and the flames lit up their faces, some apprehensive, others clearly excited by the drama. His mother, already lit to the gills, climbed up on the sofa and held up a bottle of wine with cobwebs still clinging to it. "While we wait for the light, let's give a toast to Slocum and his recipe for jellyfish plastic! *Ganbei* and good luck!"

As the crowd lifted their glasses, a roar of weather shook the house down to its rocky foundations. The windows rattled, and the wind howled in the chimney like a ghost. No one moved. The trees creaked and groaned as a wall of tide reached up from the beach and landed on the lawn with a crash of water within inches of the house. Above the sound of the wind they heard the deafening sound of a wave building strength as it rolled in from the sea, then listened to it crash onto the land. Before anyone realized that the water was upon them, it rushed across the porch, bursting the lawn furniture out from its ropes. A metal chair tumbled over itself three times before it came crashing through one of the windows. As everyone tried to crowd onto the furniture, Chandu barked and snapped at their heels to herd them to safety.

sixteen

The party was over. As Duncan fumbled with the flashlight in the basement, trying to resuscitate the antiquated fuse box, he heard the sounds of footfalls, breaking plates, and furniture being scraped across the floor as people exited blindly in the dark over his head. The floorboards bowed and creaked under the pressure of the departing crowd, loosening dust and debris that rained down upon his head. He heard Slocum scrambling for the Chinese gong in the dining room, and then he heard him whack it with a metal object, most likely the Crustastun.

"Abandon ship!" Slocum shouted. "Grab food and head for Ten

Bells." Ten Bells was on the next street up from Manavilins, high enough above sea level that they wouldn't have to move again. The guests hooted and cheered. These were men and women on speaking terms with the outdoors, and they loved nothing better than a good blow. They would have been game to stay on if it weren't for the possibility of being stranded out on the Cove after the beer had run out. One by one Duncan heard the cars and pickups grind into gear. He looked up at the basement window and saw headlights shine weakly through the storm, then fade away, leaving a teeming black void with nothing to distinguish between the elements. Water, earth, air—it was all the same now. It might be the beginning of the world, or the end of it.

As he stood contemplating the intensity of nature, a wave pounced on the house, letting in gushes of water along the basement window seams, and he got back to business. His hands were unsteady as he replaced one fuse, then another, amazed to find a carton of replacements within easy reach. The lights came on, and he exhaled in relief. There was hope. The blackout had been an internal problem, not an act of God. If the utility lines had been knocked down by trees, he would be unable to leave his mother sitting alone in a dark house, and she would never leave that house with him. Now he could go to Cora with a clear conscience, and who knew—maybe Nod would show up to keep his mother company.

Well, he knew. He just didn't want to admit it. The very thought of where his brother might be at that moment caused a surge of foreboding to rise up in his chest, but that got pushed back by the demands at hand. With electricity restored, it was probably not safe to be standing in water, not with the building's history of loose wires. He started wading back to the steps, and as he reached for the banister he noticed that the wine barrels, stored on their sides under the stairwell, were beginning to jiggle as the water rose. It was not unusual after a nor'easter to find that the barrels had floated to different corners of the cellar. He would take a hatchet to them in the morning and chalk it up to the storm.

By the time Duncan returned from the flooded basement, everyone was gone. The rogue tide had retreated as well, leaving the floor soaked and the fire out. There was no human noise, only the deep howling of the hurricane as the wind shook the house like a tambourine. It was now two hours until high tide. Two more hours of increasing assault upon the house. The odds were not good.

"Mom! Where are you?"

He had to wander through the rooms; the storm was too loud to be heard. She was not on the first floor, or the second. For one brief moment he thought she might actually have left with the crowd, but he found her in the epicenter of her insanity, the war room on the third floor.

"Isn't this exciting!" She held her velvet push-stick with both hands as she shoved the little boats around the painted harbor as if she were playing championship shuffleboard. Chandu paced the perimeter of the octagonal room, pausing at every window to look down at the harbor spreading out over the lawn and tickling the foundation. The noise outside was frightening.

"It's not exciting for everyone," said Duncan. "Certainly not for Nod."

"Nonsense." She stopped her playing for a moment and looked outside. "It's in the winds of change that we find our true direction, and he's finding his. You and me, Duncan, we've become fearful of losing sight of the shore, and it holds us back in life. Not so your brother. He's going to break through, just like your father."

"Dad didn't 'break through,' Mom. He died." Duncan picked up her glass from the ship log stand. "How much of this have you had today?"

"It's an invigorating restorative in tough times."

"It's not a restorative, it's a hallucinogen, and you have to stop."

She had her back to him as she tapped the glass tube of a barometer on the wall. "Tonic, hallucinogen—we live in mystery one way or another."

"You live in oblivion, not mystery, and at the cost of not ever leaving this house."

She turned and flipped her braid over her shoulder. "Look who's talking. When you showed up at the door a few weeks ago it was like finding a sailboat adrift. Not only have you lost your compass, Duncan, dear, but your binnacle is cracked."

The wind belted the house, and it shuddered as if it were spinning on its axis. He knew he should see this conversation to its end, but as she would say, this was no time. He had to get to Cora's while he still could. "I'm going," he said, and he turned away before realizing he had to at least *ask* the obvious question. "Do you want to come with me?"

Chandu stood still and seemed to be listening for something beyond the storm. His mother fiddled with the end of her braid as she studied the harbor on the floor. "Did you know that the word *hurricane* comes from a Mexican god of storm called *hurakon*?"

"Okay, then, you stay right here and placate your Mexican god. I'm going."

"Go, but remember this," she said as she peered closely at the Log. "You can't change the direction of the wind, but you can adjust your sails."

"I'll go by the harbor road in case Nod has pulled up somewhere along the shore," he said as he headed to the door.

"Wait." His mother held up a hand and studied the boats. Chandu settled on the floor and rested his head on a stack of Pilot Rules and sighed. "He won't be along the harbor. If my calculations are correct, he should have been pushed up onto the opposite shore."

Duncan patted his clothes for his cell phone. "I wonder if the Coast Guard has started an official search-and-rescue for him yet."

"Don't bother them," she said. "They have enough on their plates. Look at this." She gently shoved a little white boat. "With the flat bottom of the inflatable, Nod should have landed right here, and fairly smoothly at that. He's probably waiting it out now in someone's garden shed." She waved at all the other boats with her stick. "But the rest all have keels and rudders, and they're going to keep on going with a fury."

A wave reverberated against the house. "I think I'll just keep on going, too," said Duncan. "You know how to reach me if you hear anything about Nod, and I'll call you if I do. Stay by the phone."

"'You have to go out, and that's a fact. Nothing says you have to come back,'" she murmured to herself as she took a sip of her wine. "Remember that? The motto of the old life-saving organization in town."

"What's that supposed to mean?"

"Enough of that for now, Duncan, dear." She moved a cell phone aside and started paging back through the Log furiously, until she got to the year 1913. Duncan picked up the phone and turned it over.

"This is a pretty kettle of fish," she said. "This could be a hundred-year tide. That changes everything." She downed the rest of her glass and, armed with her stick, began to push the boats in all directions until they were collected in a tight bundle in the middle of the harbor.

Duncan opened the phone. "This is Nod's."

She didn't look up from her work. "Yes. He must have left it behind when he came up to get your father's compass."

"Why would he need a compass to go around the corner?"

"Duncan, dear, use your eyes! It's a hurricane out there. When you can't see the nose in front of your face, you have to rely on the magnetism of the universe to find your way."

Duncan put the phone back on the stand. "Then you shouldn't have sent him out as the storm was coming in."

"I'm his mother. I did what was best and gave him what he needed—a little *push*." And with that she putted Nod's white boat like a golf ball and let it skid off the land and across the harbor, gliding over the islands and out to the painted sea, where monsters be. "Hmm," she said. Outside came a crash of water so thundering that Duncan felt it through the bottom of his bare feet.

"What do you mean, he needed a little push?"

"To grow up! 'Put out into deep water,' as your father used to say." She clenched her fist and looked outside at the world, which in its current chaos could not be fathomed for more than a foot or two. "He's in his element now. Water! Unknown and unknowable to those on the outside, it reveals a man to himself when he becomes immersed."

"Or it kills him," said Duncan.

"Duncan, dear, leading a timid life cannot help you avoid the inevitable doom that waits for us. The grappling claw of the sea-puss gets us all in the end."

"Mom, you need help."

"As do you. Nod isn't the only one who needs a little push around here." She pointed the stick at him. "It's why I invited Syrie. I found her Dirty Talk mask in your jacket pocket, along with an incriminating photo of you with birds. I wanted to see what was going on between you two. I wanted Cora to know what she had on her hands before she got any deeper into the soup. You're more at sea than Nod is right now. In fact, you've become a navigational hazard."

"Nothing is going on. Why would you complicate my life like that?"

"To get you out of this house! You can't follow in my wake, boy. You haven't the temperament."

Outside, there was another huge crash of water that shook the house. Chandu stood up again and started pacing. His mother looked out of the window, where, in the complete and utter darkness, inexhaustible waves were rolling in over the miles toward them.

"Well, if you're really going to go, go," she said. "Don't stand here talking to me about it—do it. And you'd better take the Duck, or you'll never get across the causeway."

Duncan looked down at where the driveway used to be, now under a foot of water. His mother's old Jaguar was still there, with water gushing up over its wheel wells. His truck was gone. Syrie must have taken it, trying to keep him from getting to Cora.

"I'll get to her in spite of you," he said.

Behind him he heard his mother's footsteps pounding on the floor, and he turned. Her neck chords stood out like a ship's rigging as she raised her stick over her head. She had such a look of fatal determination in her eyes that for one horrific moment he thought she meant to kill him. But she continued past him, nimble in her bare feet over the painted coves and inlets, skipping over the submerged pier toward the cluster of boats. Then she held her stick above her head with one hand like a harpooner and released it with a single powerful blow. The stick slid across the painted water, taking the boats with it to the inner harbor, where they skidded and tumbled past the shore and did not stop until they hit the wall.

She put her hands on her hips. "Doesn't look good."

"What do you mean?"

"The boats and the tide will be hitting Seacrest's beach in about an hour." She consulted the tide chart. "One hour, eight minutes, and forty-seven seconds."

"What?"

"Use your eyes, Duncan! Look at the floor! When the tide goes out, it's going to take Seacrest's with it. Annihilated. Gone. And to think of all the time you used to waste worrying about it going bankrupt. You've set yourself on a wrong course, my son."

Duncan listened to the roaring ocean, and it seemed to be coming from inside his head. "You're wide of the mark, Mom," he said. "You can't predict that."

She stood at the window and leaned on her stick, but there was nothing to see but pillars of rain slamming on the glass. "It's the way the old building would want to go," she said. "I think your father would agree with me on this one. Now leave. At times like this a woman should be alone with her own soul."

seventeen

funny

The lobsters were running free in the house, either abandoned by Slocum or liberated by Marney during the confusion of packing up and getting out. While Duncan suited up with rain gear and boots, he nearly tripped over one pulling itself across the living room floor. Freed of their claw bands in prep for their date with the Crustastun, they were now trying to find their way home, nosing about at the bottom of the French windows where seawater alternately puddled and poured into the house. One daredevil hung by a single claw from the heavy drapes. As for the smashed window, someone had thought to barricade it with an upended table, then braced it with the metal lawn chair that had acted as a missile. The wind blew cocktail napkins around the room, where they settled and dissolved like jellyfish on the wet floor. Duncan picked up a couple of the lobsters for Cora and stuck them in his slicker pockets. He should have thought of flowers—he should have thought of a lot of things—but there was nothing wrong with a gift of lobsters. He and Cora might just have a romantic lobster dinner after all—it would just be without the lollypop glaze.

"Good luck, bugs," he said to the rest of them. "Turn out the lights on your way out."

After struggling with a ferocious wind that almost ripped the front door out of his hand, he stood on the porch and faced the wild, wet darkness, eerily lit by the glowing bait under the eaves. The sticks shuddered violently on the line, looking like St. Elmo's fire. At the rate the water was rising, the swordfish might soon be able to reach them. Duncan peeked around the corner where the outdoor furniture had been stored, and it was all gone—gone along with the banister it had been loosely tied to; gone, too, was the box of framed seaweed. A family history in bladderwrack, gone. He huddled against the wind for a moment, letting the storm beat upon him, then he removed his glasses, pulled his hood tight, and turned to make a mad dash to the garage. The wind was right in his teeth. The water was up to his ankles one moment, his shins the next as the wind pushed and pulled the newly formed lake around the lawn. Water began to slosh into his boots, and as he bent to adjust his rain pants over the tops, a great strip of seaweed came flying through the darkness and slapped him on the cheek.

"Damn." He was peeling it away from his face when the tree under which he stood groaned in a sort of "I'm going to drop this limb on you now" way, so he continued his rapid slosh toward safety.

The front path ended, and he had to step into the rushing water of the driveway, pulling himself along by grabbing onto shrubs before making it to the garage, that vast edifice originally built for horses, carriages, and boats. He pushed the heavy sliding door open, and there was the Duck, his one portal to the outside world. He climbed up to the driver's seat and fumbled under the steering column in the dark and found the key, exactly where it should be. "Thank you, Nod."

He took the lobsters out of his pocket and settled them on the floor behind his seat. He wiped his glasses dry with a tissue he found in the glove compartment and put them back, then undid his hood for better visibility, releasing a pool of water around him. He secured all the plastic side windows of the driver's cab. It was not a waterproof seal by any means, and he felt he was facing a hurricane in a pup tent. But it was better than no tent. He turned on the ignition and found the wipers, which he needed even in the garage, what with the rain slamming horizontally through the open doors. He looked over at the house, which was now surrounded by water on all eight sides. On the third floor, the war room's light shone weakly through the rain, and he saw the silhouette of his mother pass by, her stick on her shoulder.

He shoved the Duck into gear. It was time to move forward. He would drive by Seacrest's on his way to Cora, on the off chance his mother was right about the building coming down. In many ways, it would be a blessing if it did because then he would be free from Osbert and he could start anew, with Cora, somewhere far away. But he could not think of any of that now. The noise of the drumming rain on the cab's roof was deafening, and water started to spit in at him from the window seams. His visibility was limited to the few feet that the headlights managed to illuminate, so he had to follow the flooded road by memory. The only indication that he was where he should be was the occasional mailbox lifting its head out of the

 # great descrip

suvs

water like a sea monster. He looked in the rearview mirror but could see nothing, not even to the end of the Duck. He hoped the scuppers were open so the vehicle would not fill with water and slow him down. Or pull him down. And yet, it felt heady to be driving so high up, in such a strong metal beast. It made him feel invincible.

He turned a corner, out from behind the protection of the houses, and immediately felt the wind slam into the Duck, which shook but did not slide across the road. Duncan grasped the wheel tighter. The trees on either side of him swayed back and forth like underwater plants. Out in the darkness he heard but could not see the harbor. The sea continued to boil, undoubtedly crunching vessels lying at anchor and absorbing the debris into its unfathomable maw. Nod, Nod, Nod. Nothing could save him from this storm. The time to save him had been before he'd even left, and Duncan had failed at so simple a task.

Water poured down the windshield in sheets so thick that he had only a second of visibility after the wipers cleared the view, like watching photos being flipped by an unseen thumb. He braked with a lurch when the thumb stopped at the flooded causeway. His headlights shone on the debris washing past with the tide and spilling over into the salt marsh, which was indistinguishable now from the ocean that fed it. Logs, nets, shreds of hulls, lobster traps, plastic fish boxes, small appliances—off they went. Duncan half-expected to see Nod sweep by in the inflatable, and then he thought how easy it would be to get washed away himself. He hoped the Duck's engine was up to this.

He looked at the fuel gauge. "Almost empty," he said out loud. He wanted to be angry with Nod, but what with him missing at sea, it seemed a petty thing to contemplate. In truth, he had only himself to blame. He should have checked the gauge before he left. He could have siphoned oil from the home's heating system. His own bad decisions had led him right to where he was at that moment, out in a hurricane, caught between his childhood home and his marital bed, with only a teaspoon full of diesel to see him through.

It would have to be enough. He only had to get to Seacrest's, where there was plenty of fuel to be had. He inched the Duck into the water until he felt the tires lift from the pavement, then switched on the propeller. The Duck jerked alarmingly to the right, but it quickly regained its stability and began to chug over the washed-out section of the road to the other side. The wild screaming of the gale made him want to scream himself, but he could not afford to lose concentration as he tried to keep a straight path. He felt a hard bump underneath the Duck and realized he had made it across, even managing to arrive more or less back on the road. He paused to reflect on his success when, off to his left in the harbor, a white fishing boat appeared, lifted from a furrow by a large wave, then disappeared again. Its estimated landfall would be ...

He slammed the Duck into gear and did not look back. He rounded the corner into town and was just about to take a breath when he had to brake again. A splintered oak had fallen across the road, exposing a gothic cathedral of jagged roots and taking the electric lines with it. Houses nearby were dark behind their high fences, and their lawns were underwater. He could see the road on the other side of the tree, but there was no way to it. He'd have to take High Ridge into town and hope that the Duck could squeeze through its narrow lanes and negotiate its sharp turns.

He backed up to change direction but was soon stopped again. Another tree, more downed wires. A garage by the road was missing its roof. A car was tipped over on its side. He could wait it out where he was, sitting in the Duck until the roads were opened, or he could try to get back to where he came from. His mother's house.

"No," he said. "No, no, no, *no*." With some difficulty, he turned the Duck around, back to the harbor road, and stopped. He closed his eyes and imagined the short bit of coastline from where he was to Seacrest's, and he realized that if he could just navigate the Duck the few hundred yards past the stony lump of land that bulged out into the water, he could ride the tide onto Seacrest's beach. He could do it. He could. He opened his eyes and saw the rolling green tides batter the shore.

"I can't do this." And it wasn't fear of the water that made him say it. The Duck could navigate land and sea, but it could not fly over the walls that stood between him and the water. Right ahead was the "Lightkeeper's House," whose raw plywood was swollen with rain and bowing out from the frame. The roof on the fake lighthouse was gone, and he imagined the tower filling with the sea. Usually surrounded by weeds, the house was now surrounded by water. The gate was swinging open and closed, open and closed.

Duncan looked around, tapped the fuel gauge, said a prayer, and gunned the motor. He waited for his moment when the gate slammed open, then steered the Duck into the driveway, scraping both sides of the vessel against the pillars. The gate and the fence were so rotted they just gave way. The driveway turned into lawn that sloped down to the water and became a launch, letting the Duck roll into the harbor. It immediately began rocking and snorting. He was water-borne, and then airborne as a wave picked him up. In that moment he did not think "death" but "life," and then he could think of nothing through the pumping of blood in his head. The Duck belly flopped back on the water without splitting in half, and Duncan choked out a little laugh.

The compass on the dashboard glowed a fluorescent direction that he could not read because the needle was too jittery. He would have to steer by his gut. If only he hadn't shied away from the water these past few years, he might have more confidence. He was as bad as his mother. He thought of his father, clinging to his little boat when the squall came up, with nature leaving no options. Duncan hoped that when his father got swept overboard, he did not linger long. That was the worst part. The suffering. The lungs filling with water even as the brain remained on. It was why Clyde Harmon talked about keeping a gun on board. And yet, knowing his father, he would never have equated sinking with drowning. He would have remained positive even as the pressurized world turned slow, dark, then quietly black.

Duncan felt the surf twisting the Duck's screw, but on it chugged. Off to his lee side, he saw a boat rear up like a great sea beast, leaping clear out of the water then dropping sideways. He thought of his mother's warning that all the boats were heading this way, toward Seacrest's, but he could not see through the walls of water that surrounded him. His amphibious vessel powered on without sinking, even as he jerked it back and forth to avoid the rocks and the heaving navigational markers, which appeared and disappeared like deathly phantoms. He thought of his father. "You have to just hunker down and ride out the storm, son," he used to say in the face of any problem that Duncan brought to him, whether it was math homework as a child or girl problems later in life. He never offered any specifics on these matters, only the one piece of advice: perseverance. Then from nowhere, other words shot through his brain, sounding very much like Winston Churchill: "If you're going through hell, keep going."

He stepped on the accelerator and kept going, buffeted by the storm, which soon felt like an extension of himself, something not to be fought but to be accepted. Since he could not change the water, he would change himself. He would enjoy it, lost in a wild ride into the darkness, thrilling, frightening, and brief though it was. It might be all there was.

The Duck, amazingly, cleared the rocky point without crashing, and almost immediately got swept sideways on a massive swell, propelled toward what Duncan could only hope was Seacrest's beach. The boat went down on its ear before righting itself. Mountains of black water surrounded him. No lights shone through the mountains, but that could be because there was no electricity in town. Noah's dove could not find land in this storm, but Duncan refused to panic. His shoulders ached from holding the wheel so hard, and he wanted to let go, at least long enough to put on a life jacket, which was something he should have thought about much sooner than this.

It became clear he would have to do more than just hold on. He could not just ride the wave and hope for the best any longer. Even if he was going in the right direction, the chances of a smooth landing in this storm were nil. He would be battered to pieces on the shore—if not here, then elsewhere. He opened the throttle all the way, even at the risk of running out of fuel, so that he could steer the Duck perpendicular to the waves so it would not get rolled over. The windshield wipers continued to work furiously against the onslaught of water, and there was a brief moment when he was lifted up, as if by a hand, and held aloft long enough to see the glimmer of a light on shore. Seacrest's. Yes, it was Seacrest's. He'd made it, and he began to laugh, and in it he heard the crazy laugh of his brother. It was a pure, sweet glimpse into Nod's soul, now that it was too late. For a moment it seemed as if the ocean stopped moving and the world stopped spinning. It was as if his mind cleared itself of a lifetime of accumulated debris, useless fears and damaging thoughts, and in this clearing, in this clear blue light of heightened awareness, he realized that the keys to Seacrest's were attached to the ignition keys in his pickup truck, somewhere with Syrie.

That was a problem. But it was not the problem of the very moment. Slowly, slowly, he started to rise again. He smiled at the sight of the lights returning and went higher still. As high as he was lifted, he was suddenly dropped into a valley set down among the high hills of the sea, and the boat shuddered in pain. The cabin immediately began to take on water. He held his breath when it reached his face, and then all the noise stopped as he became completely submerged. He felt his glasses slip off his face and float away, but he could not take his hands off the wheel to save them. A figure appeared before his closed eyes. He was hallucinating, but at least he knew he was. It was Cora, wrapped only in a mist. He remembered what Slocum said about gales subsiding if a naked woman appeared before a sailor. He felt saved, even as he was plunging into the night. It was very dark, but peaceful in a way he could not have anticipated. He was almost calm. He did not even panic as his lungs began to ache. He clutched the wheel tighter. What else was there to do? What went down would come back up, in theory, and at the very lowest point in the swell he felt himself lifted again and all the water drained out of the cab. He breathed. He hoarded air as he felt the vessel begin the cycle again. This happened two times more, and two times more he held his breath and refused to panic. He held on to the wheel and gunned the motor to keep her from rolling under the waves.

At the bottom of the third drop, he felt his tires bounce on sand. To keep from getting pulled back into the harbor, he struggled to get the Duck moving forward and realized the engine was dead. He'd run out of fuel and out of time and felt silly for thinking he was any match for the ruthless force of nature. He sensed the hand of the sea slip under him again, pulling him back. Then the hand disappeared as if deciding against him, and the momentum of the storm threw the Duck forward. Duncan was seized with vertigo and felt the Duck plunge downward like a diver, jerking sideways, then skidding through a vast, nameless corridor of green-black water. The last thing Duncan saw before his head hit the steering wheel was lobsters, flying through the air around him.

eighteen

Duncan sank slowly beneath the violent surface of the storm, where all was still, infusing him with an unworldly serenity. He found himself suspended in a warm saline fluid, somehow mastering the replication of his own cells, watching the expansion of veins like flooded streams along transparent limbs. The minute pulse of his multi-celled heart began to beat. Over and under he tumbled in total surrender, his feet drifting, his arms spread, his spine curved in repose. From this sweet darkness, soft hands lifted him into the light, where he sensed booming waves vaulting the seawall, a tremendous crash and a withdrawing roar. Somewhere from the edge of this watery swirl came weak flashes of red and blue lights and the muffled blare of emergency vehicles. A megaphone voice cut through the noise as if shouting down from the black heavens: *Evacuate.* As he was being stripped of his clothes, he remembered saying that the lobsters were still trapped inside the Duck, and a voice close to his ear assured him that they would all be saved.

"Lovesters," Duncan whispered before passing out again, itching to get back to the complete peace of abandon, and then he felt an annoying yank of reason on his frontal lobe.

"Don't surrender, Leland," said another voice.

The words "rapture of the deep" floated to the surface of his mind. The seductive killer, they called it, as cruel and efficient as a curvaceous shark. Deep sea divers, fooled by oxygen-deprived brains, sometimes froze in wonder at the beauty around them, convinced they were beyond the grasping tendrils of mortality, a delusion that holds them down until they drown.

"No," he said. "No." He struggled to return to the solid world, the world where Cora lived, where he used to live before he broke loose from his mooring, unable to withstand the pressure of so simple a decision as life. It was not too late to say yes. Yes to everything. Yes, yes, yes, yes, *yes.* He flapped his arms and legs, prompting his muscles to get back to work and return to physical consciousness. It was exhausting, like swimming in the air, and just when he felt he might slip back under, he felt something small and alive scamper across his chest.

"Fingers," he croaked.

He snapped upright to a seated position as if the ferret had pressed an electric buzzer on his stomach. His eyes were open wide, and he was breathing unevenly as his heart pounded. The taste of salt water was in his throat, and he could smell his own mustiness, as if he'd been stored somewhere dark and damp for a very long time. He was naked except for a scratchy blanket, which he tightened around him. At first, he didn't know where he was, but as his eyes adjusted to the dim light, he was surprised to find himself on Seacrest's factory floor. The fluorescent lights, which made the factory as bright as day in the middle of the night, were off. Only the security floodlights in the corners were lit, criss-crossing their beams in the air, casting shadows among the columns and tanks. The stainless-steel surfaces were clean, radiating a dull silver in the half-light of the room, creating the atmosphere of an empty church, or a tomb.

"Twenty-two minutes to high tide," said a familiar voice. Duncan blinked at the figure in the corner as he patted his naked body for glasses.

Beaky Harrow was sitting jackknifed on the floor a few feet away, leaning against a wall, his head sunken in the stiff carapace of a yellow raincoat, still dripping water. The ferret sat on his knees. Beaky handed it a pair of glasses. "Go ahead, Fingers. He needs these."

Fingers lifted the glasses in its mouth and ran slinky-style across the floor toward Duncan, who leaned away from the animal. It dropped the glasses within his reach and stared at Duncan with its probing little eyes.

"Beaky," said Duncan, putting on his glasses. "What are you doing here?"

Duncan once heard that businesses often got torched for insurance money during hurricanes because emergency crews couldn't get to them, and then the storm erased all the evidence. Not to mention that the wind accelerated the destruction. Had Osbert sent Beaky to do just that, using the trash company's key? Duncan couldn't remember what the contract said about who got the insurance money if something happened to the building before the loan was paid off, but he was sure it was in Osbert's favor. Then he thought about the death clause. Maybe it wasn't the building Beaky was here to destroy.

"Waiting," said Beaky, contemplating the ceiling. "Waiting for the tide to turn. What're you doing here?"

"I don't need to explain why I'm here. It's my factory. Still. In spite of you and your blackmailing photo."

Beaky turned to him with an exaggerated look of surprise, like a Kabuki actor. "Blackmail?"

"You plan to ruin me for disposing of a couple of bird bodies?" said Duncan. "Is this Osbert's plan to get control of the company? Because if that's your scheme, I intend to fight you every step of the way."

"Please, Mr. Leland." Beaky took Duncan's tie out of his pocket. It was wet, and the red stripes seemed to bleed into the yellow background. Fingers stood up on his hind legs. "We're just trying to keep you out of trouble. You've got to think of your public image. It's a valuable commodity to us all." He made a quick motion with the tie, and Fingers came scurrying to him. "I showed you the picture as a way of saying be more careful. It's my job to keep an eye on you."

"You're not going to use the photo against me?"

"If we wanted to exact harm, Leland, we would have just let nature have its way with you and let you get washed back out to sea right now. You're a lucky man." He teased the ferret with the tie. "We were pulling into the lot when we saw the Duck get tossed onto the last scratch of beach. With effort, lots of effort, we chained your axle to the Benz. There was a monumental tug of war between us and an outgoing wave, I can tell you—our boots and ears filled with water, couldn't open our lips for drowning, but we won you. Won you from the sea like a prize marlin. Lucky us. Tied your Duck to the loading dock." He flicked the tie. "Poor Fingers nearly drowned in my pocket. We had to revive him under the hand dryer in the bathroom."

"We?" Duncan stood up with a groan. He felt badly bruised all over, and his bare feet were cold against the cement floor. He wrapped the blanket around his shoulders and found his socks hanging to dry on a heat duct and put them on damp. The rest of his clothes were still too wet. He limped over to the window that faced the parking lot, and through the rain he could make out the flashing emergency vehicles in the street, trailing flood evacuation warnings behind them. On higher ground, a black Mercedes was chained to a light post to keep it from being washed away. When a wave retreated to gather strength he saw that the seawall was gone, and when the wave rushed back in it smacked hard against the sea side of the building. His mother was right. It was coming this way. Through the horizontal rain he could see the barge-like shape of the Duck floating at the dock meant for trucks. The water had to be three feet deep in the lot. It was coming in fast. Another few feet and the water would start pressing against the windows. There was no way out. He could not possibly get to Cora's from here. He went back to his dripping clothes and pulled his cell phone out of his pants to call her, and water poured from the seams. He picked up the phone on Annuncia's desk in her office, and it was dead. This meant that he couldn't even activate the alarm system to be saved by the police. He saw his wellies propped up against the wall to dry upside down, exposing the white crosses painted on the bottoms.

"Where are the lobsters?" he asked.

"Set them free," said Beaky. "That photo of your dad in your jacket pocket—I dried it off and put it on your desk. Needs new glass."

Duncan turned to him. "How do you know that was my dad? You've met him?"

"Who else would you have with you on a day like this?"

Duncan ran his hands across his face. "You people aren't supposed to have the keys to my office."

Beaky took something out of his slicker pocket and handed it to Fingers, who came jingling over to Duncan with the goods. "Very funny," Duncan said as he picked up the keys at his feet. They were not his keys; his keys were off somewhere with Syrie and her little dog. These were Annuncia's keys. They were all there: one to her office, one to his, one to the storeroom, and one for the loading dock door. The one to the building itself wasn't there. "Did Osbert give you the trash company's key to get in the building?"

"The trash company," said Beaky. "There's an interesting subject."

Duncan followed Beaky's eyes to the far end of the room and saw someone move in the shadows. His waterlogged brain made out the figure of a man staring out the window, facing the storm head-on from the sea. He twisted slowly around, like a creature on the bottom of the ocean.

"Osbert?" said Duncan.

Using his walking stick, the man took a step out into the half-light of the room. "Don't come any closer," Duncan said. "If anything happens to me, they'll know it was you."

"But it's not me. And it never was." Osbert's severe black suit made his body disappear in the darkness and cast his face in shadowy contrasts, making him look like an Old Masters portrait. It was the first time Duncan had ever seen him without his sunglasses. "Call me Adoniram."

"Adoniram?" The roar of the storm accelerated, and Duncan felt his voice get suctioned out of the room. "*Adoniram?*" He tried to remember what the artist looked like in the old clips he'd seen on the New Adoniram Project website—the gangly, bearded young artist with a ponytail down his back. His hair had covered most of his face, so it was hard to tell. And yet. Thirty years, a shaved face, a wider girth, and a shorter ponytail—this was the same man who scratched words into the sand with a stick and called it art.

"I thought you were dead."

"There are always two deaths," said Beaky, without looking up from Fingers, who was executing some sort of a leaping war dance at his feet. "The one the world imagines, and the one you keep to yourself."

"When you start to believe your own PR, it's time to leave," said Adoniram, the man formerly known as Osbert. "I grew sick and cynical with the world, and death seemed like the ultimate peace at the time. I was young. I should have been braver and just admitted what I thought of my art instead of running away from it."

"I don't understand," said Duncan, shivering slightly under his blanket.

"I shouldn't have filmed the happenings," said Adoniram, studying the knobs on his stick. "The integrity of time-based art is inseparable from its transience and its embrace of loss. Record-keeping intellectualized the experience and made it a commodity, and it became part of the culture industry. But all negatives have some positives, and documentation kept the happenings alive all these years, and that I don't regret. When the film clips surfaced on YouTube, they sparked a revival of my work by way of the New Adoniram Project, of which you became unknowingly, but significantly, involved."

Duncan struggled to let this information sink in. The sight of Osbert being no longer Osbert threw him off, and he was still not sure if his life wasn't in danger. "Why haven't you revealed yourself? You'd be a huge hit."

Adoniram looked up from his stick and smiled. "They would say I rose from the dead, and we all know where that leads to. Having said that, I am intrigued by the New Adoniram Project. It's fascinating to see how theory evolves, and this whole business has helped move my new work forward. When I saw you and the factory on YouTube, I saw that Seacrest's would have a significant role in it. The timing coincided with a breakthrough for me, and I could see what had to be done."

"Done?" Duncan didn't like the sound of that. He turned to Beaky, half-expecting to see a revolver trained on him, but he was tickling the ferret's stomach with the tie. "What does Beaky have to do with all this? Is he your hired gun?"

"Beaky is my art dealer," said Adoniram, and the two men exchanged a smile. "It was always tricky work, asking patrons to fund art that can't be owned, and once I was dead, it made his job even harder. He went back to New York City to represent a new generation of artists."

Beaky choked out a little laugh, and Fingers jumped sideways on the floor. Duncan looked at them all. "You're not the mob? What about the trash company?"

"Rumor and fiction mixed with garbage. Although there's really no reason why we couldn't process municipal food waste along with the fish waste. Faster and cleaner than composting. Could be quite profitable. It's something to consider."

"Eight minutes to high tide," said Beaky, studying his watch. "Another ten or so after that before it turns."

"So what did you want Seacrest's for if there's no garbage?"

"Access to your equipment." Adoniram held out his stick to a blue barrel in the corner. "Come closer, Duncan. Let us look out upon the great mystery while I tell you a story."

The building shuddered from the force of the storm. There was no way out right now, no escape to Cora or Ten Bells, but if anything happened, at least it could be said he went down with his ship. He stepped around Beaky and the ferret and ducked under a conveyor belt to reach Adoniram. They stood side by side at the window, with the full power of the storm only inches from their faces on the other side of the glass. The sea had risen to right below the panes. The tight new energy-efficient windows were keeping even a drop of the waves from entering, but when the sea itself got past the sill, the glass could not possibly withstand the pressure. It would give.

"I think we should go upstairs to my office," said Duncan. "It'll be safer there."

"Don't think." Adoniram touched his chest with the stick handle. "In art, the trick is to go directly from the eye to the heart, skipping the brain altogether. The words I used to write on the beach were merely forms, symbols of our culture—it was immaterial what the words meant. My goal was to bear witness to time and tide washing away the foul human stamp on nature."

Duncan flinched when a wave slammed against the glass then disappeared into the night. "Were the words immaterial even in your last work, 'God Help Us'?"

Adoniram looked out at the wild storm for a minute and shook his head. "No," he said. "Those mattered. But they got washed away as easily as the words that didn't. It is an unfeeling and undiscriminating force out there."

"I wish I could be so unfeeling," Duncan said, a bit stove in with emotion.

"No, you don't. Feeling is the portal to experience. There can never be enough." Adoniram raised his voice to be heard over the mounting wind. "After I rowed away from this very beach in 1977, I set out to stage my death. I was disgusted with art and I was disgusted with the world. New life comes to those who give it up, as my evangelist father used to say, so I made a leather coracle with my own two hands, stretching layers of goat leather over a wooden frame, whipping the skins together. I sewed the sails myself and cut down a small oak tree for a mast, then headed for the jagged cliffs of Western

Ireland. I set the boat free to wash up on the rocks upon arrival and swam to shore with nothing but the hair on my head. I stayed there for close to twenty-five years, studying the Neolithic rock formations of a lost world, exploring the dolmens and the cromlechs, looking for answers. I lived in a stone hut I built myself in the abandoned hills. At night I read Churchill's multi-volume account of his war, which I found in the village dump. By day I earned money caddying for rich Americans at Ballynahinch, which is where Beaky found me."

Duncan stared at Beaky in disbelief. "You play golf?"

He shrugged. "I do whatever it takes to win over clients."

"He convinced me to move back," said Adoniram. "It was time."

"And it was time for me to leave New York," said Beaky. "I bought the quarry."

"As a cover, we encouraged rumors to the effect that we were refugees from the late-nineties Rhode Island mob breakup. Humans are always ready to believe the worst in others. Beaky in particular seemed to thrive in that persona."

"It wasn't all that different from the New York art scene," said Beaky.

"The quarry made money, but not enough for all that I needed to do, so Beaky started an informal loan operation to tide us over. He gained a reputation as a bit of a thug, but it couldn't be helped. Someone had to bail the boat while I rowed."

"I do whatever I have to for my artists." Beaky smiled at Adoniram.

"In the meantime, I found peace in the solidity and whiteness of the stone. This time I wasn't just rearranging the material by drawing in the sand. Now I was actually mining the material—the very earth itself—discovering its secrets, changing slab to rock and rock to gravel, performing daily the miracle of transformation. Not unlike the way you turn fish scrap into fertilizer here, in this building. Both of us, Duncan, we smash delusions about permanence and beauty that we project upon the hogwash the rest of the world calls art."

"I'm not so sure about that," said Duncan, wrapping the blanket tighter around him as the waves got stronger and higher right outside the window. "I just process fish waste."

"Don't belittle your powers." Adoniram rested his stick against the window and put both his hands on Duncan's shoulders. His face held an expression of deep concern. "Or your capacity for love."

"Love?" said Duncan, but Adoniram had already turned back to his subject.

"The quarry was my canvas," he said, holding his arms wide apart as if describing a fish he'd caught. "I wanted to find a return to meaning and remembered everything I'd learned from Churchill. He wrote that 'all the great things are simple and many can be expressed in a single word: freedom, justice, honor, duty, mercy, hope.' So for years, after the crew left for the day, I used a backhoe to arrange and rearrange the gravel into those words before the delivery trucks came to take it all away in the morning. I felt as if I was sending those sentiments out into the world. It was very satisfying. I was quite complete. I felt that it was possible for the world to be saved as long as at least one person learns something and acts on it. I called it my Churchill Series. But my education was not yet done. One day, as I was walking along a newly dynamited site, I fell into a natural split in the earth. I came very close to death, but there was a strong presence in that crevice that pulled me back to life. It pulsed with gravity. When I came to, I was a different man, transformed by my experience, the very experience I had sought but could not achieve by faking my death in 1977. It took days to crawl back up to the light, and I was dehydrated and half-mad, and I was covered in a dusty substance. Can you imagine what I found, Duncan, deep inside the earth?"

Duncan shook his head. It was hard taking in this story with the entire North Atlantic ocean banging against the building the way it was.

"*An ancient ocean bed.* A living ocean that had been transformed into a thick crust, as dried up as a dusty slab, but recognizable nonetheless. I saw the future."

A wave rose from the ocean and filled the window before them. Duncan stepped back as it slammed into the building. "Do you have a dry cell phone?" he said. "I'd like to see if my wife is okay and let her know I'm alive."

"Your wife is just fine." Adoniram took Duncan by the blanket and brought him closer to the glass. "As it happens, I'd been playing around with micro-art at the time, doing installations that could only be seen under a microscope. I was feeling guilty about the diesel I was using for the backhoe, so I wanted to explore art that had a small carbon footprint. I scraped some of the dust on a slide, and lo!"

"Lo?"

"Yes, lo. That's when I identified the dust molecules as diatoms, a type of phytoplankton which forms the basis for the entire marine food chain. A single-celled workaholic that sucks carbon dioxide from the atmosphere and, when it dies, sinks to the bottom of the ocean carrying that carbon with it, making the air fit for humans."

"Kills pests, too," said Beaky. "The cells have sharp edges that can slice through the soft underbelly of a slug."

"Slice?" Duncan's hand went to his throat.

"But like our friend the eel, this useful creature of the sea is dying off because of warming waters. What we've done to the ocean is enough, as Churchill would say, 'to disgust a sow.' But the more research I did, the more I realized I had something extraordinary on my hands. When I looked them up, I found out that they were mega-celled diatoms that hadn't been seen in the oceans in millions of years. My particular diatoms were not just dead, they were extinct."

Duncan looked outside and felt the ocean very close by. "Dead and extinct. Hmm."

"The bigger the diatom, the more carbon it absorbs—a savior in the form of a single cell. The thing to do was to reintroduce the giant diatom to the oceans, execute a truly major art installation on a global scale. No filming, no websites." He put his arms around Duncan's shoulders.

"You can't reintroduce a dead species," said Duncan, removing his arm and almost losing his blanket in the process.

"In art you can. 'Irrational judgment leads to new experience,' as Sol LeWitt, my old comrade in conceptual art used to say. The diatom died so that we could live. In return, we will symbolically restore it back to the ocean."

Duncan thought uneasily of the death clause. "What has this got to do with me and Seacrest's?"

"Transformation and distribution. I needed both of those things to complete my vision. The vein of diatomaceous material was thick. It was laborious to even retrieve it from deep in the earth, but retrieve it we did. The quarried chunks were crushed and compressed, then, bit by bit, brought here at night, where Annuncia and Wade powdered it in the grinder and integrated it into your fish scrap and seaweed powder. Come spring, it will be distributed as fertilizer, shipped out to farms and gardens and parks around the world, where drain-off will take care of the rest. Everything flows to the sea in time. It's the sea's biggest asset, and its biggest liability. I've put Beaky in charge of global marketing."

They both looked at Beaky, but he was looking at his watch as he stood up from the floor. Fingers was on his shoulder.

"Why go through all that trouble?" asked Duncan. "Just dump it in the sea."

"'Irrational thoughts should be followed absolutely and logically,' said Sol. My concept is to integrate it in a substance that will be spread haphazardly and unsuspected in different environments around the earth, and that is the path that must be followed. But dumping is also a part of the plan. Because dumping in the sea has destroyed the sea, we are going to launch the new installation by tossing a symbolic barrel into the deep tonight."

"High tide," said Beaky.

There was a symphony of violence outside, a destructive cleansing and reordering of the world from top to bottom. Duncan did not understand how the building stood the force.

"We'd better get out of here," he said, feeling his words get absorbed into the noise of weather outside. "My mother says this place is going to collapse at high tide."

"*My mother says,*" mimicked Adoniram. "But who knows? Maybe the old gal is right. Water is always trying to get back to where it came from, and it once covered the earth. It is time, perhaps, to return to being an aquatic ape, as your friend Slocum suggests."

"Not *my* friend," said Duncan. "You're the one he gave the jellyfish processing rights to."

"Jellyfish." Adoniram shook his head and turned his attention back to the sea. "Brainless and spineless, and yet we've let them take over the ocean. They adapt and reproduce quickly—far better than we do, eh Duncan?"

Duncan bristled. Was this a dig about his own reproductive problems? "I don't see how we've 'let' them do anything."

"But we have. We've killed off so many marine species we've created the empty space for jellyfish to fill. We let them spin out of control, and now we must do something to control them. Slocum's recipe is promising. The total amount of plastic trash in all the oceans is a hundred million tons. Sea turtles are eating plastic bags instead of jellyfish. If we could use jellyfish matter to replace even some of those plastics, it would create a delicious circle. While I was getting my stomach pumped at the hospital, I realized that it's not enough to work in symbols, such as words in gravel or extinct diatoms in fertilizer. Lying in the emergency room, I wanted to recreate nature's churn, restoring balance back to the universe. The Diatom Project is the artistic expression of the concept; the Jellyfish Project is the tangible application."

"The universe notwithstanding, I could have held the rights to process the tangible jellyfish as well as you," said Duncan. "You stole it out from under me."

"Not stole—protected. Annuncia convinced me that you seemed too fragile to take it on right then, and it was too important to fail. However, having seen your determination to get here, I'd have to reassess. I wouldn't have credited you with so much fire. 'Difficulties mastered are opportunities won.'"

"Sol LeWitt?"

"Churchill!"

"It's time," said Beaky as he climbed up onto the forklift.

"How did you get Annuncia to go along with all this? To betray me?" He waved one arm over his head and held onto the blanket with the other.

"There is no betrayal," said Adoniram. He carried his body like a dancer as helped Beaky maneuver the barrel onto the lift, and for a moment Duncan saw the young man on the beach. "We all have your best interests at heart. And the world's interests. Of all the people in town, only she—who would have been a young girl when I was living here—saw past the sunglasses and the age. She imagined a dense beard and knew who I was. The woman has a vision as strong as my own. I had hoped she would be here by now, but the storm must be beyond even her powers."

He wielded a metal tool to pop the top of the barrel; then, with Beaky's help, he used both hands to pry the lid off. A little wisp of grayish-white ash rose up, like a ghost.

Duncan touched the diatoms and rubbed the dust between his fingers. "So smooth. It doesn't feel as if it could cut through a slug."

"Tell that to the slug," said Adoniram. Then he picked up his stick and with elaborate care used it to write in the powder.

MERCY

They considered the word without speaking, even as the building shuddered from nature's assault.

"You can't beat a nice ritual, can you?" said Beaky, who then took over from Adoniram, pressing the barrel lid back on and hammering down the edges. Then he unscrewed a spout on the lid and set about to attach it to an exhaust hose. The waves continued to slam hard against the window.

"We really should move to the other end of the room," said Duncan.

"J. M. W. Turner, the great painter of light," said Adoniram, cleaning his hands with a Handi Wipe, "used to tie himself to the mast of a ship and sail into the middle of a raging storm so that he could thrill to its fury. He offered himself totally to the experience. To achieve greatness, we must all give ourselves over to greatness."

"I've had enough thrills for tonight."

"Time," said Beaky, tapping his watch.

"Won't your powder just settle to the bottom of the sea as soon as you shoot it out there?" asked Duncan.

"No," said Adoniram. "Dust rides the currents across the sea for a long time. When we scatter a loved one's ashes on the sea, they go farther in death than was ever possible in life. Come, Duncan. Stand next to me."

Out of the darkness, Duncan saw a sailboat rise up sideways in the harbor before being quickly yanked back down to some black, watery hell. He hoped it was just another boat that had come loose from a mooring field and not one full of crew. He thought of Nod, and his heart sank.

"Did you know," said Adoniram, gazing out at where the boat had been, "that the United Nations estimates that there are more than three million shipwrecks on the ocean floor?"

"Seems reasonable to me," said Duncan. "I was almost one of them not so long ago. Nod could already be there."

"Don't give up on your brother," said Adoniram. "There's always hope. I'd like you to do the honors of throwing the switch."

Duncan looked at himself. "I'm not dressed for the occasion."

"If that blanket was an animal skin, you'd pass as a caveman. Pre-industrial, pre-cultural, Neolithic, even pre-human. Back to before we ruined it all. It's exactly what's called for."

Beaky switched on the exterior floodlights, making circles of light in the storm. Adoniram moved closer to the window and looked out on nature's chaos, then raised both his arms, like a conductor. Or a sorcerer. The fabric of his black suit was so fine that Duncan could see the light through it.

"Ready?" asked Beaky.

Adoniram nodded. Duncan bent to turn on the exhaust vent. The sound of the storm almost drowned out its noise, but Duncan soon heard the familiar motor, and then he began to see the release of the powder into the swirling mess of water and wind outside.

Duncan could not explain why it moved him to see puffs of dust blow into the storm. But it was all rather beautiful and powerful, and in his heart he wished that Adoniram had recorded it. He would like to share this with Cora. Then he remembered the security camera, tucked way up under the exposed steel beams of the ceiling, aimed outside. The little red light was blinking, and he smiled, and as he did he caught the eye of Beaky, who winked at him. Still an art agent at heart.

Duncan continued to watch the slow display of dust mixing with the rain and felt a deep cosmic response. He felt as if he was gaining perfect clarity. How had he so muddled it all these past few months? How could he not have seen what lay all around him and in him? He felt lifted up and made whole. He was wiping tears from his face when a rush of wind tore through the room, and he steeled himself for the building to tumble beneath his feet, but the howl ended as a door slammed shut.

It was Annuncia and a police officer, peering out from their black slickers, hooded like the angels of death. "Duncan!" Annuncia shouted, "something's happened out on the Cove. You better come."

nineteen

The sun on the water's horizon cast long shadows on the land. As the harbor moved with powerful post-storm swells, the surf smashed against the shore, heaving up pieces of wreckage. The house was gone, washed away with most of the backyard sometime during the night. Duncan stared but could not comprehend the empty space. The shell grotto had crumbled away, leaving behind a spurting copper tube. The last surviving mulberry tree no longer survived. One of the tall cedars that once marked the entrance to the Drop had been hauled by the sea to the top of the garage; its mate was gone altogether. The land that held the pet graveyard had fallen away.

Corrugated pipes, ripped from the earth, lay scattered like Roman pillars, and the ancient septic tank, torn from its resting place, had cracked open against a rock like an egg, so that the scent of sewage mixed with the rotting odors of the sea. The dovecote was so much stone rubble. The wrack line, the farthest spot where seaweed had been deposited by the storm tide, was over a quarter-mile inland. The old octagonal house never had a chance, and when it disappeared, so did his mother.

A Coast Guard helicopter flew so close to the shoreline that Duncan had to back up and hold his glasses to his face. This was the only house lost on Cean Avenue, the others being somewhat protected by this spit of land. Were protected. The spit was gone. Behind him, Chief Lovasco, wearing street clothes of jeans and a windbreaker, sounded orders through a bullhorn, directing the rescue effort on the ground. Lovasco wore a "leave everything to me" expression, but Duncan worried that his enthusiasm outran his abilities. Duncan knew him from elementary school, and even though he was not a chowderhead by any means, it was a lot to keep under control. There were so many volunteers milling around it looked like a going-out-of-business sale, but they all kept their distance from Duncan. Everyone had run out of positive things to say hours ago. Even the police dogs ignored him as they crawled over the remains of his childhood. Shingles floated in puddles, and shards of glass poked through slimy mountains of seaweed. Duncan thought he recognized an arm of the Venetian chandelier. His nemesis, the front door, had been salvaged by the Red Cross to make a table from which coffee and donuts were being served. He thought of his mother's ancestor, Ethel Tarbell, who still clutched the door's key in her grave, hoping to use it on her return. "It's no use to you now, is it, Ethel?" he said out loud, not caring who heard him talking to ghosts.

He struggled to navigate around a messy slaw of yellow nautical rope, car tires, pot haulers, pumps, boat electronics, coolers, filters, gloves, boots, and lobster gear. It was as if the ocean had taken it upon itself to trade in all this junk for his family. He came across the lounge chair from the porch, where his mother would lie for hours looking out on the water, her jelly glass of mulberry wine by her side. The wicker still held the indentation of her form. He righted it and faced it to the harbor before heading to the edge of the abyss that had once been the cellar, now an octagonal body of water. A shank of chimney remained, rising up from the dark pool. The furnace was gone; the wine casks were gone. The stairs led up to nothing. A blue, felt-bottomed boat model was floating on its side.

He felt a hand on his shoulder. "Dunc."

"Josefa." She carried a five-gallon container of water and put it on the ground. He shrugged, she shook her head, and they both turned to look at the harbor so they would not have to look at each other. A Coast Guard vessel rose with the swells. On its deck, divers were suiting up. "Looks like they're going to start searching … " His voice caught on the words.

Josefa did not reassure him that they would find no bodies, and that was worst of all. "Found your stuffed marlin down the street," she said. "Lost his fin, part of his tail, and some stuffing … but he's still recognizable. Dragged him into the van."

"I should bring him down to Seacrest's to be processed."

Josefa's eyes moved across the yard like the hard sweep of a lighthouse beam. "Where's Chandu?"

Duncan shrugged. "Where's Nod? Where's my mother? You tell me."

Josefa took a breath. "Have faith. Some folks have a way of turning up like bad pennies."

They flinched at a sudden noise. Behind them, a group of men directed by Slocum had tried to raise a fallen wall and failed, so it had splintered loudly back to the ground, where the horsehair-and-seashell plaster shattered on impact. Duncan recognized the soaked wallpaper from his bedroom, silk-screened boats of an earlier time, turning in a gentle breeze. A trailer pulling a front-loader drove up into the washed-out gully of a driveway. Duncan closed his eyes to push away the image of what it might uncover.

"Odd Slocum's here," said Josefa, "and not out looking for his sister."

"Rheya still missing?"

Josepha nodded. "Syrie had the dirt right. Rheya skipped town ahead of the storm … or tried." There was a crash nearby as someone tipped over a French door. "I should go." She bent down and scooped up a wiggling shiner from a puddle with her hand and dropped the little fish into her bucket. "Got to meet the aquarium people … harp seal is tangled in line out on Colrain. I have to lead them to the poor thing."

"Nice to know that something might get saved today." Duncan was still staring at the Coast Guard cutter.

Josefa patted him on the arm and walked off to her van, pausing here and there to inspect puddles for stranded sea life, and then she stopped mid-step, staring up into a pine tree whose top third had been snapped off by the wind.

When Duncan realized she had spotted something, he felt his heart beat in his throat, and he rushed toward her. It was not impossible for someone to be washed up in a tree. In fact, considering the recent tide, it would be a logical place. He was out of breath when he got to her. "Josefa, what?"

"Look!" She pointed to the jagged mess of upper branches, and a crowd of would-be rescuers came running. She whistled a short convoluted song, then whistled again. She held an arm straight out from her body, and a sheer white parrot sailed down upon them with wings extended and landed on her sleeve, feet first.

There was a collective sigh of disappointment from the rescue workers as they returned to their tasks.

"It's okay, buddy, you're safe now." Josefa put her forehead to its beak, and it shimmied to a perch on her shoulder. "I'll take him with me. Bet he's been reported on the missing pets list. Call me if ... " She did not finish the thought.

Duncan wandered off, away from the crowd, and found a foundation stone that had separated from the others. He wiped it clean of seaweed and broken glass and sat down, feeling himself sink into loneliness. When he left Seacrest's, he had thrown on all his damp clothes, and now the stickiness of salt water drying on his skin made him itch. The constant boom of the Atlantic on the opposite shore pounded on his temples. He rested his chin in his hands and smelled the sea on his palms. Through his fingers, he watched the Coast Guard cutter plunge and rise as spray broke over its aft deck, again and again, as the crew readied to descend into the churning water. It was too painful to consider what they were looking for and what they might find, but the more he tried to think of something else, the more his mind turned to morbid images: Nod gargling sea foam out in the harbor somewhere, his mother tumbling from her war room, Chandu desperate to save her, visions of blind destruction that swamped him with agony. He closed his eyes and gave himself up to the sound of the surf, moving in and moving out, in sync with his waves of grief. He nodded off for a moment, the rhythm of the ocean having turned from an aggravation to a comfort, and jerked up with a start when he sensed someone sitting next to him.

"Cora."

She handed him a cup of coffee, and he took it from her. "I came when I heard." She put her hand on his leg. "Any news?"

He could not believe she was here. It was as if she had returned from the dead. She had on her old blue hat with ear flaps and a pom-pom on top, and her nose was red from the wind, the way it gets. Her yellow fleece jacket was new and baggy, but her jeans were warmly familiar, and her knee-high wellies were a comforting match to his.

She touched his cheek, then took a tissue out of her windbreaker pocket and wiped his face. "Your eyes and nostrils are caked with salt."

"I'm glad you're here," he said. He rested his coffee on the ground, then put his head on her shoulder. He was so violently tired that when he closed his eyes, the past twenty-four hours swept over him like a hallucination, and he had to jerk himself back up to keep from falling away. "I'm such a screw-up," he said. "I couldn't even make it home to you last night. I failed."

"You didn't fail me," she said as she stuck the tissue in her pocket, and then she inched closer to him. They gazed out at the water together, resting their weight on each other as lobster boats slowly trolled the shore looking for their traps. Fishing boats—those that had not been crushed in the storm—were taking advantage of the diminished competition and chugging out to sea through the powerful swells. It took a long time for the fury of the ocean to dissipate. Above them, hundreds of seagulls hung in a thermal, spinning in circles like buzzards. "Where do you think they all went in the hurricane?" Cora asked.

"They didn't go anywhere," he said. "Josefa says they float on the surface of the water and ride it out. She said it's what they're made for. We should be so well designed."

"From what I heard from Slocum, you did a pretty good job of riding it out, too. I'm very impressed."

He smiled, but then they both froze at the sight of the Coast Guard divers in black rubber falling backward from the fantail, one by one, into the water and disappearing into the churning sea. Cora tightened her grip on his leg.

"I killed them," Duncan said.

"Don't." She put her arm around him. "Whatever happens, don't blame yourself. Slocum told me that your mom sent Nod out into the storm, and he went. And later, she wouldn't leave with Slocum and then she wouldn't leave with you. Their decisions are not your fault. Only Nod could have saved Nod, and he chose not to. The same with your mother." She looked over at the gaping hole where the house once stood.

"I could have done a better job of talking some sense into them. I wasn't very effective."

"Who breaks the lifeline?" she asked. "The one who pulls or the one who lets go?"

He shook his head. "It doesn't matter if they're dead, does it?" He looked down at his feet and recognized a shape sticking out of the mud. He used a piece of house lathing to pry up an empty green bottle, then turned it over in his hands. "The mulberry wine is a mild hallucinogenic."

She stared at him. "What does that mean?"

"It means my family is not congenitally nuts." He held up the bottle to the light. "They make themselves nuts with this. Mom drank the wine. Nod ate the jelly. Not only that, he was conceived during a binge. Maybe he has fetal mulberry syndrome."

They both began to laugh in a high-pitched, almost hysterical way that made some rescue workers take pause.

"It's not funny," whispered Cora as she wiped tears from her eyes.

"No, it's not." Duncan turned to look out at the water.

"It's so much easier to name a problem than it is to fix it, isn't it?" she asked. "Sometimes, at work, it's all I can do. I feel like a failure every day."

236

They both contemplated the desolate landscape around them and the seeming futility of trying to help anyone or anything.

"About this baby," said Duncan.

"Well, it's about time you brought up the baby!"

"I've been an idiot. When we were about to start a family, I saw my own family from the outside for the first time, and it stopped me cold. And far worse than seeing them, I saw me."

"I've always seen your family. They display their oddities because it's never occurred to them that there's anything wrong with being odd. That's what I love about them. It's what I love about you."

Duncan looked into her face and saw the truth of their marriage. Being a family therapist, she must have been drawn to him by his flock of odd ducks, and he was drawn to her by her fascination with them. On some level, he was probably hoping she could help him figure them out or at least deal with them so he wouldn't have to. Then she could save him when he started skipping down the psycho path, too.

None of that mattered. He loved her for herself and not for how she could help him. He could help himself.

"Duncan, don't you have any questions?"

"Questions?" He closed his eyes and leaned toward her. But just as they were about to kiss, Slocum shouted at them.

"Duncan! Get a load of this!" He was waving them over to the new ledge of land.

"Oh, no," said Duncan.

"We better look," she said and took his hand to get to her feet. They maneuvered over the minefield of broken objects to Slocum and looked down at the beach with him. The tide was out, but the water was agitated enough to cast spray in their faces, misting Duncan's glasses so that he could not quite make out the massive object that had rolled on shore.

"That's astounding," said Cora.

"It's downright creepy," said Slocum.

Duncan wiped his lenses and put them back on and still had trouble absorbing the sight. It was a killer ball of plastic crap the size of a whale.

"Ghost nets," announced Marney, who'd come to help with the cleanup. "The lost nets and lines—they gather marine debris as they roll into a ball along the bottom of the sea, getting bigger and nastier every day."

Along with the lobster traps, polyethylene bottles, flip-flops, Mylar balloons, disposable diapers, and Tide detergent jugs, woven into the mess were fish of all nations, dead seagulls, other sea birds, and, worst of all, a harbor seal, drowned when it got ensnared by the netball. There were certainly many other casualties woven deep in its center, and Duncan hoped one wasn't a member of his family.

"What have we done?" asked Lovasco.

A small tug boat turned the corner of the Cove, chugging close to the shoreline, and in a moment Duncan recognized Adoniram, dressed in a fresh, well-fitted suit and tie. Beaky was standing on the deck.

"Isn't that Osbert Marpol, from the Club?" asked Cora.

"Yes. No. It's Adoniram. When I got washed up in the Duck on Seacrest's beach last night, he saved me."

"Adoniram?" She gave Duncan a worried look.

Duncan waved at the boat, and Adoniram waved back with his stick. "Do you have a dry cell phone?" he asked her.

She dug through her pocket and handed him her phone. He dialed Adoniram's phone number from memory and watched as Adoniram took his cell out of his suit and clicked it on.

"Duncan!" he shouted over the sound of surf. "You and I send diatoms to the sea in a symbolic cleansing gesture, and the ocean regurgitates a giant netball back at us, in our faces where it belongs. It is one of the side effects that the artist cannot imagine."

"What are you doing out there?"

"The ocean has encountered another world. Look at all that plastic. Look at the nets, how they've strangled every living thing they've encountered. From my side I see a dead sea turtle."

"What's the plan?"

"We're going to bring it to the attention of our world. Who is it who said that the sea is forever asking questions and writing them aloud on the shore?"

"Churchill?" asked Duncan.

"Why not? We'll display this creation of death on your parking lot. It will be the first of many installations I'll create there."

"Are you coming out as yourself, then?"

"Back to life. And back to work. Talk later."

Duncan put the phone back in Cora's pocket and put his arms around her. They watched as Adoniram joined Beaky in the task of uncoiling rope on the deck.

"I thought you and Osbert were enemies," she said. "I thought you were afraid he was going to kill you."

"I used to think many things that turned out to be wrong. For one thing, he's not even Osbert, so how could he kill me? From a false equation you get only a chain of errors."

"Have you been eating the mulberries?"

He smiled and did not answer. They watched as Beaky handed Adoniram an iron fishing spear attached to a rope, then Adoniram raised the instrument over his head and lunged it at the plastic ball, à la Ahab. After the spear hit its mark, Beaky leaned out from the bow and tossed a grappling hook on the line and pulled it tight, securing the boat to the ball. He gave a tug to test it, then motioned to Adoniram that they were ready to go. Fingers moved from Beaky's pocket to his shoulder.

The crowd on land applauded when the tugboat slowly edged the plastic ball off the beach, then began to cheer when the ball began to sink below the surface of the water, threatening to pull Adoniram and the boat down with it. But he revved up the tugboat and got enough momentum going to keep the ball floating along behind them as they disappeared into the rising light of day, around the tip of the Cove.

"God help us," said Cora.

Duncan waved at the tug as it disappeared. "Maybe instead of worrying about bringing my fucked-up genes into the world, I should have been worrying about the fucked-up world."

"It's too late to worry now."

They stood there for a while as the others returned to the cleanup and search efforts. Duncan looked down to inspect the new landscape of the beach, which had expanded as the yard contracted. He saw pieces of their old rickety dock, along with the crumpled hull of *Ariel,* Nod's catboat. There was no sign of the inflatable—no motor, no seats, no shreds of rubber. He looked down at the steep wall beneath them, which had been sliced off so neatly by the sea that it read like a geological chart. Horizontal layers of dirt were squeezed in between thick strata of compressed sand streaked with rust. Roots, rocks, and odd subterranean life saw light for the first time in millennia. If a mammoth tusk fell out of the wall at that moment, Duncan would not have been surprised.

When he looked back up, Slocum was standing next to them, with his arm wrapped around Gabriella, the figurehead from his mother's living room.

"I think she'll clean up pretty good, don't you?" said Slocum. "The fallen angel."

"Slocum, any word on your sister?" asked Cora.

Slocum arranged a grim look on his face and shook his head.

"No word," he said. "We'll just have to keep looking. Judson Drake is gone, too. Heard he might have been on *L'ark* when she came loose. Poor bastard."

Duncan touched Gabriella's splintered face. "This isn't the first time the old girl has had her troubles on the sea. In spite of what my mother said about the U.S. Navy sending it to the family in appreciation of some relative's valor in the Napoleonic wars—in which, mind you, America was not even involved—Lucius found her right on the beach after a storm in 1882. Where'd she wash up this time?"

"Behind the lighthouse, on the rocks." Slocum turned and pointed over at the stone beacon, which stood twenty feet closer to the water than it had before the storm. "Not too far from where they found your mother."

"My mother?"

twenty

Chandu, dripping and swaying like a surfacing sea god, was hoarse from howling as he stood guard by Duncan's mother on the war room floor. It was, amazingly, still in one octagonal piece, somewhat lathered in dirty sea foam but perfectly balanced on a chest-high pile of trash at the Boat Club beach. It had been yanked to shore by a boat lift after a commercial charter had towed it to the basin. Emergency workers were now trying to entice his mother to leave the floor and come to the ambulance for treatment, but she pushed them away with her bare feet as she clung to the prow of the old bookstand bolted to the floor. The platform tipped gently back and forth as they struggled, as if it were still at sea. Chandu stopped making his mournful sound when he saw Duncan.

"Duncan!" his mother shouted. "Thank goodness you're here. Tell these people to leave me alone."

"Mom, you're alive." He pulled himself up onto the floor.

"Of course I am." She raised the trophy that held his caul. "I grabbed this when the walls started to bow out. Here, help with these knots."

She and Chandu were lashed by their waists to the bookstand. There was so much rope twisted around them that Duncan didn't even know where to begin. To make matters worse, a line of swordfish bait was entwined in the mess. The plastic glow-sticks still held light. Chandu licked his face when he knelt down.

"Old man," said Duncan, rubbing his shaggy head with both hands. "You did it." Never did an animal smell so thoroughly like the ocean, or smell so good. He was alive. They were both alive. "Were you on this floor during the storm?" he asked his mother. "Out on the water?"

"It was no bed of owl feathers, I can tell you."

Duncan shook his head. She was one tough bird, he had to give her that. He examined the rope and attempted to pry a line loose from the Gordian knot that held them to their raft. He felt his mother's hand on his shoulder.

"Duncan, dear, I have bad news."

The crowd surrounding the floor became quiet and apprehensive. Duncan couldn't imagine what would constitute "bad news" in the face of all this destruction. He assumed ... Nod.

"Gone," she said, and she ran her hand over the empty book-stand. "One hundred and forty years of work, gone. I held onto it as long as I could, but it dissolved in my arms. Leaf by leaf, it pulled away in the wind and the water, until finally the covers held nothing, and then they, too, fell apart and my hands were empty."

"It?" asked Duncan.

"The Log," she said. "Gone."

The crowd looked at one another in confused silence, and Duncan went back to the knot. The Log. Maybe that would be the end of her obsessive race planning. But of course, if Nod was gone, it was the end of it anyway, wasn't it? "Well, you saved the caul, Mom. That's something."

"No, the caul saved me." She held the loving cup like a baby. "It kept me from drowning, but it could not keep the Log safe from the ravages of water. 'Full fathom five thy father lies; Of his bones are coral made ...'"

"You'll get by without the Log," he said. "It's going to be harder to get by without a house." He sat back on his ankles, and his wet boots felt cold against his body. He wanted to add " ... or Nod," but he could not bring himself to say his brother's name. "This knot is too tight." He turned to see Slocum arriving with his arms full of his mother's things, picked up on the walk over. "Slocum, do you have a knife on you?"

"Are you mad?" his mother said. "That will be the day when a son of mine can't release a sheepshank. There"—she tucked the loving cup under her arm and pointed at a line—"pull hard on that one, and it will all fall away."

He did, and it did, and his mother and Chandu stepped out of their restraints.

"Now get off that floor," shouted a woman standing nearby. She was very short, so that her head barely cleared the edge of the floor, and she had a fiercely determined look to her face. She didn't seem to be an emergency worker, dressed as she was in a damp but tailored pantsuit.

"Who's that?" Duncan asked.

"Ignore her," said his mother.

A young man with an ambulance badge snuck up behind his mother and threw a silver blanket around her shoulders. "Mrs. Leland, you've got hypothermia. Come with me, and we'll get you warmed up in the ambulance."

"She wouldn't have hypothermia if she had more fat," said Slocum as he made a neat pile of rescued objects on the ground. "This storm was just a warning. A new aquatic phase has arrived, and we must adapt with fat!"

"I'm not going anywhere until my floor is safe from the grasping hands of those people. They didn't come to rescue me—they want this!" And with that, she stomped the floor with her foot. Her toenails were still perfectly trimmed in scarlet.

"Don't do that!" said a man standing next to the woman. He had keen eyes and gray hair neatly cut. He wore a dark suit that looked as if it had been slept in, and Duncan realized who they were. "Those people" were the two museum representatives that his mother had chased from the house the day before.

His mother stomped again. "I'll do whatever I want to *my* floor."

"It's our floor now," said the man. He strained his neck forward like a sea turtle. "We found it."

"I never abandoned it!" shouted his mother. "Go away, you wreckers!"

"Mrs. Leland is right," said Chief Lovasco, and everyone turned to him for guidance. "She is still in possession of her vessel."

"We claim salvage rights." With her short, raptorial arms, the museum woman waved a sheath of papers over her head. "It's not a boat. It's a major work of American art. We saved it, so it's ours. She just happened to be on it."

"You see, Duncan, dear," said his mother, whose lips were turning blue. "I can't go anywhere."

"You two"—Lovasco motioned to the museum people—"leave her alone until we get her stabilized. Come with us, Mrs. Leland."

"It's ours!" they shouted, and they grabbed hold of the splintered edge of the floor.

"How did it even survive in one piece?" asked Cora. Slocum pushed her up onto the floor, then a Red Cross worker handed her a stack of towels.

"The wine saved us," said his mother.

"The casks," said Slocum, picking up a metal barrel hoop from the ground. He stuck his head through it and wore it like a necklace.

"From what we can make out," said Lovasco, "when the walls gave out, the floor launched into the water below and landed on the wine casks floating in the yard."

"Off we went!" said his mother. Cora wrapped her mother-in-law's single braid in a towel and wrung it out. "We caught hold of the line of swordfish bait when we passed the porch, and then we sailed out of danger."

"They lodged in the teeth of the old pier. These folks"—Lovasco gestured at the museum people—"were out on a vessel as the storm was winding down, and they saw the lights in the dark and heard the howling of the dog. They were able to tow her here to the Boat Club."

"It's a miracle," said Slocum.

"It might be a miracle," said the museum woman, "but it was no accident. When we got the news that the house fell into the ocean, we risked our lives in that charter boat to search for the Dodge floor. We hadn't intended to find *her,* too. We don't want *her.*"

"Now here we are, and no one will give way," said Lovasco.

"I should have left the house earlier," Duncan's mother told Cora. "I had some dark thoughts out there in the storm. Some regrets and misgivings."

Duncan wondered if this was the start of her life without an hallucinogenic crutch.

"It's hard leaving something you love," said Cora. "The important thing is that you got out alive."

"It was a matter of interpretation," his mother mused. "My actions were based on bad information. All these years I've been reading the wrong columns, so I was miscalculating the wind and tide projections." She shook her head, and her heavy braid swung a bit. "When the first wall went down, I thought some abnormal wind must have turned the tide before its time. But I still thought the house would hold. When the next wall went down, I said, 'Impossible.' I grabbed the loving cup anyway and tied myself to the bookstand with Chandu and a flashlight. I went over the numbers again, and that's when I realized my mistake, but it was too late. Next thing I know, I'm at sea."

"Well, if it's any consolation," said Duncan, "Seacrest's is still standing."

"Of course it is. I was using a bad equation." She squinted as she looked around her. "The worst thing is, now that I know where I went wrong, I no longer have the Log to guide me. Maybe Nod knows what we should do next. He's always been so good that way. Where is he?"

Duncan and Cora exchanged looks, then Cora put her hand on his mother's arm. "Annabel, they haven't found him ... yet."

His mother stared out at the sea, and a pained expression crossed her face. The sun, cleared of the horizon, shone a white brilliant light. It was difficult even to look in that direction.

"Nod might not come back," his mother said, tightening the silver blanket around her. "But he'll be okay. Nothing would have stopped him from surviving."

The Coast Guard cutter motored loudly around the corner, and for a moment, Duncan thought this was it. They had Nod, one way or another. But no. The crew was suiting up and checking tanks, which meant a new batch of divers was preparing to go under. A red-and-white helicopter swept close to the waterline. For a moment, he wished for his mother's sake that she had her war room back. It was obsessive, but it gave her life meaning and made it seem not so sad. And he felt she was going to be very sad very soon.

"The great tomb of the sailors," said Slocum, shading his eyes with his hand as he looked out to sea.

"He was a man who knew his bowline from a sheepshank," said Duncan's mother.

"It's a little early to be using past tense," said Duncan, stinging with what felt like an attack on his knotting ability, while marveling at her ability to accept the worst and move right along. "There's still hope," he said. "Plenty of hope. Let's first get you settled, Mom. You're shivering."

"Duncan, dear, this is no time."

Cora put her arms around her mother-in-law. "Come on, Annabel. You've got to warm up. Duncan will guard the floor for you."

"Cora, how are you doing? I don't know how Duncan could have walked away from you at a time like this." She patted Cora's hand and turned to Duncan. "I'll go inside if you stay here and maintain the family claim. You'll have to commit to stay put, for once."

"Should I tie myself to the mast?" he asked.

She didn't answer but allowed Cora and a rescue worker to help her to the edge of the floor, where Slocum picked her up and stood her on the ground. She staggered as if still on her life raft, then bent over to pick up a cracked stave of a wine cask.

"Those idiots," she said, addressing her anger now at the crane operator who lifted the floor to shore. "Don't know the proper way to beach a vessel. Maybe the other casks have washed up safely elsewhere. We've got to go looking for them, Slocum. Let's hurry before more wreckers arrive."

A wave, pushed by one behind it, slid so far up the slant of sand and rock that their feet were unexpectedly soaked. A thin coat of petroleum was left on the land as the water retreated, creating rainbows in the dark pools cupped among the descending slabs of shale.

"Dry clothes first," said Lovasco. "I don't want any more fatalities than necessary."

"I wouldn't have thought any were *necessary,*" said Cora, her arm through her mother-in-law's, treading carefully through the mess.

"That's where you're wrong," said Slocum, who was on her other side. "They're absolutely necessary."

"Amen," said Annabel Leland. "If there wasn't death, how would we know what to do with life?"

Duncan watched as they walked away, led by Chandu, who sniffed out the easiest passage through the chaos for them. The rescue team followed behind in twos like a funeral procession. The sun was heating up the earth now, and the moisture on the black roofs of the boat sheds was beginning to evaporate in wisps. It looked as if the world was dissolving in a slow burn. His mother stopped to look at smashed pieces of casks, but Cora kept pulling her forward. Chief Lovasco directed his officers to continue searching for Nod, and the museum people stood firmly with their hands clasped on the floor. Their charter boat knocked against the Club's wooden pier as the captain waited for further instruction, and a lobster boat pulled up behind it. Annuncia and Wade. Duncan watched them intently for a moment to see if they knew something about Nod, but they moved slowly as they tied up, too slowly to have any news, and when they saw him they looked at him for an answer. He had none.

He sat down as heavily as a body bag and leaned against the book stand. It seemed strange that Nod was not with him now, Nod who had spent so much of his life here on the Club waterfront. Duncan kept expecting him to pop up from behind an upturned boat and give his slightly manic, breezy laugh, making death seem like a sick joke. His eyes scanned the boatyard, trashed not just with garbage but with yachts stove in on their sides, pleasure boats still attached to their moorings dragged from the sea, and dinghies blown in a pile against the shuttered porch of the old clubhouse. The building was still standing, somewhat, but looked as if it were being held together with string and tar. Enormous mounds of seaweed and weathered planks and lobster pots created a labyrinth around it, and in this mess he saw their float. Nod had never even made it this far to collect it. He must have been lost as soon as he stepped onto the inflatable, swept out of the cove and through the jagged teeth of the sunken pier where he was swallowed by the sea.

Annuncia and Wade appeared by the floor and stared at it and him, as if they were both already museum pieces. "Look. It's the racing map," said Wade, using his arm to wipe a strand of seaweed off the floor.

"Keep your hands off," said the museum woman.

"Coastal Bank & Trust washed into the water," said Annuncia, ignoring the woman altogether. "We went to have a look. What a crowd. People must think money is going to float to the surface. Feds are there—National Guard, too. Then we heard the news about your mom on the Coast Guard channel."

"No word on Nod?" Wade asked. They leaned their chests against the floor and rested their arms on the floor as if they were settling down for a long night at Ten Bells. Both the museum people groaned.

"No Nod, but no body either," Duncan said.

"Doesn't mean anything," said Annuncia. "The crabs and the

gulls will make a swift and environmentally friendly end to him if he doesn't show up soon."

"There are worse graves than the clean, green sea," said Wade, touching the painted expanse of water on the floor.

"Stop that," said the museum man.

"Yes, stop it." Duncan rested his forehead on his knees and felt very tired. As soon as his eyes closed, he dropped into wakeful REM dreams and had a vision of Nod, arms and legs extended, drifting and twirling down to the depths of the ocean like a leaf, through an autumn forest of coral and anemone. Cod the size of babies nosed at him as he came to rest at the bottom with their father.

"Was Nod wearing a gold earring?" asked Wade.

Duncan snapped awake again. "Why? Has someone been found with an earring?"

"No," said Wade. "Just the polite thing to do. If he washes up on shore he should have enough gold on his person to bury him."

"Used to be law," said Annuncia.

Duncan just stared at them. In all this commotion, he'd forgotten he was mad at Annuncia. "You missed quite the happening last night at Seacrest's with your buddy."

Wade looked away and whistled, and Annuncia shrugged without changing the neutral expression on her face. She pushed herself away from the floor as if she were leaving the dinner table. "Speaking of which, we've got to head over there now. He called to ask for help with the netball installation."

"Why didn't you just tell me what he wanted the factory for?"

"That would have meant revealing his identity. That was for him to do, not me."

"Besides, Mr. Leland, you would have said no," said Wade. "It's pretty far out. I was skeptical myself, all these art shenanigans."

"I had to save the factory for a higher purpose," said Annuncia.

"You had to sign a contract so he could have access to a processing plant to fulfill his contract."

"His contract?"

"An artist says he is going to do something, and he carries it out. That is the contract. Phase One of the Diatom Project was completed last night. Phase Two begins in the spring when we start shipping out the product. Phase Three is when the customers start spreading it in the soil. The fourth and final phase is when the rains wash it back to the seas. The idea comes from Adoniram, but we are all involved in the execution of his idea, as we were all involved in destroying the oceans in the first place."

"Adoniram?" asked the museum man. "*The* Adoniram? The conceptual artist?"

"He's alive?" asked the woman.

"Down at the Seacrest's parking lot right now beaching a new installation," said Annuncia. "The ugly consequences of human excess."

"You can't quite get it out of your mind once you seen it," said Wade. "Smells, too, as the day warms up. Full of dead things."

The woman turned to her associate. "You stay here and guard this. I'm going to Seacrest's."

"Adoniram," the man said. "It's a miracle."

They all watched as the museum woman headed for the dock, tripping over all kinds of seaweed in her heels, and, with a raised arm, she motioned to the captain to start up his engine.

"Mr. Leland," said the museum man. "Do you think you could remove yourselves from our painting now?"

"Please," said Duncan. "Go home. This floor hasn't been abandoned. It is not yours, it is ours. If you want to buy it, we'll talk about that later. Right now, we have to concentrate on my brother."

"But in the likely event that the floor is going to be ours, one way or another, I'd like to see to its safe storage."

Duncan closed his eyes tightly. He heard the seagulls come to life directly over him, making a raucous noise, hanging in a current that Duncan could not feel. He sensed that they were looking down at him as they soared and circled, absorbing the big picture in a way that he could not. He wished he had that sort of distance. The tide was coming in, and he heard the grinding of stones as the water moved forward and then relaxed.

Chief Lovasco pulled himself up onto the floor without speaking. He was stern-faced, and Duncan could guess what that meant. When Lovasco knelt next to him, Duncan could smell coffee on his breath and the drying weeds of the ocean that were stuck on his rain gear.

"Duncan," he said. "I just got a call. You'd better come to Colrain with me. They've found a body."

Even though Duncan knew that this was going to be the end to the search, he longed for uncertainty again. "Nod?"

"No, we think it's your father. And we have quite a few questions for your mother."

Killed him? a double surprise!

twenty-one

"Things have a way of washing up there, don't they?" said Chief Lovasco, his voice muffled as it came through the opening of the glass divider in the police cruiser. Duncan was squeezed in the backseat between his mother and Cora, on their way to Colrain Beach on the windward shore on the wild Atlantic, unsheltered by the bay or any nearby islands. It was a stretch of land famous for beachcombing.

"A dead whale rolled up on it when I was a kid," said Duncan, wondering at his ability to chitchat on this grim occasion. But what else was there to do? Lovasco refused to talk about the body, and Duncan could not put his thoughts into words. That they should think they found his father after all this time was absurd—no flesh would have survived ten years at sea. Not even bones. Teeth, maybe. In all likelihood they'd found Nod, but to consider this option was to acknowledge that his brother was actually dead.

"You could smell the rot from the house," said his mother, who was gazing at the passing scene from her window, the first time she'd seen this much of the world in years. When they had pulled out of the Boat Club driveway, then past the empty space that was once her house, Duncan braced himself, thinking they were in for a bit of rough weather from her, but no. She was acting as if a road trip around town in the back of a police car was an everyday event. It was strange that she did not even comment on how the landscape had changed since she'd last seen it, but then again, it was totally different from when he last saw it. Trees were missing, roofs were sitting in washed-out streets, and the very coastline was rearranged, as chipped and gouged out as if the earth were made of Styrofoam.

"Please," said Cora, slumping down in her seat. "Let's not talk about rot."

Duncan put his arm around her and she closed her eyes, but as tired as he was, he could not close his. He could not even imagine sleep. His mind was so wired he was experiencing the world as one of those dreams where you can't get to where you're going. Only instead of the inexplicable barriers of the sleeping brain, such as giant frogs leaping at your head or your Spanish teacher holding a stop sign in the middle of the road—bizarre obstructions that make you forget just what it was you were looking to find—their delays were all too explicable. Flooding and utility work forced them to detour again and again, and even where the roads were open, Lovasco had to maneuver around workers trying to restore power.

"The world just picks up and moves on, doesn't it?" Lovasco said, as a woman in a bright orange vest waved him around a fallen tree and sparking wires.

"What choice is there?" asked Cora, without opening her eyes.

"Are you sure this is my father?" Duncan asked, but Lovasco tightened his lips.

"I don't think you have anybody's body," his mother said, leaning forward to lecture Lovasco. She was bundled up in a mishmash of Red Cross handouts, topped off with a shiny raincoat in zebra print. Her feet were still bare. "You certainly didn't do a very good job of finding mine. A couple of museum curators with a charter did that, and now they're going to snatch the floor while you hold me hostage. How much have they paid you to conspire with them on this ruse?"

"Don't make things worse," said Duncan, although he couldn't actually imagine what would constitute worse. He lowered his voice. "Mom, let's say he's right and this is Dad's body. Why does he want you for questioning?"

"I don't think we need to go into it now," she said and sat back in her seat to admire the passing scenery.

Cora leaned toward the open divider. "Could you roll down a window back here?" she asked Lovasco. "I'm feeling carsick."

"Sorry, Mrs. Leland," he said, squeezing the car past a boulder that had been tossed onto the road by a wave. "I can't take the risk of the other Mrs. Leland escaping."

"Escaping?" said Duncan. "From a moving car? Is she under arrest?"

"Duncan, dear," his mother said. "This is no time."

"Just a precautionary measure," said Lovasco.

"I shouldn't have had that coffee," said Cora. "I thought I could get away with decaf."

"It's good to be a little seasick," said Duncan's mother, patting Cora on the leg. "Shows you're catching enough air to steer clear of the rocks and shoals of the early weeks."

"Early weeks?" asked Duncan.

His mother tossed up her hands. "Duncan, please, stop asking so many questions."

"Yes," said Cora. "The early weeks of pregnancy." She put both hands on her stomach. "Not that you've asked how the appointment went. It's the one question you haven't thought to ask these days."

"What? *What?*"

"You know what," she said. "The insemination appointment a few weeks ago. You've never asked about it."

The walls of Duncan's throat went dry as the news swept through him like a hot wind. He tried to stand up in the police car, but the roof forced him to sit back down. He took off his glasses, then put them on again. He felt for Cora's hand and tightened his grip on it until it seemed as if he could feel the ridges of her fingerprints on his palms. As this stunning piece of information slowly seeped into his brain, he felt his body flooding with sensation.

"I don't know what happened," he said at last. "I guess I assumed you weren't going to go through with it while we were fighting."

"We weren't fighting. Not then, anyway. I just needed to be calm for the implantation, and that wasn't going to happen with you hanging around fretting about blimps and death. So I sent you to Slocum's for a few days, and you never came back. Then we *were* fighting because you hadn't bothered to ask how it went, or what the results were, or anything. I thought it was your way of bugging out. I thought I was going to have to be a single mom."

He placed his hand on her stomach. "Why didn't you just tell me? You know I'm an idiot. I thought I wasn't supposed to come back until I worked out my problems. I thought you didn't think I was sane enough to have children."

"Duncan. Really. You're sane enough. If I suggested that you see someone, it's only because I wanted you to get help for you, not me.

I want you to be happy when the baby comes, not tied up in knots about it. You'll only raise a Nod that way."

Lovasco whistled.

Cora bit her lip. "I'm sorry. That's my hormones talking. I'd love a Nod baby as much as any other baby. *Any* baby. I can't believe, after all we'd been through to get to implantation and what we paid for it so far, you thought I wasn't going to have it done. Was that wishful thinking? Are you really ready for this?"

He pulled her close. "I'm ready. I just wish I could have been there."

"No, you would have been too tense, and you would have made me tense, and then my uterus would be too tense for a zygote to hang on. Besides, I didn't want to make a big deal about the appointment. It's rarely a success the first try. But it turned out there was nothing particularly wrong with your sperm or my eggs—they just needed a little *push* to get them together."

"That's the spirit," said his mother. "Take determined action, I always say."

"Did you know?" Duncan asked her.

"Of course I knew," she said. "Cora told me when I called to invite her to the party, but I'd already heard the rumors from Mrs. McNordfy. Even Noddy, who never leaves town, saw her going into a fertility clinic in Portland when he went to buy *Sea Turtle*. You have got to start paying more attention to the world around you, Duncan!"

There was some silence as Duncan considered the source of this accusation, and then he considered that she still might be right. He had not been paying attention to the important things around him. "Was I really so stupid?" he asked Cora.

She leaned her head back and groaned. "Duncan, please, this isn't the time."

"What a mess," said Lovasco, and for a moment, Duncan

thought he was referring to their lives. But no, he was talking about the mountains of trash deposited by the storm that were increasing in height and frequency as they got closer to Colrain. The road, puddled and scarred, looked freshly reopened. On one side was the ocean, still white-tipped and wild, and on the other side were the battered marshlands. They were designed by nature to help absorb flooding, but nature could not have foreseen all the indigestible trash in modern water. The exposed mudflats were covered with so much shredded polystyrene it looked as if a dirty blizzard had swept in from the sea along with the pieces of boats, and of those, it seemed no size or class was spared. There were modest wooden boats and immodest fiberglass yachts, working vessels and Boston Whalers. But no deflated bodies of inflatables. Not yet.

Lovasco turned into the parking lot and headed to the far corner, where an ambulance, two fire trucks, and a half-dozen police cruisers waited, all in a hyper sense of emergency with a full spectrum of lights blinking. As Duncan helped Cora out of the car, Lovasco took his mother's elbow, but she shook him off. He motioned to two officers, who approached with their hands resting on their holsters, to stay on either side of her while he walked ahead, leading them over the dunes to the beach where they came upon the full expression of the storm's wrath. It looked as if half of Port Ellery had gotten sucked into its vortex and been left there to die. Scattered along its length were gray plastic fish bins, kitchen countertops, aluminum siding, and mooring balls, and at the end of the beach, where the sand changed to rocky cliff, the sea was still worrying a lobster boat against the piles of broken and eroded stone. A long tangle of traps and buoys rolled back and forth at the tide line, out of reach of the lobstermen who were lined up to sort them out, held back by a labyrinth of yellow police tape. It was a crime scene. On the other side of the tape stood Josefa, holding a subdued seagull under her arms as she talked to the police.

He heard her say, "There they are … " She and everyone else stopped talking when Duncan and his family came into view. His mother stepped around a boat pump that had been ripped from a hold of some ill-fated boat. Yards of snapped wire sprang out from all four sides.

"Looks like a giant spider, doesn't it?" his mother asked of no one, and the instant the officers turned to look, she struck off. At first, Duncan thought she was on the lam, but she wasn't running away from the crime scene; she was heading toward whatever it was that awaited them all behind the yellow tape. Duncan could see a pile of broken staves.

"It's one of her wine casks," he said, not bothering to chase after her but continuing to pick his way through the mess with Cora, conscious now of the dangers of stumbling. "Cracked open like an egg."

"She seems so desperate about the loss of her wine," said Cora. "I wonder if she shouldn't go into detox."

"That would take care of her housing problem for a while." They almost started to laugh, then Duncan stopped when he saw a human shape on the ground next to the broken barrel. "Stay here," he said. "Don't look." He lifted the tape over his head, then stopped, unable to fully register the sight before him. His mother, on her knees, was by the side of the body.

"Brendan," she said.

"So it's true," said Lovasco. "You can identify this man as Brendan Leland?"

Duncan went momentarily deaf at the mention of his father's name. He looked at Josefa, who gave a little shrug and clutched her seagull. She must have found the body, and she would have known exactly who it was.

"Who else would it be?" his mother asked impatiently, and she took her husband's purple hand into hers.

Duncan heard Cora gasp, and in a minute she was by his side. They both stared. His father's form was strange and unearthly. He was in the sailing shorts and T-shirt he'd worn his last day on earth, but now, along with his clothes, his bare arms and legs were pickled and dyed purple from the mulberry wine. He was not perfectly preserved—the wine was not high enough in alcohol for that—but it had kept the body from decaying altogether. He was considerably shrunken and folded up as tight as a fetus.

"He saved my life," his mother said, smiling.

"Your life?" Lovasco asked, and Duncan noticed an officer taking down notes. His mother was in serious trouble. For all he knew, she'd killed him and hidden the body in the cellar all these years. He wondered how far they could go on an insanity plea.

"That's what I said, isn't it?" his mother said peevishly. "He saved me and Chandu. We were in death's hands when the house fell out from under us, but when the floor landed on the casks, I knew Brendan would keep us afloat. He always has. It's been such a comfort all these years knowing he was beneath my feet. I couldn't bear to leave him. Neither could Nod."

"Nod?" asked Cora.

"Noddy found him that day on the beach. He was such a help. I'm not sure I could have done it on my own. It's not easy squeezing a man into a barrel. But of course, they used to do it all the time in the golden age of sail, packing their captains in alcohol rather than feeding them to the sharks. They got them home that way."

"But he was already home," said Lovasco. "If what you say is true, he washed up practically at your back door."

She stood up. "What do you mean, 'if what I say is true'?"

"Poor Nod," whispered Duncan. If, in fact, what his mother said was true—always a dubious proposition—then it wasn't the death of their father that had kept Nod at home—it was finding his body and stuffing him into the barrel that had sent him over the edge. He must have felt implicated and decided to stand watch all those years.

Duncan put his arm around Cora. "So, you still think we're not any worse than any other family?"

She touched her stomach, and a worried look came over her face. "You win."

"Mrs. Leland." Lovasco took a step toward his mother. "You've got to come to the station with me for questioning. You have the right to remain silent—"

"Don't be absurd," his mother interrupted. "I've told you what happened, and that's all you need to know." She used both hands to wipe her pink pants of sand. They were too short for her by far, and now the knees were soaked through. She could get more clothes from the Red Cross to hold her over, but Duncan could not let her go into a shelter. Here he was, finally about to go back to his own home, ready to start a family, and he'd be taking his mother back with him. Unless, of course, she was locked up.

"Mom, I think you should do what the chief says."

She turned to Lovasco and pointed to her husband's body. "Chief Lovasco, if you want to be of any use, you can find an empty cask for me. This one won't do."

Duncan saw the other officers exchange looks that made him think they were going to jump her with a straitjacket, but instead they all turned to watch a mud-splattered Land Rover slide down off the sand dune and onto the beach, heading right toward them before stopping at the yellow tape.

"Everard Blue," said Josefa.

"Who?" asked Cora.

"It's that man," said his mother, with a venomous look. "I don't care for him very much. Duncan, tell him to go away."

"He's a retired admiralty lawyer from New York," Duncan told Cora, ignoring his mother. "He just moved to Port Ellery, and Slocum invited him to the party last night." Duncan lowered his voice. "I think they have some chemistry."

Cora raised her eyebrows.

Everard Blue waved away the officers who tried to keep him from crossing the tape. Chandu jumped out of the car and ran ahead.

"Out of my way!" Everard said. "I am Mrs. Leland's attorney."

"I don't need a lawyer," said his mother, bending to hug Chandu, who stiffened at the sight of the body on the ground, his former master. "What are you doing with my dog?"

"My dear Mrs. Leland," Everard said, bowing deeply. He wore khakis and a waxed overcoat, with old-fashioned galoshes on his feet with the metal clasps undone. He looked at the body and shook his head. "I stopped by the Boat Club to check on my *Avocet* and heard about your problems. This fine animal insisted he come along with me, as I must insist now on coming along with you to the station."

He reached out to her, and after a mild squirmish during which she kicked sand at him, he got hold of her hand and kissed it. His mustache brushed up against her skin, and she stood very still.

She looked at Duncan for guidance. "You do need a lawyer," he said. "And Judson is still missing."

"Judson?" She looked out at the water. "With *L'ark*?"

"Fool," said Josefa. "Must've tried to save her by bringing her out to sea to ride out the storm … him knowing squat about boats."

His mother continued to study the water until Everard pulled her closer to him by her hand.

"It's a sad fact, Mrs. Leland, that when a body is involved, the law must be involved." He rested his other hand on top of hers. "There are details that must be gotten out of the way. First they'll want to do an autopsy to confirm he died of drowning."

"What else would he have died of?" she asked. "He was DD when he washed up on the beach."

"DD?" asked Cora.

"British navy designation for Discharged Dead," said Duncan, who knew this bit of arcana because DD was carved on some of the family members' ancient gravestones, in spite of the fact that none of them had ever served in the British Navy. Or were, for that matter, British.

"*We* know that," Everard said to his mother in a conspiratorial tone, "but we must be patient with the authorities. They have their jobs to do, and after a few formalities, the body will be released back in your care."

"I'll need a cask," she said.

"You have no wine, no cellar, and no house," Duncan said, wondering if a psychiatric evaluation would be one of those formalities the lawyer spoke of. "And even if you did, you're not putting Dad back in a barrel."

Everard smiled. "Let's get the paperwork behind us first." He held out his arm to her. "It's time, Mrs. Leland."

She looked around at the beach and the water, then at her husband. Chandu was sitting by him. Duncan would have thought his hackles would be up, or that he'd be howling at the sight, but he seemed to be simply observing a silence.

His mother raised her hand. "Good-bye, Brendan darling." And then she took Everard's arm. "Yes," she said. "On we go." And arm in arm they headed toward Everard's Land Rover, cautiously scaling the garbage and seaweed, with Chandu right behind and, behind him, the police.

"Do you have a boat?" his mother asked Everard.

"Indeed," he said, assisting her over a fish tub. "*Avocet,* a Crowningshield."

"Gaf-rigged or marconi?"

"Gaf-rigged, of course."

A muffled sound of approval came from his mother, and then Duncan lost the thread of their conversation as they loaded Chandu into the backseat, got into the car, and slammed the doors. When the Land Rover drove away in a spray of wet sand, the ambulance crew brought out a stretcher and set about to take the body away. One of the EMTs shook out a sheet. "Wait," said Duncan, and he knelt down next to his father.

Josefa came over. "What a mess."

"Poor Dad," he said, and he felt a decade of unspent grief well up inside of him. It had been so easy to think of his father as being somewhere out there all these years while there was no body to prove otherwise. But here he was, in the wasted flesh, the man who had taught him how to measure danger by the sound of waves on the shore and showed him how much easier it was to right a boat when it was pointed into the wind. He'd told him how to take conditions as they come and make the best of them, and that one day he would have to learn to deal with uncertainties he would rather avoid. This was the man who believed that to harvest something from the sea, you first had to love the sea. And as for a sudden violent squall that could end a life in a nanosecond, there was sometimes nothing to be done.

All these lessons, and yet he had learned nothing. Cora stood behind him and rested her hand on his shoulder. The seagull struggled in Josefa's arms, so she put it down, and it limped away. They all watched for a moment, then the EMTs went back to work and took the body away.

twenty-two

By ancient proclaim, the third Sunday in October was set aside every year by the early settlers of Port Ellery to give thanks to the fish for food before hunkering down for the harsh New England winter. All adults and children of a certain age, led by the mayor, would dress in robes of cod skins trimmed in lobster claws and run into the sea. This practice continued well into the nineteenth century and was still unknowingly observed by the dozen or so hale citizens who took a ritual plunge into the icy Atlantic every New Year's Day. But the old date was still remembered by some, so Josefa chose it for Kelp Day. A cold front was moving in later that week, but that was later. For now, the day was unseasonably warm, and the air was filled with the salty breath of the sea. Everyone in town who still had a boat in the water was motoring, sailing, or rowing out for the celebration. Fueled by used cooking oil from Manavilins, *Sea Turtle* was in service again, even though her propeller shaft was still a bit out of truth after her rough beach landing at Seacrest's. She led the fleet outward bound with the tide to the mouth of the bay, near Chester Island, where Kelp and a few other birds would be released. The old sea-worthy hulk had lost her plastic canopy and a few rows of seats, but that suited the day's purposes just fine, as it created an open staging area for the event, with room for tables and a grill for a party afterward.

Tucked in a shady corner of the Duck, the newest reiteration of "Kelp" stood watch in a cage, suspiciously eyeing the hoopla building up around him. Stacked alongside were four other cages, the other seagulls and seabirds rescued and rehabilitated in the wake of the storm. The ones that survived. Josefa, Slocum, Clover, and Harley fussed about in the stern setting up tables, while Duncan sat at the wheel in the deck house with Cora. It had only been two weeks since he had sat in that very seat, prepared for the Duck to morph into his coffin, but it turned out to be his kind of vessel: solid, dependable, and willing to adjust to a rapidly changing environment. It had restored his love of the sea.

"On such a beautiful day it doesn't seem possible to have bad weather again," said Cora. A film of autumnal gold reflected off the smooth water and made her glow. Then she crinkled her face and turned her nose to the back of the boat, where fishy exhaust fumes rose up from the engine below. "If only it didn't smell so bad."

"Smells better than diesel," Duncan said, with one hand on the wheel and the other resting lightly on her leg.

"Better than old fried clams?" Her hair was tied up in a ruby-red scarf to keep it from blowing around, and she wore large sunglasses so that in profile she looked like some starlet from an old movie magazine, only with a tint of early pregnancy in her complexion. He crept his hand up over her nylon windbreaker. It would not be long before he could feel the baby floating inside. He had gone with Cora for her first real obstetric appointment a few days before to view the fishlike shape on the ultrasound screen. Dr. Zander had explained that humans revisited stages of evolution during gestation, and their baby was still working its way through the Paleozoic Era. "We begin our lives as saltwater animals," he'd said, "suspended for nine months in a saline fluid in the womb. Then *poof!* We're forced out into the air to suck oxygen, and any water in the lungs will kill us. What a system."

Duncan thought of the gill on Nod's ear and felt a rush of sadness. He gazed back at Port Ellery's harbor, whose edge was thick again with lobster buoys, most of which had been recovered on distant shores in the days after the storm, but others were replacements for the ones lost forever. All the washed-up trash was pretty much gone now, too, returned to the sea by the constant repetition of tides, out of sight and out of mind until the next time. Even the massive ball of plastic and sea flesh that had settled on the beach would have rolled back to the ocean floor by now if it hadn't been for Adoniram pulling it up onto the earth and calling it art.

Sea Turtle clanked solemnly past the Cove, and everyone went silent as they passed his mother's house with its lone chimney still standing, like an ancient obelisk. It was not being rebuilt. There was simply not enough stable land. While his mother waited for the insurance company to arrive at a figure, she planned to sail the Caribbean on Everard Blue's yacht for the winter, and in the spring she was coming back to run the Duck, even going so far as to talk with Slocum about doing sunset barbecue Duck tours. "Charred Charters," Cora joked. In any event, his mother was leaving the property to return to the sea. If she missed the old house, she did not say it. Duncan, on the other hand, felt its loss immensely. When he told Annuncia what the plan was, she said, apparently by way of consolation, "Humans and their creations are the aberrations of nature, Dun'n. Good-bye and good riddance is how I see it."

She was wrong, but he did not argue the point. Humans were part of nature, and their inventions were, too. It was just that nature was not all deer frolicking in the woods or the sun rising over a perfect sea. Sometimes it was brutal, if not bizarre, in its capacity for destruction and disorder. Annuncia was right about one thing, though: He should not dwell too long in the land of painful memories of the past. He wouldn't. With a baby coming, he was already feeling nostalgic about the promise of the future. He could not wait.

As the Duck sputtered through the gray-blue waters, they moved between small piney islands whose brittle trees were jagged and raw from the gale-force winds. Wet blobs of seals sunned themselves on the surrounding rocks. A whiskered seal glared at them, raised its flippered tail, and slid off its rock into the water. Duncan watched the streamlined body move just under the surface, gliding forward before disappearing into the unknown darkness below.

"I think I might take up diving next summer," he said.

Cora sucked in the corner of her mouth for a moment as she stared at him. "You won't find Nod that way," she said, softly.

"I know," he said. "I just want to see what's under it all." And he spread a hand out in a hopeless gesture.

"I'm not sure that's possible," she said. "I think it's like a therapist trying to unlock the human mind. Even after years of sessions, we can only understand the teeniest bit of someone, and that probably none too well. The ocean is not only stranger than we think, it's stranger than we *can* think."

"I'm pretty good at thinking strange," he said.

269

Cora nodded without comment, and they both went back to studying the backwaters among the islands, lost in separate thoughts. A moment later the harbor suddenly opened up around them, and Duncan felt a shiver of belonging. Here he was, part of the scene he had so long pondered from the lofty distance of his office window, where it had seemed as if the water had nothing to do with him.

"Look," said Cora. "You can see that nasty ball from way out here."

The Sphere, as Adoniram called it, was still in Seacrest's parking lot and had become the poster child of the green seas movement, attracting crowds and media. Adoniram, now that he was officially alive again, was a Happening unto himself. Duncan was going to ask Adoniram to sit on Seacrest's board. He would be the first non-family member in that position, but considering how involved he was in the new product line, it only made sense. He was an investor, after all, but no longer an ominous one. Apparently, the ashes from their contract had been in the barrel with the diatom dust.

"The contract was an interesting exercise in words," said Adoniram. "As Sir Winston Churchill said, 'Play the game for more than you can afford to lose … only then will you learn the game.' I'd say you learned, Duncan. You'll learn more. Success is not final, failure is not fatal: It is the courage to continue that counts."

In exchange for going along with the Diatom Project, "Go Kelp!" was to be properly labeled, saying that it contained diatom dust. Marketing was playing the dust up as a bonus slug control, not conceptual art, as Adoniram was pushing for. Duncan trusted that word about the Diatom Project would leak out on its own, and that whatever the benefits or repercussions that resulted would just happen, with or without his worrying about it.

"I'll miss the Sphere when it's gone," said Duncan. Beaky had sold the Sphere to the museum curators who had rescued his mother, but they did not get the Dodge floor, which was safe in storage.

Adoniram had convinced Duncan's mother that it should be the star exhibit in a proposed regional museum for the Adoniram archives, such as they were. The two of them had become as thick as thieves since he'd come "alive." It seemed she'd been a huge fan of his early work. Who knew? The museum might help keep Port Ellery's head above water until the fish stocks revived. If they didn't—well, then. Well, then.

"You're just a sentimental fool." Cora rubbed her stomach. "I won't miss the Sphere; it stinks."

"That's the point, according to Adoniram. What we've done to the ocean stinks. He's going to install it outside on the museum plaza in Boston next week so everyone can smell the marine animals decompose. A webcam is already recording the process as it slowly reduces to a pile of dust and irreducible plastic bits. I think he's going to scratch *God Help Us* on the pavement around it."

"Tack, Everard! Hard to port!"

"Your mother," said Cora. "I'm still not used to seeing her out in the world."

Everard Blue's rather spiffy yacht, *Avocet,* was coming up on the starboard side of the Duck with intent to pass. Annabel Leland blew twice into the whistle around her neck, then resumed barking like a coxswain to Everard, as if she could propel the boat forward by the force of her blistering words. She was enjoying the intoxication of unleashed wrath. She yelled against the wind and against the sea, but Everard, for one, remained unmoved as he stood at the varnished wheel, calmly smiling ahead. The wind picked up its pace, and the boards creaked as the sails began to bellow out with success.

"What a couple," said Duncan.

"Whatever works," said Cora. "That's my motto at the office these days. Whatever works." And with this she reached over and patted his leg. "Like us."

Avocet tacked in front of them with a sheetful of air that sent them across Duncan's bow.

"Annabel, my ducky, what was our time from the red nun?" Everard shouted. Chandu looked up from where he was lying on the deck, letting the spray hit his face.

"Seven minutes, thirty-eight seconds," she shouted back. She was in fine feather in her new clothes, a green racing jacket with white cropped pants. Her feet were bare, and on her head was a first mate's cap, under which her orange-gray braid swung like a pendulum in the middle of her back. "Not good enough," she shouted. "Come about and do it again!"

Chandu stood up and resettled himself away from her fury, but he could not escape the coil of rope she tossed on his broad back for safekeeping. He looked at it, then let his drooling head relax back down to the deck.

"It's going to be interesting to see how much of her old personality was the mulberry wine, and how much was just her," said Cora. "If she was self-medicating all these years, she could turn stranger now than she was before. There's always that danger when you remove someone's crutch."

"The silt is still settling to the bottom on that one," said Duncan. "At least she's out of the house."

"That's because there is no house."

"True, but she could be living in the ruins, like a hermit."

As it was, she was living under Everard's roof, and Duncan didn't want to know the sleeping arrangements. He was grateful that Everard, who'd been a hammer-thrower in college and ran a successful admiralty legal practice in his working years, had come along when he did to retire in Port Ellery. As Cora said, it would have been too psychologically complex for Duncan to have finally left his childhood home only to take his mother with him. But Everard had done more than give her a roof—he gave her back some meaning and purpose to her days, without which any life might seem pretty colorless. She waved at them as the yacht tacked again, ducking under the swinging boom without even glancing at it, then blew the whistle twice.

Everard tipped his white captain's hat as they circled around *Sea Turtle*, returning on the port side, and Duncan tapped his horn hello. Apart from escorting his mother back into the world, Everard had been a huge help in sorting out the legal problems surrounding his father's body and expediting the autopsy. At the hearing, he brought in chemists to testify that the wine had hallucinogenic qualities which would have led to warped decisions on his mother's part, and a psychiatrist testified that the trauma of finding his father dead on the beach would have distorted Nod's cognitive ability as well, making him susceptible to his mother's order to stuff his father into a cask. The autopsy confirmed that Brendan Leland had died of accidental drowning ten years before. In the end, no charges were brought against his mother. The body had been released back to the family earlier in the week, and they had held a private burial at the family plot across town, finally laying him to rest under a stone erected a decade before.

"He would rather have had a burial at sea," his mother said when it was done. "I never thought of him as a man buried under green grass."

"I want him where I can keep an eye on him," said Duncan, who had gone to the funeral home before the burial to peek in the casket to make sure he was there. As for Nod, who knew where his body was? His mother believed he was still alive, and if that kept her going, so be it. It wasn't particularly necessary for her mind to exactly mesh with reality as she floated though the rest of her life. Stranger still, whenever his name came up, she quoted the Koran:

"Put your child in the ark and let him be carried away by the river." It was anyone's guess how she had happened upon that, or why it gave her any comfort. Still, according to custom, in three months' time, the family would bury an empty coffin in Nod's name and call him dead.

Adoniram and Beaky, another couple for whom the words *whatever works* sprang to mind, came bobbing alongside the Duck in a raft created from remnants of vessels that had washed up in the storm, lashed together with odd bits of rope. The raft was being propelled by a strange makeshift engine, fueled by some unknown substance that smelled of garbage. Two deck chairs were balanced on the uneven surface for sunbathing, and the two men raised their hands in greeting as they passed. Adoniram was well dressed in a pressed suit, as usual, but wore no tie. He had an unlit cigar in his mouth and looked extremely self-satisfied. Fingers sat on Beaky's stomach and stretched in the warmth of the sun.

Annuncia, who was wearing her red Seacrest's smock "for the publicity," sailed behind them in a small boat, with one hand on the rudder stick as if it grew out of her arm. In her other hand she held a long-handled net with which she collected bits of floating debris. Duncan still wasn't happy that she'd been manipulating him like a puppet in the past couple of months, but maybe he was, as she claimed, not in any shape to save his business on his own. She gave him a rare smile, and he waved.

Duncan hummed to himself as he continued to steer the Duck to its destination, nodding to people in boats as they passed. The mayor's motor yacht, *Flask*, suddenly cut through the space between them all, churning up the water in its wake and sending Adoniram and Beaky bobbing one way and Annuncia the other. The TV crew was setting up its camera on *Flask*'s foredeck while the mayor chatted up the pretty newscaster in the wheelhouse. Duncan hoped they were watching the time. Weaving in between all the different vessels were Harvey Storer and Syrie, in wet suits, riding a jet ski. Storer was at the wheel, and Syrie had her arms wrapped around him. This was the banker who had refused to lend Duncan money for payroll almost two months before, accusing Duncan of owing more on Seacrest's than it was worth. Now it was Storer's company that was underwater, Coastal Bank & Trust having slipped into the harbor during the hurricane. Rumor had it that Storer had gone off the deep end in the aftermath, and maybe this was proof of that. As for Syrie, she waved vigorously at Duncan as the jet ski passed, sending up a spray of water between them and the sun, creating a small rainbow as a shower sprinkled down on all their heads.

"I heard about the kiss, you know," Cora said to Duncan. "Were you really going to regress to high school and start over?"

They smiled without looking at each other. He notched up the Duck's speed a knot or two to get to the meeting place on time, and as the water burst smoothly at the bow, Duncan felt life breaking against his own. He had run aground, but he felt he was finally off the rocks, and this made him feel buoyant and full of life, instead of the unsalvageable wreck full of free-floating anxiety he seemed to be not so long ago.

"What's that smell?" asked Cora. She sat up straight and looked around as the color drained from her face.

"Lunch," said Duncan. Slocum was starting up the oil barrel grill that he'd hung over the stern, using a squirt of his jellyfish soup as a propellant for the fire. Yet another use. His jellyfish plastic was moving along through the lab, but it would take time to produce anything close to a product. Adoniram still held the processing rights for it, if and when that time finally came—a good reason to have him on board at Seacrest's. He'd even been hinting that he might give the rights to Duncan's unborn child as a baby present. Another Leland saddled with the business, born with a silver thorn in his side. But at least he or she would have a business. Much better to have something to worry about than nothing at all.

Josefa came up to the bridge. "Almost to Chester," she said, and she handed Cora a can of ginger ale with a straw.

"Why did we have to come all the way out here?" asked Cora, taking a sip. "Couldn't we have done this from the beach?"

"Gulls roost on that island at night. If Kelp and the others can figure out where they're going to sleep tonight, they'll be more relaxed."

"Not to mention that Chester Island is a pretty sweet backdrop for the six o'clock news," said Duncan.

"Doesn't hurt to think of these things," said Josefa, looking out at the island.

"What deserving Kelp is this, Josefa?" asked Duncan. "Number three? Four?"

She kept her eyes on the horizon. "I've got a new van, new cages, soon even a new shelter. Can't say it hasn't all been worth it."

No, he couldn't. Whereas earlier he'd been disgusted that Josefa was replacing dead Kelps with live ones, after his experience with Adoniram he now understood that the symbolic rendering of an object could substitute for the real thing, sometimes even more so. The important thing was the idea. Get the idea right first: Birds needed to be helped back to health; the world needed to be saved with giant diatoms—if not diatoms, then something; it hardly mattered that this was not the original Kelp or that those particular diatoms were extinct. Executing a well-planned, bizarre gesture made people curious, and it made them feel. As Adoniram said, there was not nearly enough feeling in the world.

"You below the mark, Cora?" asked Josefa.

"Bleh."

Josefa patted her on the shoulder. "Rheya was sick like that, too."

They were all quiet and did not look at one another. Slocum's sister had not been found after the storm, nor had her dory. Suspiciously, Slocum did not seem overly concerned, which confirmed rumors that she was alive and just hiding from the law. It would not be the first time a storm had been used as a cover to fake a death and start a new life. But it was a very fine line between faking death and death itself.

"I wish Nod would show up, one way or another," said Duncan. He scanned the rocky shore, and he knew that for the rest of his days, he would always be expecting to see a waterlogged body washed up on every cove and inlet.

"There are some who just can't be saved," said Cora.

"Could be he didn't want to be saved," said Josefa. "We can't judge."

"He had problems," said Cora, sitting herself upright again, "but I never really thought of him as suicidal."

"I'll just have to find a way to live with the fact that he died proving how fatal it is to be a fool," Duncan said, and no one argued the point. He remembered what Adoniram had said to him when the Coast Guard abandoned the search on the third day: "Self-destructive behavior is as close to self-sacrifice as you can get, my friend. Try to think of Nod in that way."

Thinking of Nod in that way hadn't really changed the pain he felt when he thought of him at all, but it kept his mind busy when the dark times came on him.

Again they heard his mother's voice travel across the water as *Avocet* came sailing back. "You're luffing, Everard! Head down! Down!"

"She really needs to work on her emotional management," said Cora.

"Annabel is certainly a strong cup of grog," said Josefa as they watched the boat move up on them.

Cora put her hand on her forehead. "Please, don't say the word grog."

The mayor's boat sounded a horn, which started all the other boats going like a pack of dogs.

"It's time," said Josefa. "I'll go get Kelp."

"Off we go," said Duncan. He pointed the Duck into the drowsy breeze, turned off the engine, and helped Cora stand.

"I can get up by myself," she said.

"Drop sail!" his mother shouted as Everard's boat swept right up next to *Sea Turtle*. "Bumpers!" She ran to the port rail and threw rubber cylinders over the side to protect it from the Duck as her long braid whipped the air.

Cora went to help Josefa carry Kelp's cage onto the open bow of the boat, forward of the wheelhouse. "You stay," Josefa said to Duncan. "Help your mother tie up."

"The drogue!" his mother shouted. "Throw the drogue in the water!"

Duncan watched Everard toss the floating sea-anchor overboard. Then his mother picked up the coil of line that had been stored on Chandu and yelled "Catch!" to Duncan. He had to lean out over the water to grab it; then he tied it to the rail so they could raft together. Other boats nosed in closer, each tying up to the other, until they formed a long line of boats, from the largest, like the Duck, to the middling sailing yachts and lobster boats, to a wide assortment of Boston Whalers and rowing dinghies, but there was no hierarchy among them. In Port Ellery, people were not judged by their boats but the way they handled them. After lines were secured, people began to move freely from deck to deck and ladder to ladder until they were close enough to the Duck to see the birds set free.

As the boats swapped slaps with the water, Slocum and his

family opened coolers of beer and soda and threw food on the grill: marinated calamari, pumpkin slices, roast oysters, lamb kidneys wrapped in bacon, whole whiting, pale seafood sausage, and suspicious sauces and condiments of Slocum's own making. It looked and smelled unusually appetizing to Duncan, but Cora, even upwind in the bow, was in no mood.

"I'm going to be sick," she said.

He got her another ginger ale and sat down beside her on the deck, their legs hanging over the sides. They rested their arms on the low rail that edged the bow, whose deck was heavily ridged, like the throat of a whale.

Josefa was behind them, getting Kelp out of the cage, while Clover held the door open. "There you go honey," she said as she helped tuck Kelp attractively in Josefa's arms. "You two look like a postcard."

The mayor sounded another horn and, with the help of an address system, gave a speech on the maritime history of Port Ellery and the importance of fighting to keep the industry afloat, while somehow avoiding the paradox of wanting to save the oceans and still needing to fish from them, before finally turning to the subject of how all of Josefa's years of "broken wing" work were about to pay off.

As he continued to babble, Slocum wandered to the bow with a platter of grilled whiting, and three gulls swept down from the sky to get them. Clover's son, Harley, came running from the stern with a mooring stick raised over his head and chased them off.

"Good boy," said Clover. "It'll be your job to keep those flying rats away from the food."

"The birds are just jealous," said Slocum. "You think they like eating raw fish? They want what we have—a cuisine. We are the only cooks on the planet!"

"Thank God for that," said Cora.

The boaters must have felt the mayor had talked quite long enough because they began to honk their horns, and he wrapped up his speech with a heartfelt thank you. After a brief moment of confusion about what to do next, the TV crew gave the signal to Josefa, who gave her assistants the nod. She opened her arms and released Kelp into the air, and then Clover, Slocum, and Harley tossed the other saved birds aloft with a cheer. The birds all faltered a bit—one small tern almost dropped in the water—but they all regained their wings and soared up, soon becoming bright white spots in the sky. A breeze rose at the same time, and all the boats shifted as one, moved by the unseen hand of the wind.

The boaters cheered. "Fly free, Kelp!" "We love you!"

"What is your mother doing, Duncan?" asked Cora.

On the deck of the yacht, his mother was directing Everard in maneuvering a small signal canon to the fore. When the birds were fully airborne, she shouted "Now!" and Everard lit the fuse. When the canon erupted, the noise sent the terrified birds out over the sea.

There was a moment of stunned silence, then more cheers. Chandu stood up and began to bark. "At least she didn't kill them," said Josefa.

"That's a start," said Duncan. He took Cora's hand as they watched Kelp float away on a current, until he was just a speck in the sky. Maybe Nod had floated away, too. Maybe he had concocted an elaborate scheme to leave Port Ellery forever with Rheya and Judson on *L'Ark*. It could be he just pretended to go out on the water to do his mother's bidding as the storm came in, but instead had already made plans to meet up with Rheya out in the bay. They could have helped each other, the dory pulling the inflatable, the inflatable pushing the dory, struggling through the rising waves to *L'Ark* outside the harbor. It would have been a stiff pull, but it was possible. Maybe Judson had managed to get the yacht safely from the Boat Club to deep water on his own and was there waiting for his captain and crew. Judson would have had a few suitcases of cash on board and three forged passports in his briefcase. Duncan imagined them spending the rest of their lives in gray water, one step ahead of the law. Maybe Nod was in love with Rheya, maybe he was in love with *L'Ark,* or maybe he was just in love with the sea. It didn't matter. Duncan could keep Nod alive this way forever, sailing in the warm trade winds, finally free with his own life, a baby coming, blue skies, tropical bays. Why not? They had the means, and they had the will. Between them all, they could be content; they could even be happy. What else was there, really?

As the excitement of the release ebbed, people began to crowd up on the Duck. Slocum and Clover passed some trays down the sides to the attached vessels and sent Harley around the deck with a cart. Out of deference to Cora, Duncan waved the food away, then checked his watch. The tide would be turning before they knew it. He was already feeling the tug of it, pulling them back to land. It would mean a smooth ride home for Cora's stomach. He gazed out at the vastness of the ocean where Kelp and the others had flown, unidentifiable now from the thousands of others in the sky, and let them all go.

great last sentence!

People Who Live
by Erica Jong

People who live by the sea
understand eternity.
They copy the curves of the waves,
their hearts beat with the tides,
& the saltiness of their blood
corresponds with the sea.

They know that the house of flesh
is only a sandcastle
built on the shore,
that skin breaks
under the waves
like sand under the soles
of the first walker on the beach
when the tide recedes.

Each of us walks there once,
watching the bubbles
rise up through the sand
like ascending souls,
tracing the line of the foam,
drawing our index fingers
along the horizon
pointing home.

Acknowledgments

The author is indebted to the artist Sol LeWitt for his 1969 manifesto "Sentences on Conceptual Art."

Excerpts of *Float* in various forms have been previously published. The first two chapters appeared as the short story "Float" in the *Bear Deluxe Magazine*, #31, Winter 2010–2011. "Float" won the Doug Fir Fiction Award sponsored by the magazine and its parent organization, Orlo, a nonprofit group that uses the creative arts to explore environmental issues. Chapter Eight was published as "Infinite Kingdom" in *Precipitate, Journal of the New Environmental Imagination* (now called *Newfound*), Winter 2011/12. A portion adapted from Chapter Six was featured on the DimeStories Virtual Open Mic in November of 2012, and a modified Chapter Four appears as "Lost Point" in the anthology *Imagination & Place: Cartography*, published by the Imagination & Place Press, 2013.

Many thanks to the Dorland Mountain Arts Colony for the gift of unfettered time to edit the final manuscript.

Appreciation goes to the Dana Awards for recognizing *Float* as a finalist in the 2011 Dana Award in the Novel.

A shout-out to Karen Ristuben, whose environmental artwork graces the cover of *Float*. She spreads the word on the catastrophic dangers of plastics in the oceans through her multimedia presentations.

Finally, deep gratitude to the Raymond Street Writers, especially Judy Salzman, whose spirit hovers over every word.

About the Author

JoeAnn Hart lives in Gloucester, Massachusetts, America's oldest seaport, where fishing regulations, the health of the ocean, and the natural beauty of the world are the daily topics of wonder and concern. She is the author of the novel *Addled* (Little, Brown, 2007), a social satire that intertwines animal rights with the politics of food.

Her essays, articles, and short fiction have appeared in a wide variety of literary journals and national publications, and she is a regular contributor to the *Boston Globe Magazine*. Her work has won a number of awards, including the PEN New England Discovery Award in Fiction. She and her husband tend a few farm animals, including two donkeys from Save Your Ass Rescue. In fair weather, Hart rows a dory around the harbor.

Float was a finalist for the Dana Award in the Novel, and the first two chapters, slightly modified, won the Doug Fir Fiction Award for a short story relating to environmental issues.

About the Cover Artist

Karen Ristuben is an artist and educator living in her hometown of Gloucester, Massachusetts. She received her Master of Fine Arts from the Vermont College of Fine Arts, her BFA and teaching degree from the School of the Museum of Fine Arts/Tufts University, and her JD from Suffolk University Law School.

Her art practice is environmental advocacy at its core. She believes that real change toward a healthier planet calls for knowledge, then caring, then action. Through multimedia, she bridges the disciplines of art, environmental science, and education for the sake of our shared planet.

Karen is currently leading the Rocky Neck Art Colony, one of the nation's oldest art communities, through a time of growth as it develops its programming and infrastructure for the benefit of future generations of artists, residents, and visitors.

Ashland
Creek
Press

Ashland Creek Press is an independent publisher of
books with a world view. From travel narratives to
eco-literature, our mission is to publish a range of
books that foster an appreciation for worlds outside
our own, for nature and the animal kingdom, and for
the ways in which we all connect. To keep up-to-date
on new and forthcoming books, subscribe to our free
newsletter at www.AshlandCreekPress.com.

CPSIA information can be obtained at www.ICGtesting.com
Printed in the USA
BVOW021513180213

313573BV00001B/1/P